BRITAIN IN OLD PHOTOGRAPHS

TORQUAY

CW00823377

South Devon Technical College School of Arts, *c.* 1966. The Torquay Art School was built by Robert Stark as the Salem Chapel, and he ministered here until his death in 1854. Robert Stark was born at Chelston on 17 April 1788, and although brought up in the doctrines of the Church of England joined a body of dissenters of the Calvinistic persuasion. A few years after his death the chapel was converted into the School of Science and Art under the name of the Vivian Institute. In 1887 it was enlarged by taking over the house on the right, and became the town's memorial of the Queen's golden jubilee; in 1918 it became the School of Arts and Crafts.

BRITAIN IN OLD PHOTOGRAPHS

TORQUAY

TED GOSLING

SUTTON PUBLISHING LIMITED

Sutton Publishing Limited
Phoenix Mill · Thrupp · Stroud
Gloucestershire · GL5 2BU

First published 1996

Copyright © Ted Gosling , 1996

Cover photographs: *front*: Meadfoot Road, 1907; *back*:the old dairy, 1871. *Title page picture*: John Fry Rockhey JP was Mayor of Torquay on two occasions, during the year of Queen Victoria's diamond jubilee and at King Edward VII's coronation.

British Library Cataloguing in Publication Data
A catalogue record for this book is available from the British Library.

ISBN 0-7509-0730-4

Typeset in 10/12 Perpetua. Typesetting and origination by Sutton Publishing Limited. Printed in Great Britain by Ebenezer Baylis, Worcester.

Torquay Museum, from whose collections the photographs for this book were taken, is run by the Torquay Natural History Society (founded in 1844), and is the oldest museum in Devon still in existence today.

The Museum's collections cover a wealth of subjects including geology, natural history, archaeology, ethnography, social history and local history. Its collection of pictorial records numbers about 40,000 items. These are mostly photographs, but there are also prints, drawings, and watercolours. These predominantly feature Torbay and the surrounding area, but there are also many photographs of other Devon localities, especially Dartmoor.

The Museum is open throughout the year and enquiries about the collections for research or other purposes can be made to the Curator, Torquay Museum, Babbacombe Road, Torquay, TQ1 1HG.

CONTENTS

INTRODUCTION

From the earliest times Torquay has been famous as a shelter for shipping from the Atlantic gales coming from the south-west. During the Napoleonic Wars the fleet anchored here regularly and Earl St Vincent occupied Torre Abbey as his naval headquarters. As a result, the officers had their wives and families brought down to stay at the hamlet of Tor Quay. This was the start of the rapid growth of the popular seaside resort we know today.

In 1821 the population was still less than 2,000 but by 1841 it had risen to 6,000. The railway came soon after and by 1850 the town was known as the 'Queen of Watering Places'. The expansion was well planned and the new town abounds in fine Victorian architecture, the layout being in many terraces and wooded drives following the contours of its seven hills. Sir Lawrence Palk owned much of the land and he wisely developed it with an upper-class clientele in mind. The harbour was extended and Torquay was incorporated as a Municipal Borough in 1892, taking in Babbacombe, Chelston, Ilsham, and St Marychurch. The picturesque village of Cockington was added in 1928, and fortunately the village remains unspoilt.

Cockington Court, which now belongs to the Corporation, was the home of the Cary family from the time of Richard II until they were forced to sell out to the Mallock family in 1654. It remained with them until 1927.

Torre Abbey and its grounds extending to the seafront are also the property of the Corporation, having been purchased from the Cary family in 1930 for £40,000. They had been the owners for almost 300 years. The Mansion House had been rebuilt and extended by the Cary's in about 1750 and was used by Earl St Vincent when he was the naval commander here in 1800. On his birthday, 9 January 1801, there was a great celebration in the ballroom, where Admiral Lord Nelson danced before leaving for the battle of Copenhagen. The Spanish Barn is an ancient tithe barn and was used to imprison 397 Spanish seamen after the defeat of the Spanish Armada. The impressive gatehouse was built in the early part of the fourteenth century.

Today Torquay is the best known of all the Devon seaside resorts and this new collection of pictures provides a unique history. Included in its pages are photographs drawn from family albums, local collections and professional photographers. Many have never been published before and they will take the reader on a fascinating journey through the more recent history of the Torquay area.

Once again, Ted Gosling has assembled a notable collection and it is a worthy addition to the ever increasing series of his pictorial books covering the seaboard of both Dorset and Devon.

ROY F. CHAPPLE
former Devon County Councillor

E. P. BOVEY,

BUILDER & CONTRACTOR

TORQUAY.

Painting and Decorating   ✳   Plumbing and Gas-fitting

PAPER HANGING, WHITING & COLOURING.

GENERAL REPAIRS AND CLEANING IN ALL BRANCHES
BY EXPERIENCED WORKMEN.

✳

Office and Works near the Museum, TORWOOD.

Although there were improvements for those who served on board in the Royal Navy the rates of pay were low by any standard. Places like the Torquay Sailors Rest, pictured here just after it opened in 1903, provided accommodation and meals for men of the Royal Navy, and although a temperance restaurant it must have been popular with matelots.

Chapel Hill, *c.* 1900.

THE EARLY DAYS

Waldon Hill and the inner harbour, after the widening of the Strand, c. 1870. At the top of the Hill is Waldon Castle. On the lower slope and appearing here over Vaughan Parade is Rock House. In 1832 Mr Gladstone and several members of his family, including W.E. Gladstone, resided at Rock House, and it was here that the latter received his call to parliamentary life as a candidate for Newark.

Warberry Hill, as seen from Park Hill, 1878. This fine view was taken by Francis Frith of Reigate. The east side of the Braddons is being excavated for the building of the Winter Garden. The site is below the Wesleyan church and the museum.

Warberry Hill, as seen from Woodfield Road, 1878. This is another view photographed by Francis Frith. Frith, who was born in 1822, settled in Reigate and opened a photographic business there in 1860. With his associate photographers he photographed hundreds of thousands of familiar places such as this, then sold prints or postcards at a modest price.

Topographical photographs are among the most interesting of old photographs, and this Torquay view from above Livermead taken in 1870 is an exceptionally fine example. In the centre foreground note the single-line railway bridge. The railway to Torquay and Paignton was opened on 1 August 1859, and by 1870 the railways were making popular travel possible for the first time in history. Torquay was linked to a growing national railway network which helped determine her role as a leading seaside resort.

The · Watcombe · Terra-Cotta · Co.

LIMITED,

ST. MARY-CHURCH, TORQUAY.

THE Company manufacture Art Pottery of very high class, in great variety, both glazed and unglazed. Amongst the former are some

just brought out, well deserving the attention of the Public.

The Works at Watcombe may be seen by Visitors on application to Mr. CHAS. BROCK, the Manager.

The Watcombe Terra-Cotta Co. advertisement of 1878.

Torquay Harbour, *c.* 1880.

Torquay Harbour from Vane Hill, *c.* 1880.

The front of Millers Cottage, with the photographer's back to the Old Dairy (now Chelston Square), 1870. This is on the site of West Dale and Sunnyvale.

The back of the Chelston Millers Cottage and granary for the mill, 1870. The mill is on the right side of the road; the mill wheel is hidden by brambles. Nos 1, 2 and 3 Brooklet Villas were built on the site of the old mill, which was known as Heron's Mill.

This interesting old print of 1821 shows the Torquay waterfront as seen from below the Rock Walk. This was a time of growth in the town. A new market house had been erected and private houses were multiplying apace. Here in this print the row of houses on Victoria Parade is terminated at the south end on the seaward side by the pier, which was erected by Sir Lawrence Palk in 1806 to protect the harbour. The little promontory with the pathway known as Beacon Hill was cut back in the 1860s for the building of Haldon Pier, and the baths were built at an earlier date over the stone archway seen here on the right. This also meant cutting away part of Beacon Hill.

ESTABLISHED 1815.

WILKINSON & CO.,

Wine and Brandy Merchants,

24 VICTORIA PARADE,

TORQUAY.

As nearly the whole of our Wines are specially selected and shipped direct to our Bonded Stores, whence they are bottled here (Sparkling excepted) by most experienced cellar-men, under our personal supervision, we are enabled to give the best possible value.

Wilkinson & Co. of 24 Victoria Parade used this advertisement in 1875.

Shipping in the outer harbour.

Torquay from Waldon Castle, probably 1885. This was the year in which the tower was added to St John's Church, seen here on the left.

Here is a wonderful view of Torquay's sea road in 1866, showing how quickly and immensely things change. Note the two toll houses near the end of King's Drive and to the right of Abbey Crescent.

View of Corbyn Head from the beach, *c.* 1870.

The old dairy, 1871.

The Old Mill and granary for the mill, Chelston, *c*. 1890.

A charming picture from the Brown and Rawcliffe camera series showing Torquay from Waldon Hill, 1900.

Torquay from the Rock Walk, c. 1900: another view of the Princess Gardens as they appeared at the turn of the century. These gardens were built on 3½ acres of reclaimed marshland and were opened to the public in 1894. Note the complete lack of traffic then in comparison with the same scene today.

The Rock Walk, *c.* 1900.

No book on Torquay would be complete without a photograph of the old forge in the picture-postcard village of Cockington. Taken at the turn of the century, the picture has managed to preserve for us something of the unhurried pace of life in what was then a rural area, not the busy tourist attraction of today.

The Ilsham Road junction with Asheldon Road near Kents Cavern: a peaceful street scene, 1897.

Chelston was formerly part of Cockington parish, and pictured here in Chelston are the old dairy with Walnut Cottage. The walnut tree was removed during 1881, so this photograph was taken before that date.

Torquay from Corbyn Sands, *c.* 1900. Although the children playing on the beach have hats on and the older people are wearing hats and coats this has no seasonal significance. In those days it was the custom for dress in warm weather as well as cold to conform to the strict social formalities. Note the remains of the old stone breakwater, which protected the tiny harbour used by the monks of Torre Abbey.

Torquay from Vane Hill, *c.* 1870. Waldon Hill dominates the centre of this early photograph with Torbay Road running around its base.

Reading the Charter of Incorporation, September 1892. This must relate to the group of people in the right-hand corner of this picture. The account of the day's proceedings in the Torquay Directory for 7 September included such phrases as 'enormous concourse of people' and 'profusion of decorations on every hand', and certainly flags were flying in the harbour.

Construction of the Princess Gardens, 1890. These gardens, which cost £4,290, were formally opened by the Mayor in 1894.

THE TOWN
&
THE NEIGHBOURHOOD

Torquay panorama, looking west, 1959. The long hill in the distance on the left is Warren Hill, and in the right foreground is part of Beausite in Hillesdon Road. Abbey Road is shown on the right, stretching towards Chelston in the distance.

Melville Lane, 1959. These houses were built in about 1850 and by 1954 had become so derelict that the Town Council submitted plans for the compulsory purchase of sixteen unfit houses in order to clear the site for a car park. The bottom photograph, taken in October 1959, shows the workshop and store of no. 24, whose owner was the last to resist the purchase order. Master Plumber F.C. Day had lived in no. 24 for the past thirty years. The premises had been in his family for 110 years and had been built by his grandfather.

Fore Street, St Marychurch, 1969. The street was so narrow that the car and bus in this picture could only pass each other with care. As street improvements were urgently required a cutting was made through land behind shops on the left of this photograph.

A start was made by demolition of part of Hampton Court, September 1969.

Sun Temple in Tessier Gardens, erected by the Corporation of Torquay in October 1933, in appreciation of the gift of the garden by Mrs A.A.E. Tessier.

The fountain on Babbacombe Downs erected by her many friends in memory of Georgina, Baroness Mount-Temple, who died on 17 October 1901. She had lived at Babbacombe Cliff for many years and had done much philanthropic work. She also worked to protect wild birds and animals. The fine statuette in bronze of Lady Mount-Temple was by Mr A.G. Walker.

Terraces of houses are a feature of Torquay, and this example of mid-nineteenth century architecture is Wellswood Park, a terrace of houses facing the north and west sides of a large open space – The Park.

Lisburne Crescent, which borders the road linking Babbacombe Road with the Lincombes. It faces south over Torbay and is named after the first Earl of Lisburne, into whose family Sir Lawrence Palk married in 1792.

This interior view of the Roman Catholic Church in St Marychurch was taken by J. Blampey of Ashburton in 1891. This church, dedicated to Our Lady, help of Christians and St Denis, was built in 1860–70 at the sole cost of William John Potts Chatto Esq. of the Daison, St Marychurch. He is buried in the crypt below the lady chapel.

The Roman Catholic Church, St Marychurch: another fine photograph taken by J. Blampey of Ashburton in 1891. When the parish church of St Marychurch was destroyed during an air raid on 30 May 1943, one of the enemy planes struck and dislodged the large top stone of the spire, and then fell in the Teignmouth road.

St Luke's Church, *c.* 1890. This church was consecrated in November 1862. The original panels in the canopy over the altar, decorated in colour, are shown here. Directly over the central window the light shines on three words from the Te Deum: 'Heaven and earth are full of the majesty of thy glory'. In the porch above, subjects from the same canticle, such as angels and prophets, are depicted.

Cary Park in Babbacombe was dedicated to the public for ever in the sixtieth year of the reign of Queen Victoria, 1892, by Robert S.S. Cary of Torre Abbey. Pictured here in Cary Park is the memorial erected in his memory by his widow in 1903.

Torquay Meadfoot, *c.* 1890. The view remained unchanged from 1878, when the sea wall was built, until June 1960, when Kilmorie (the large house on the hill in the centre) was demolished to provide a site for a block of flats. Kilmorie was built for Robert Dykes, who took up residence in 1851.

The block of flats which was built on the site of Kilmorie House, pictured here near completion, 1962. The flats represented a triumph of architects and builders over barriers of natural land formation. Set into the beautiful wooded slopes of Kilmorie on a hillside above the cliff face, the flats looked right down to the sea below. Privacy was the key idea in designing these fifty-four super-luxury flats. The slow radius curve of the block meant that the elegant recessed balcony could be used without fear of being overlooked by neighbours.

Lloyds Bank at the junction of Vaughan Parade and Lawrence Place, 1932. Local solicitor Mr W. Kitson came to live in Vaughan Parade in 1832, and with Capt. W. Vivian and Mr E. Vivian founded a bank in 1854 called Torquay Bank, which in 1900 became Lloyds. The Palk Arch on the right was built in 1832 and survived until February 1962. The building to the left of Lloyds is that of Kitson, Hutchings, Easterbrook and Co., a firm of solicitors.

Entrance to Pimlico with the post office on the right, June 1964. On the left is the former Christian Alliance Club of Women and Girls (CAWG), whose motto 'By love serve one another' survived the period when it housed a bookmaker, but eventually succumbed to the bulldozer.

Demolition of CAWG for a new roundabout at the road junction, January 1965.

The wall of the old CAWG being pushed down, January 1965.

Long Park Pottery *c*. 1900.

Torbay Road at the Paignton end, *c*. 1906. One of the first horseless carriages is parked against the pavement. The cyclist sporting the boater is passing Dellers Supply Store at nos 8 to 12 Torbay Road, which at that time was owned by a Mr William Lambshead of Palace Avenue. The shop on the extreme right was occupied by the Irish Linen Company.

An aerial view of Torquay, looking north from Princess Gardens, 1947.

Cary Parade, with the church of St John the Evangelist standing in Montpelier Place in the background, *c*. 1965. This church, formerly a Proprietory Chapel, was rebuilt in 1865–71 in the Gothic style from the designs of G.E. Street RA.

Marine Spa, 1960. This was a popular venue for tourists and visitors. It had a ballroom, seawater swimming pool and large sun lounge, and offered many health treatments. It was eventually demolished in the 1970s to make room for that white elephant of all white elephants, the Coral Island entertainment complex.

Mr P. Turnbull, the County Planning Officer, is seen here with the draft town map for Torquay at the start of Borough status negotiation, 1960.

By the 1960s motorists and non-motorists alike were complaining about the clogging of town centres by cars, with shoppers becoming wearied by the problem of finding parking spaces. This photograph, taken during the summer of 1961, shows the traffic hold-ups in Castle Circus.

Union Street, 1961–2. The redevelopment of this area was taking place, and the Prince of Wales Inn had already gone.

Old Town Hall, 3 August 1962. The pole on the right marks the reconstruction of shops in Union Street. It stands on the site of the new Woolworths store.

Watcombe Hall, December 1963. The Hall stands on the seaward side of St Mary's Church in Shaldon Road. It is well placed in the valley overlooking the sea, and is under the shelter of Echo Rock. It was formerly the home of financier Mr C.W. Bashchwitz. On 6 December 1963 it was opened by the Electrical Trades Union as a convalescent home for members. Pictured here is the Warden Mr A. Woodcock, who was responsible for twenty-four patients, each of them staying for two weeks.

The Killester Hotel, Lower Warberry Road, 1960. From 1910 this had been the home of Oliver Heaviside, the sixty-year-old mathematician and scientist; at this time it was a private house called Homefield. Heaviside died in a Torquay nursing home on 3 February 1925, and there is a plaque to his memory in the entrance to the Town Hall.

Hatley St George, built by Mr Harvey in Lincombe Drive in 1846.

Castle Circus, November 1967. This fine press photo was taken by a Mr John Beale who perched 90 ft above the ground on a crane erected on the triangle between Union Street and Tor Hill Road at the start of the rebuilding. The site known as Brock's Corner, occupied by a furniture store of that name and other business premises, had been cleared to provide space for sheds and offices. Union Street passes the electricity showroom in the left foreground and continues down to Fleet Street. In Castle Circus the Town Hall faces the cinema. In the distance is Stentiford Hill, approached from Castle Circus by Castle Road.

Torquay panorama, 1959. In the left foreground is the other part of Beausite with Union Street stretching towards Torre. The spire of Upton Church is in the centre with Belgrave Church to the left of it. On the extreme right is Stentiford Hill, with Queen Street at its foot.

This splendid photograph shows how the Imperial Hotel looked in 1885. The foundation stone of this luxury hotel was laid on 25 March 1864 by Lady Palk and the hotel opened for business in November 1866. Since that date many rich and famous people have stayed in the hotel enjoying a service second to none.

JUST PEOPLE

Three former mayors of Torquay are seen here at the Town Hall after a ceremony in which they were made Freemen of the Borough, 5 April 1961. Since 1892, when Torquay received its Charter of Incorporation, only twenty-two names, including those of the present recipients, had appeared on the list of honorary freemen, and it was the most honourable distinction any town could confer. On the left is Councillor F.J. March Snr, member of the Council, who was Mayor from 1949 to 1950. In the centre is Col. Rowland Ward, a former Borough Alderman and Mayor from 1935 to 1936. On the right is Councillor C.T. Bowden, first elected to the council in 1932, twenty-one days after Mr March's election; he was Mayor from 1945 to 1946.

Hatfield, a two-storey home standing beside flats for the elderly, was built by Torquay Borough Council and opened on 12 April 1967 by Miss F.M. Pugh, Chairwoman of the Welfare Committee of Devon County Council. She is seen here standing left of centre at the opening ceremony; standing in the centre is Alderman Gerald Whitmarsh, Chairman of Devon County Council.

Hatfield was built at a cost of £87,000 by Devon County Council, and here are some of the residents in the dining room just after the opening in 1967.

A potter in the Long Park Pottery dipping vases to glaze them, *c.* 1900.

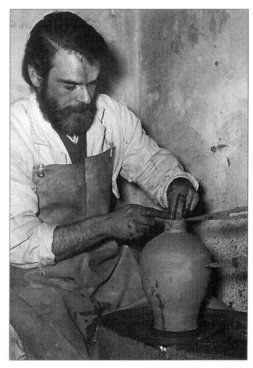

St Marychurch Fore Street Pottery came to
101 Fore Street in 1964, and used the traditional
methods and equipment of the Royal Watcombe
Pottery. It then employed a staff of nineteen to
produce giftware for the holiday trade. Here is
bearded Mr Cyril Wilson at the throwing wheel
in 1966.

In 1966, when this photograph was taken, the St Marychurch Pottery still had a staff of nineteen, including two part-time workers. Pictured here is one of the girls slip-dipping the ware into desired colours.

St Marychurch Pottery, 1966. When the ware comes off the throwing wheel and jolly machine, it is sponged and fettled to remove rough parts. The pieces are dipped in whichever colour is required. They are then ready for decoration, and in this picture the artists are at work.

Former Royal Watcombe worker, who had spent most of his life in the craft, was Arthur Cole, who is seen here placing the trays ready for decoration.

In 1966 the St Marychurch Potteries were busy producing traditional Devon designs, including Cottage Ware, and also the firm's own development – a line called Petit Tor Ware. Here we see kiln operator George Hall stacking a small kiln.

Terry Burke, the artist, settles
himself in the inner harbour at low
tide, May 1960.

Civil Defence personnel marching up Fore Street in the Mayoral Sunday parade at St Marychurch,
20 May 1963.

Kents Cavern, the excavation by members of the Natural History Society during the winter of 1938–9. Pictured here we see Miss E.A. Webb sitting between the Misses Dicks with the Revd Mr Shooter and Mr E.H. Rogers on the right.

The gambling craze reached Babbacombe in 1962 and pictured here in the lounge of the Academy Club we see the first session to be held under the new Gaming Law.

A few days before the drama and pageantry of Queen
Elizabeth's coronation on 2 June 1953, the whole country
was thrilled by the news that Edmund Hillary and Sherpa
Tensing had climbed Mount Everest. Torquay man M.H.
Westmacott was one of the British Commonwealth team
that took part in the ascent. At 11.30 a.m. on Friday 29 May
the summit of the world's highest mountain (29,002 ft) was
reached for the first time. These two photographs show Mr
Westmacott's reception at Torquay station, with his mother
and with a group of holiday-makers.

Celebration of the coronation of Queen Elizabeth II, 2 June 1953. The people of Torquay had joined whole-heartedly in the festivities of the day, and in each district of the borough committees were formed to collect funds for parties for the children and in some cases for the old people also. Each Upton Hill child received a coronation book as a memento of the occasion, and there were pirates at the Strand party held in the alpine playground. These colourful costumes were worn by Chairman Mr Bert Medway and other helpers. In this picture is the party held at Compton Place, St Marychurch, which was one of the thirty-seven street groups visited by the mayoral party on that day.

The Revd W. Kitson had assembled his family with staff to pose for this picture on the lawn of Shiphay House. It was 1865, and they sat for a minute or two in the sunshine to have this photograph taken, leaving behind a charming reminder of a day caught from time. It was taken on a summer day, and proves that our ancestors really did wear those incredibly hot clothes in warm weather. Revd W. Kitson is the patriarchal figure seated in the middle of the group with the stove-pipe hat.

The Randell family of St Marychurch, c. 1900. This is an excellent group photograph – well arranged with the family facing the camera in an alert and confident manner. Richard Randell, the family patriarch seated on the right, was the last man in Torbay to shoe oxen.

Miss Jessie Coombes, the chief donor of the Young Womens Christian Association, Torquay branch. She served as the Hon. Secretary until December 1901, six months before her death.

Philip Henry Gosse was a noted scientist who came to Torquay in search of health, and in 1857 settled in St Marychurch at a house called Sandhurst. His book *Land and Sea*, first published in 1864, shows how closely he studied the natural history of Torquay – bringing his powers of keen perception and exact investigation to bear on all natural objects.

John Lane, the son of a baker, was born in Abbey Road, Torquay in 1843. He left school at the age of eleven and was apprenticed to an attorney. He died in 1899 at the age of fifty-six, a chartered accountant and secretary to many of the projects that grew up in Torquay at that time of rapid expansion. John Lane left manuscript notes of his public, social and literary activities, and during his life amassed a great collection of engravings of Torquay.

Harry Green JP, CC, Mayor of Torquay, Recorder of Poole and a President of the Torquay Natural History Society. In 1928, as mayor, he opened the museum extension. This was his first connection with the Natural History Society, but from 1929 to 1931 he served on its committee. Green was appointed President in 1937 but died during his second year of office.

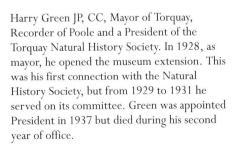

Torquay's first Girl Guide Company was formed on 9 June 1912. The founder of this company was its first Captain, Miss C.M.S. Bishop (centre). Back row, left to right: Lt. Miss Nissa Compton, Gwen Rawlings, Nora Brook, Lt. Miss Kathleen Allams. Centre row: -?-, Freda Barnett, Gladys Young, Kathleen Mohan, PL Ethel Vickery, Katie Smith, PL Annie Gove, Dorothy Westaway. Front row: PL Dorothy Milden, Miss Bishop, PL Ethel Barnett. Foreground: Ethel Williams and her sister.

The horse gave employment to a large number of people in the town, not only wheelwrights, blacksmiths, saddlers, stablemen and harness-makers, but also firms like the Torbay Mill Co. Ltd, who traded at 175 Union Street, supplying hay, corn and other requisites to the equine world.

Digging deep into the past below Union Street, December 1959. The men pictured here were 20 ft below Castle Circus, drilling and digging a tunnel to house a section of Torquay's main drainage scheme, when they found an old culvert. This culvert did not appear on the drainage charts of the Borough but an account written by Joseph Hall, who was a surveyor to the Local Board, suggested that it may have been part of a scheme devised in 1881–2 for carrying off storm water and so preventing the flooding of Union Street and Fleet Street. The stonework of the culvert was sound and obviously the work of an expert mason.

Sifam Electrical Instrument Co. Ltd, December 1960. This factory, in Woodland Road, was opened by Mr F.M. Bennett, MP for Torquay and Parliamentary Private Secretary to the President of the Board of Trade, on 9 December 1960. The aim was to provide employment all year and to expand the export trade without spoiling the amenities of the town.

During his time as Mayor, Ald. J.F. Haarer was called on to perform many civic duties in the borough. Here we see him undertaking what must have been one of the more unusual tasks during his mayoral term. It was 1960, and he was inspecting the progress of work under Union Street in the main drainage tunnel.

The Salvation Army, 7 April 1964. The twenty members of the band are seen here with new instruments, and their leader is being congratulated on their acquisition. This ceremony shows the change in public opinion since William Booth visited Torquay in 1882 to launch his mission and was met with public hostility. Four years after his visit the Salvationists were attacked by a mob as they marched, and thirty of them were prosecuted for preaching and playing musical instruments in the streets.

Rose Cottages, Parkhill Road, Upton – also called Penny's Cottages, c. 1950. Standing at his gate is Mr J. Hooke aged ninety-seven. Having a wonderful memory, he could recall the days of stage coaches, pack horses, smuggling and sailing ships, and was fond of telling people that 'the Doctor says I be like leather and leather be good stuff'.

TORQUAY
&
THE SEA

Meadfoot Road, 1907. It is interesting to note that ladies' bathing machines were still operating on the beach. These bathing machines had two compartments, one for disrobing and a wet section for putting on the costumes. The machine was wheeled down to the sea until the wheels were half submerged; the ladies then went down three steps to stand in the sea.

Babbacombe beach, *c.* 1890.

A wonderfully atmospheric photograph of Oddicombe beach by J. Blampey of Ashburton, 1891.

Oddicombe Beach, *c.* 1905. A day at the seaside has been a distinctive feature of English life since railways made journeys to the coast possible for the majority of people. The rapid development of Torbay resulted in beaches like Oddicombe becoming popular. In 1926 access to this delightful beach was made easier by the opening of the cliff railway, and since that date millions of people have travelled in this conveyance.

Torquay Harbour, 1895. Then, as today, the sight, the sound and the smell of the sea are everywhere in Torbay, and this delightful photograph pictures a typical nineteenth-century scene.

Centenary of Torbay Royal Regatta, 25–7 August 1913. Competing yachts included King George V's *Britannia* and the Emperor of Germany's *Meteor*. Owing to the war no regatta was held for the next six years.

Torquay Harbour, 22 July 1934. A schooner, the *Mary Miller* of Dublin, and a steamer are evidence of maritime activity here at a comparatively recent date.

Torquay inner harbour entrance, 27 June 1895.

Spectators who had gathered for the opening of Babbacombe Pier, 1889.

Opening of Babbacombe Pier, 1889. This pier was built by Leveson Vernon Harcourt for the benefit of the fishermen and boatmen of the beach. The Cary Arms pub sits on a ledge in the background.

Inner harbour, April 1959. From the harbour side Torquay spectators watch efforts to salvage the 70 ft motor-launch *Zephyrus* after she had been towed into the inner harbour. The launch sank in the outer harbour after water had entered through the exhaust ports. The boat, which was being fitted out for a trip to the Mediterranean, belonged to a Mr Richards, a Cheshire businessman. In charge of the lifting operation was Captain Jim Dale of the Torbay Marine Services Ltd.

The replica of Drake's ship, the *Golden Hind*, in the inner harbour, April 1962. It was built to appear in Westward Television's series 'Life of Drake'. The boys of the Brixham Seamen's Orphan home are drawn up on Haldon Pier to welcome it. Colin Smith, the Drum-Major, aged nine, is on the left.

Mending nets, Beacon Quay, 1960. This photograph shows fishermen against the background of the new harbour and the Haldon Pier.

The result of a storm in Torbay, December 1959. Seen here is a capsized barge off Daddy Hole Plain. She was one of three being towed by a Dutch tug when great waves broke the tow on the evening of 7 December and one of the two men aboard was lost. By the 8th the barge had capsized, and was kept afloat by trapped air. Later she was carried past Haldon Pier and drifted near Palm Court Hotel, where she was sunk by frogmen.

A picture taken for the *Torquay Times* in November 1959 shows the harbourside.

Princess Gardens and Vane Hill from the west, 1920. The Princess Gardens and Pavilion are on land reclaimed from the sea. The Princess Gardens were named after Princess Louise, who visited the town in 1890 to lay the foundation stone of the Princess Pier.

An aerial view of Torquay, 1965.

SPORTING EVENTS

Men's bathing place near Beacon Cove, 1960. Here we see the start of the long-distance swim from Torquay to Brixham and back.

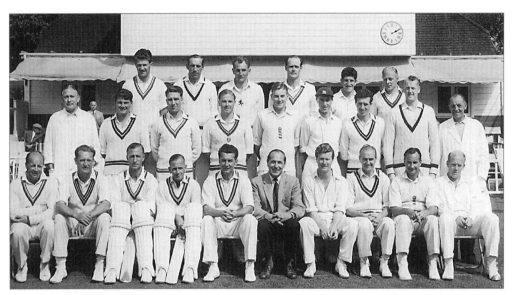

Torquay Cricket Festival, North versus South, 6, 8, 9 September 1958. Back row, left to right: I. Thompson (Sussex), L. Jackson (Derbys), D. Halfgard (Kent), B. Close (Yorks), K. Barrington (Surrey), G. Dews (Worcs). Second row: S. Buller (Umpire), M. Allen (Northants), B. Taylor (Essex), M. Horton (Worcs), R. Illingworth (Yorks), K. Andrews (Northants), F. Titmus (Middx), C. Gladwin (Derbys), F. Price (Umpire). Third row: R. Watkins (Glam), M. Tremlett (Som), J. Robertson (Middx), G. Emmett (Glos), R.T. Simpson (Notts), D. Haines (Hon. Sec.), C. Ingleby-McKenzie (Hants), D. Brookes (Northants), D. Kenyon (Worcs), T. Lock (Surrey).

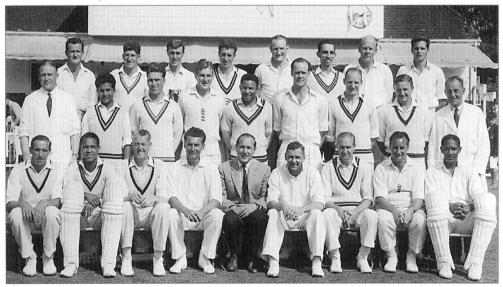

Torquay Cricket Festival, England XI versus Commonwealth XI, 10, 11, 12 September 1958. Back row, left to right: J. Manning (Aust.), K. Barrington (Surrey), K. Andrew (Northants), F. Titmus (Middx), F. Titmus (Middx), P. Wight (WI), T. Lock (Surrey), R. Willson (Torquay Pro.). Second row: S. Buller (Umpire), Hamil Mohammed (Pakistan), B. Taylor (Essex), R. Illingworth (Yorks), C. Smith (WI), B. Close (Yorks), L. Fuller (S. Africa), C. McCool (Aust.), ? Price (Umpire). Third row: L. Jackson (Derbys), G. Sobers (WI), C. Gladwin (Derby), R.T. Simpson (Notts), D. Haines (Hon. Sec.), V. Jackson (Aust.), D. Brookes (Northants), D. Kenyon (Worcs), F. Worrell (WI).

Walls Hill, Babbacombe, August 1965. Spectators gather to watch the regatta sports, which are taking place in the fine natural stadium.

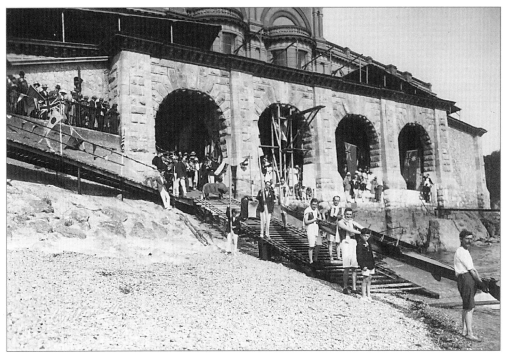

Torquay Rowing Club, 1923. The christening and launching of the new boat *Lady Betty*. In the background of the top picture are the arches under the Marine Spa. The bottom picture was taken after the launching from the short gangway. The crew were A. Martyn (Stroke), R.H. Reed (3), S. Bindon (2), N. Bindon (bow), W. Wicks Jnr (Coxswain). Dimly seen in the background are ships of the fleet.

Torquay Rowing Club, 1923. Members of the crew pose for this picture at the christening and launching of *Lady Betty* from the slipway below the Marine Spa.

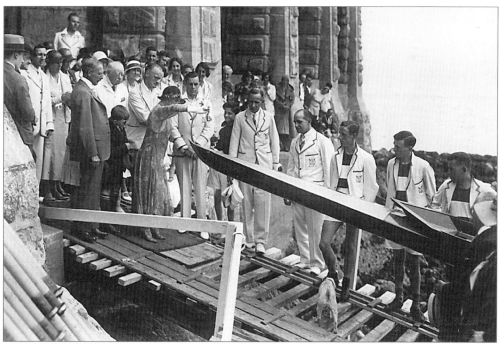

Torquay Rowing Club: the christening of the new boat *Ida* by Mrs Iredale, wife of Councillor Iredale, sometime Mayor of Torquay and President of the Club, 1935. She is shown pouring champagne from a silver cup over the bow of the boat, which was then launched.

Petitor racecourse and golf links, St Marychurch, July 1914. The first steeplechases were held in 1864 and, except for a temporary break after 1877 when the Petitor road was being developed for building, continued each year until Easter 1939. The Torquay and South Devon Golf Course opened on the racecourse in 1909. Note the square tower of St Mary's Church and the steeple of the Roman Catholic Church of Our Lady and St Denis.

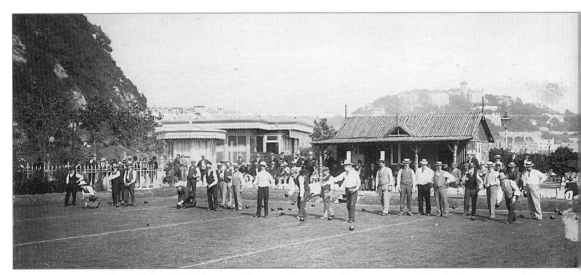

Torquay Bowling Club, 1913. The contribution of sport to Torquay is surprisingly important and its various branches have done much to encourage the growth of the town. The Torquay Bowling Club pictured here began in 1892, and played on the Recreation Ground until an elephant which had escaped from Wombwell's Menagerie completely wrecked the green. The Club was then transferred to the Princess Gardens in 1913.

Croquet tournament, 11 September 1901. The sunshine was truly golden during those Edwardian summers, with a lightness of heart for those who belonged to the upper middle class. The spectators seen here in all their splendour would have belonged to that privileged order. Croquet was entirely a middle and upper class game, only played in restricted circles. In Torquay the croquet ground adjoined the tennis courts in Belgrave Road and this tournament attracted a list of 100 entries. Three events were played in four courts and the referee was a Captain Dixon Green, seen here in the top picture wearing a white cap and standing on the left.

Torquay Rowing Club, crews and trophies, 1935. Below the trophies won at regattas during that season is the West of England Senior Championship Shield, which was regained for Torquay after a lapse of twenty-nine years. The pride of their achievement is reflected in the faces of the ladies' and men's teams, who are pictured here. Back row, left to right: H. Grant, C. Chamson, K. Lander, H. Ball, J. Altonson, L. Dyer, W. Pridham, ? Godfrey, ? Grant, B. Dewar. Second row: Mrs Stranger, ? Evans, ? Bindon, Miss Wipperman, Miss Oliver, R. Reed, C. Rowe, C. Newlyn, R. Pringle, J. Heale, W. Stranger. Front row: Mrs Cotton, Miss Monk, ? Whitwell, ? Peek, Col. Luxmore (President), G. Fleet (Coach), K. Ireland, G. Fleet, L. Pook, F. Clark. Sitting in front: M. Plowman and G. Luxton.

The junior crew in *Lady Betty*, Torquay Rowing Club, 1926. This photograph was taken at low tide, and the difference in levels between high and low water can be seen on the rock behind.

Torquay Rowing Club Ladies' Crew seen here after winning a race at Totnes Regatta, July 1932. The crew was trained by Mr W.R.H. Stranger, at whose insistence ladies were admitted to the Club. Left to right: Miss V. Kellow (Coxswain), Miss E. Knight (Stroke), Miss B. Knight) (3), Miss D. Hogarth (2) and Miss M. Williams (Bow).

Beacon Cove in the winter of 1958, showing six intrepid bathers on a Boxing Day swim, and the hundreds of onlookers who cheered them on from the beach and from the gallery above.

Torre Abbey Sands at high tide, showing the crowds of holiday-makers enjoying the sun, summer 1959.

HIGH DAYS
&
EVENTS

The start of the waiters' race at the Strand, Torquay Carnival, 1958. These waiters' races were always a big attraction during the Torquay Hotels week, when the catering industry staged a busy programme of events in the town. Note the Nottingham and Welsh jewellers displaying their well-known Rolex watches' sign.

Mayoral procession, Queen Victoria's diamond jubilee, 22 June 1897. The possibilities of a great celebration in 1897 were first discussed after the golden jubilee of Queen Victoria in 1887. Public interest was thoroughly aroused and events were organised throughout the country to celebrate the sixtieth year of her reign. These two photographs show the mayoral procession that day passing through Union Street. The weather during the week before the jubilee had been unsettled and stormy, and although the morning was dull and overcast on the great day, by mid-morning the sunshine burst through as if to give emphasis to the popular term 'Queen's Weather'. Note Benjamin Knight's pharmaceutical chemist's shop on the right at 67 Union Street.

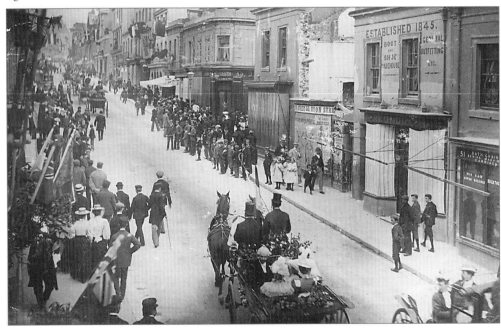

Celebration of the jubilee of Queen Victoria, 21 June 1887. After thanksgiving services in all the churches a royal salute was fired from the pier. The representatives of all the trades and public services paraded in order to testify to Torquay loyalty. This is the start of the long procession headed by the brass band of the firemen.

Events were organized throughout the country to celebrate the completion of the fiftieth year of Queen Victoria's reign. The weather throughout the summer months was of exceptional splendour. Pictured here are the Yeoman Cavalry in the jubilee procession, with the lifeboat in the background on a cart drawn by a horse.

The Royal Yacht *Victoria and Albert* arrived in Torbay on Tuesday 26 July 1910 with the King and Queen on board to inspect thirty-seven battleships and twenty-seven cruisers of the Fleet. When George V came to the throne the sovereignty of the British Fleet over the seas was far reaching and absolute, as shown in this review, when over 150 warships manned by 40,000 officers and men rode at ease in Torbay. The naval review attracted a large number of spectators, who no doubt looked with pride at these steel-clad champions of the nation's honour, aware that a great navy was then a paramount condition of national existence.

On 29 July 1910 their majesties landed at the Princess Pier where the Mayor, Brigadier General Spragge, escorted them to the pier pavilion, where a loyal address was presented.

The Duke of Connaught is seen here inspecting veterans on the pier, *c.* 1910. The ships of the Mediterranean and Home Fleet are seen in Tor Bay.

The coronation procession of the children consisted of 5,500 children with 500 teachers and helpers on 22 June 1911. The children from different schools are seen passing the Old Toll House in Torbay Road. George V was crowned king on this day, and with Queen Mary, quickly gained a firm hold on the people's hearts. Those who came into contact with them discovered that they had an unrivalled capacity for putting people at their ease, and their coronation was celebrated throughout the country.

Celebration for George V's coronation day, 21 June 1911. The sky was black indeed when King George V came to the throne. At home there was fierce conflict between the political parties, the question of Home Rule for Ireland and the veto of the House of Lords. In Europe there were signs of growing tension with the German powers, but despite all this the country celebrated the coronation in a grand style.

Over 5,000 children were entertained to tea on the Recreation Ground. The empty place on the left-hand end of the second row shows that long plank seats had been provided. Just for the record the feast consisted of 50 quartern loaves, 8,000 splits, 7,000 rock buns, 2,464 lbs of cake, 112 lbs of butter, 112 lbs of jam, 150 lbs of cream, 60 lbs of tea, 336 lbs of sugar and 60 gallons of milk: it must have been a Devon cream tea to beat all cream teas!

The coronation celebrations, 22 June 1911.
Every town and village in England had its own
celebration, its own procession, its own feast
for the poor, its sports and its firework display.
Here we see more of the 5,500 schoolchildren
in procession with teachers and helpers,
passing the old Toll House.

One of the entries in the Water Carnival is seen here in the inner harbour with Victoria Parade in the
background, c. 1910. The florist's shop belonged to Mr Burridge, who traded from 8 Victoria Parade.
Next door on the left, at no. 7, was the tobacconist's shop of James Douglas and Sons.

Sunday School Jubilee, Ellacombe, Torquay. One of the frustrating features of collecting old photographs for a book like this is the number one finds with no date and little description. Any information on this occasion, and the date, would be welcome.

The Strand, 1905. The occasion was the procession of schoolchildren on Empire Day. Five thousand children marched or were brought in coaches from every part of Torquay, and were afterwards entertained on the Recreation Ground. The clock tower was Torquay's memorial to Richard Mallock, the owner of Cockington, MP for Torquay Division from 1886 to 1895, and a great benefactor to the town. Note the three lamps, which were unfortunately not sufficient to illuminate the clock faces, as intended.

The Incorporation of the Borough, 1 September 1892. A royal charter was granted to the town on 15 August 1892 for the incorporation of the town as a municipal borough. The new corporation superseded the local board which had existed since 1850. The charter bearing the Queen's signature was brought to the town by special train and was accompanied by a procession to the Strand. Here it is being read to a large crowd from the balcony of the Queen's Hotel.

The first Mayor of Torquay was Councillor Splatt, who is seen here in the centre of this group planting a commemorative tree in the Rock Gardens, c. 1895.

The Western Hospital, October 1917. This hospital on the Warberries (now demolished) was one of those used for the nursing of wounded soldiers during the First World War. In addition some seven large private houses were opened as Red Cross hospitals. Most of the nursing was carried out by members of the VAD, who although entirely voluntary were much involved in the hard reality of wartime nursing. They were much loved by the convalescing soldiers who nicknamed these angels with red crosses on their uniforms 'Very Artful Darlings' or 'Victim Always Dies'.

The great victory march past held in London on 12 July 1919 formed part of the nation's peace celebrations; similar activities on a smaller scale were held in every town and village throughout the country. In Torquay there was a procession with wreaths to the temporary war memorial, and it is seen here on the Strand. The weather was so wet that other arrangements had to be altered. The permanent war memorial was unveiled by Col. Sir Charles R. Burn OBE, MP, for the Borough in Princess Gardens on St George's Day 1921.

On Walls Hill, Babbacombe, spring 1959. Pictured here are men surveying the rock overlooking Long Quarry Point from a height of 200 ft. In the foreground is the gash made by a natural landslip. The remaining rock was considered unsafe until blasting removed the surrounding portion, including the wall which had been a part of the artillery range. This had been erected in 1876.

Torquay Remembrance service at the Cenotaph, November 1964. The Mayor Alderman R.P. Williams steps down after laying a wreath in memory of the fallen in two World Wars.

The arrival at Torquay Pavilion of 200–300 wounded soldiers, 22 June 1915. They had come from Exeter in 100 motor cars to be entertained on behalf of the town by the Mayor and Mayoress, Mr and Mrs C.T. Towell. After entertainment in the Pavilion the men had tea in the café, and afterwards were taken in two batches for short steamer trips. There was a great deal of rushing forward on the part of the crowd to wish the boys good luck, and everybody felt like shaking them by the hand.

Pictured here is the arch erected in Victoria Parade on the occasion of the laying of the foundation stone of Princess Pier. The Princess Pier and groyne were erected by the Corporation at a cost exceeding £50,000. The foundation stone was laid by HRH Princess Louise on 6 May 1890 and the pier was opened by the Mayor, Alderman Dr Richardson, on 23 July 1895.

Torquay Boy Scouts on parade – Baden Powell Inspection, *c.* 1933. In August 1907 twenty boys led by two men pitched their tents on Brownsea Island in Dorset. The boys were gathered from all works of life and for two weeks they learned to live in the open and to cultivate comradeship. From this small beginning the Boy Scout movement was born and Baden Powell, their leader, was on his way to becoming a world figure.

Flooding in Torquay after the storm of 1938.

Empire Day at Torquay, 24 May 1905. Before the First World War this was a school holiday and an occasion of much rejoicing. Empire Day was held on Queen Victoria's birthday, 24 May, and originated in commemoration of the assistance given by the Colonies in the Boer War (1899–1902). The townspeople always assembled to celebrate Empire Day and flags were hung from first-floor windows along the streets. Here we see schoolchildren gathering on the Recreation Ground in Torquay to be entertained by the Mayor and Mayoress.

Colonel Burn MP, The Hon. Mrs Burn and Mr Aubrey Bateman in the procession outside the Grand Hotel after the Declaration of Poll, 13 December 1910.

This large crowd on the beach indicates some kind of event. Any information on the occasion would be welcome.

Laying of the foundation stone, St Martin's Church, Barton, *c.* 1938. The stone was laid by Miss Kekewich, who is seen here with the Rt Revd Charles Edward Curzon, Bishop of Exeter (1936–49). The church was consecrated in 1939 as a daughter church to St Marychurch. Barton was growing rapidly and became a separate parish in 1960. Miss Kekewich lived in Berrington Tromlands Road, and in her garden were preserved the remains of the old tower of St Marychurch.

William Froude plaque-unveiling ceremony, 20 September 1954. William Froude was born in 1810 at Dartington and lived at Chelston Cross from 1867 until his death in 1879. His outstanding contributions to the science of naval architecture brought him world-wide renown. He was the pioneer of ship model research and in 1872 built the first experimental tank in the world on the site of this plaque in Seaway Lane, Chelston. Seen on the left is Professor H.F. Nordstrom of Gothenburg; standing in front are three of Froude's descendants with the Mayor Cllr W.H. White; and in the background is Viscount Runciman, who unveiled the plaque.

Torquay's impressive £33,000 new Court House was opened on 11 April 1960. It was the result of four years' planning and over one year's building work. It was erected on a site which had served the Borough in various roles since 1871, first as a school and during the war years as the Civil Defence Headquarters. Seen here outside the Court, with Lord Morris in the centre, are the Mayor, Alderman J.F. Haarer, Deputy Mayor, Major H. Stanway, the Chaplain Canon Boers, Town Clerk Mr T.E. Williams, Mr T. Adams and Mr W. Bourne.

Torquay's new Court House opening ceremony, 11 April 1960. The Mayor hands Lord Morris, a Lord Advocate of Appeal, a copy of Anthony Eden's *Memoirs* to give to Lord Kilmuir, the Lord High Chancellor of Great Britain, for whom he had deputised. On the extreme left is Councillor K.R. Bryant, Chairman of the General Purposes Committee, and on the extreme right is Lord Roborough, the Lord Lieutenant of Devon.

Interior view of the headquarters of the 11th Barton Scout Group, 25 June 1960.

Platform party at the official opening of the 11th Barton Scout Group headquarters. Left to right: Councillor E.G. Milford (first patron of the project), R.W. Castle (District Commissioner), Mrs Milford and Mrs H. Ward (Chairman of the Parents and Supporters Association) J.F. Haarer JP, CC, (The Mayor and patron of the project), J.D. Bose (Group Chairman), Miss E.E. Steed (Lady Cubmaster), Brig. G.L. Appleton CB, OBE, JP, CC (County Commissioner), Mrs Haarer and Mrs Appleton.

Opening of the 11th Barton Scout Group headquarters, 25 June 1960.

The headquarters of the 11th Barton Scout Group was the outcome of two years' work by officials and boys of the Group with the support of the general public. The hut cost nearly £2,250 and is on Barton Down, with its entrance near Lummaton Cross.

Scouts line up for inspection at the opening ceremony of the 11th Barton Scout Group new headquarters, June 1960. Left to right: Chris Woodford, Peter Passmore, Geoffrey Porter, Derek Marden, Paul Bate, John Grills, Chris Davies, Colin Gay, P/L Michael Fleet, Jim Smith. The party of officials are, left to right; Group Scoutmaster Mr C.A. Harverson, the Mayor, Ald. J.F. Haarer, ASM Mr W. Schneider, the County Commissioner Brig. G.L. Appleton.

The Lady Cubmaster Miss E.E. Steed is seen here talking to the Mayor, Alderman J.F. Haarer, during his inspection of the Cubs at the opening ceremony of the Barton Scout Group new headquarters.

Peaceful and quiet, 30 May 1943 was a typical sleepy Sunday afternoon until twenty-one enemy aircraft sped in from the sea on a hit-and-run raid. Sweeping over Petitor, where golfers dropped behind the bunkers, one plane pressed home an attack on the parish church of St Marychurch, despite the fact that its tail had been nearly severed by gun fire. The plane crashed and the pilot was killed, but so were children attending a Rogation Sunday service in the church. The pictures here show the destruction of the church, and the rescue parties carefully digging over the piles of shattered masonry.

The rescue parties pictured here included airmen
stationed in Torbay, who worked throughout one
night to dig out the young bodies.

IN LOVING
AND ENDURING MEMORY
OF TWENTY-ONE CHILDREN
WHO LOST THEIR LIVES IN THE
PARISH CHURCH OF ST MARYCHURCH
IN THE AIR RAID OF
MAY 30, 1943.

BLESSED ARE THE PURE IN HEART
FOR THEY SHALL SEE GOD.
MATTHEW 5. 8,

GLADYS BEALE	12
PHOEBE LOUISA COOK	12
MARGARET COOKE	11
IRENE DAVIES	9
JOYCE SYLVIA GIFFORD	11
EILEEN FLORENCE HARE	10
JOAN MARGARET LOVEDAY	13
KATHLEEN McDONALD	11

FROM THE
ERSKINE HOME, BABBACOMBE,
WHO LIE HERE, AND –

| GERALD BABBAGE | 9 |
| PETER BARBER | 9 |

AUBREY HAROLD BROWN	13
EDWARD CHARLES W. BURN.	10
SYLVIA MARY DANIEL	9
KENNETH NORMAN HELLIER	12
DONALD THOMAS J. HEXT	10
GEORGE HORACE LAVERS	12
MARY LILIAN PERROTT	12
MICHAEL FRANK PERROTT	12
BETTY EDWINA REES	13
PAULINE CYNTHIA RYDER	12
VALERIE GRACE TAYLOR	14

WHO WERE
LAID TO REST ELSEWHERE.

This memorial was erected through the subscriptions raised by *Torquay Times* readers, and commemorated
the Erskine Home children killed in the St Marychurch air raid, May 1943. On the simple stone panels
are inscribed the names of the eight Erskine Home casualties and the thirteen other children who lost
their lives at the same time. Within a week of the Appeal £165 was received. Erection of the memorial
cost £132 and the balance was handed to the Mayor's St Marychurch restoration fund.

Laying the stones of the restored south aisle, St Mary's Church. This shows the three carved stones over the doorway. The nearest one is inscribed 30 May 1943, the date when the bombs razed the church, killing twenty-six children and teachers. The keystone which the Bishop of Exeter, the Rt Revd R.C. Mortimer, is laying is carved with the arms of the see. The further one reads '25 March 1952 Ald. E. Ely JP, Mayor of Torquay set this stone and began restoration'. On the left is seen the foreman of the builders, Mr Puddicombe.

St Mary's Church, 25 March 1952. Aldermen, councillors and others attended the service which marked the start of rebuilding the church.

Coronation Walk, Babbacombe. The ground lying to the north and west of Babbacombe Church was leased in 1952 to the Corporation for twenty-one years by the Church Council at a low rate. It was laid out as an extension to Cary Park and here on 19 November 1952 the Mayor of Torquay Alderman T.J. Reeves Taylor is seen planting one of an avenue of nearly forty flowering trees. Mr Ross Young, the Parks Superintendent, is seen helping the Mayor.

Although the Torbay road was widened at the end of the nineteenth century, by 1930 it was too narrow and had become dangerous for pedestrians. In 1933 the road was improved and a new promenade was constructed. In the picture we see the opening ceremony of the new road taking place opposite the Palm Court Hotel in about 1934.

Mayoral Sunday Parade in St Marychurch, 26 May 1963. The parade was led by the new Mayor, Cllr R.W. Kellow, the Town Clerk, the Deputy Mayor and the ex-Mayor. Carrying the standard for the Torbay Branch of the WRNS is Mrs J. Dobson.

Opening of the new First Aid Post, *c*. 1959. The building, erected by the Torquay Corporation, was in the Abbey Park Gardens near the sea-front. On the left of the door is Mr Goodrich (Mayor from 1958 to 1959), supported by Mr Knapman (Chairman of the Ambulance Association), Mrs Goodrich, Miss Collihole, Mrs Currie and Mrs Harvey. On the right of the door are Divisional Surgeon A.V. Currie and Supt. Diamond.

Kitson Park, Shiphay. Before 1964 this 2-acre park was a derelict orchard sloping down to a small stream. It was opened on 17 May 1966 and included a modern play area. Laid out at a cost of £4,000, it was named in memory of Major Robert Paul Kitson, whose family had been closely associated with the town over many years. Pictured here we see Major Kitson's widow unveiling a commemorative tablet at the opening ceremony.

Local children gather to read the inscription on the commemorative tablet after the opening ceremony of Kitson Park.

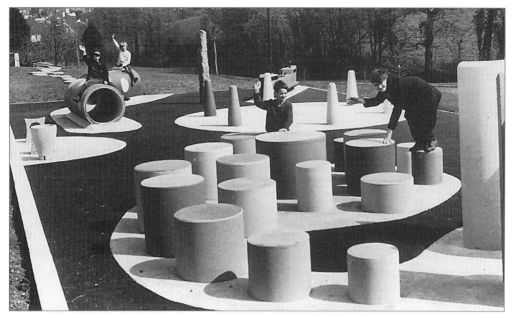

The modern play area in Kitson Park was bordered on two sides by a low retaining wall which had geometrical forms painted in pastel shades. The play area included stepping stones and lengths of sewer pipe to stimulate the imagination of younger children. Here children are playing in the park just after the opening in 1966.

The Torquay Open Air Theatre was established in 1950 and lasted until 1958; during this time it provided a season of four and a half weeks each year, usually in July and August. The Spanish Barn seen in the background was where performances were held in wet weather. It was originally the tithe barn of Torre Abbey, and became known as the Spanish Barn after it had been used to hold 400 captive prisoners from a galleon following the defeat of the Spanish Armada in 1588.

The tablet which records the opening of the Sherwell Valley housing estate, January 1953.

The Sherwell Valley housing estate was a part of the great building scheme carried out by the Town Council after the Second World War. Here we see the Mayor of Torquay, Alderman T.J. Reeves Taylor, unveiling the tablet which records the opening. On the extreme right can be seen Mr Rooke, who acted as secretary to many successive mayors.

Visit to Torquay to the anti-submarine Frigate HMS *Torquay*, 29 September 1965. Commander J.B. Rumble is standing beside the Mayor E.A. Elson outside the Town Hall. Drawn up in ranks are cadets from the frigate.

Pictured here in 1961 is a contingent from the frigate HMS *Torquay*, which had been adopted by the town a year before. Bad weather ruined HMS *Torquay*'s first official visit to the town; nearly all the official programme had to be cancelled, although this march up Union Street to the Town Hall did take place.

British Medical Association meeting, 20 June 1962. The Duke of Edinburgh steps out with Sir Arthur Thomson, acting President of the BMA, after their annual meeting at which the Duke had presided. The procession is crossing Lymington Road from the doorway of the Town Hall to the Scientific Exhibition, which was held in the Baptist School Hall opposite.

The Queen's visit to the Western Fleet: the departure of the royal family from Haldon Pier, Monday morning, 28 July 1969. Her Majesty is escorted by Lord Roborough, Lord Lieutenant of Devon, and followed by the Duke of Edinburgh in the uniform of Admiral of the Fleet. Behind their father are Prince Charles and Princess Anne. The Royal Barge will take them to *Britannia*.

Opening of Sherwell Valley County Infant School, 1960. The school was opened by Sir Ronald Gould, the General Secretary of the National Union of Teachers. Sir Ronald Gould is seen here wielding a spade when he planted a tree to commemorate the opening. Also in the picture is the Chairman of Devon Education Committee, Alderman B.G. Lampard-Vanchell and the Chairman of Devon County Council, Sir George Hayter-Hames.

Local division of the Torquay St John Ambulance Brigade marching to the Marine Spa after their annual service at Holy Trinity Church, 19 June 1966. The address that day had been given by the Very Revd Marcus Knight, who spoke of the completion of sixty years' service of the division.

The Declaration of the Poll, General
Election October, 1959. Seen here on the
balcony of the Town Hall are, left to right,
Mr W.V. Cooper (Labour), Mr F.M.
Bennett (Conservative) and Mr T. Kellock
(Liberal). The result was F.M. Bennett
(Con.) elected, 29, 527; W.V. Cooper
(Lab.), 11,784; T. Kellock (Lib.) 10,685;
a Conservative majority of 17,743.

Elizabeth II coronation decorations, 2 June
1953. The exterior stonework of the Town
Hall had been subjected to a very thorough
spring cleaning. The town council took on
the responsibility for decorating the public
buildings, and the Chamber of Trade and
Commerce for that of the main shopping
streets.

Babbacombe Model Village, 1964. The site of this tourist attraction was a grassy hillside lying to the north of Babbacombe Downs. The photographer is Gulliver among the Lilliputians during the second season of this model village.

The Princess Pier Concert Hall after preparations for a special event, 1910. It could have been part of the royal visit in July 1910, when King George V and Queen Mary came to review the Fleet. The Pier Concert Hall lasted until 17 April 1974, when it was destroyed by fire.

The South Devon Technical College was visited by the Duchess of Kent on 15 October 1958, when she opened the new hotel and catering department. The new building erected on the site of The Elms, Barton Road, is seen here being admired by staff members.

The restaurant in the hotel and catering department of the South Devon Technical College, *c.* 1958.

TRANSPORT

Messrs Grist's Dartmoor coaching excursion from Torquay, c. 1905. In these days of easy travel and communication it is difficult to envisage that except for the railway the horse was the main way to travel. The Grist family were much involved in this mode of transport. John Grist and his son were postmasters in Grafton Mews and William Grist and Sons were in Lisburne Square. Another Grist, John, was a fly proprietor with livery stables in Grafton Road, so this might have been his coach.

Electric tramways were constructed in 1906 connecting Babbacombe, St Marychurch, Tor and Torquay station, with an extension to Paignton being completed in 1910. Pictured here is the tramway under construction in Union Street with Upton Church and Brock's Corner in the background.

Laying tramlines at the clock tower in the Strand, 1906.

Laying tram lines in Union Street, c. 1905. At the time of these photographs the tramcar was in its heyday. Between 1900 and 1910 the country's tramway system had doubled in size and the new electric trams were firmly established on most city streets. In the long run the speed and flexibility of the motor bus would win, but in 1905 the tram was in the most vigorous phase of its brief existence.

Laying tram lines in higher Union Street, 1905–6.

The first electric tram in Devon had run in Plymouth in 1899. Exeter followed in 1905 and the only other Devon town to have a tramway system was Torquay. Pictured here in 1906 are the workmen laying tramlines along the Strand. The trams paid their way for some time but finally closed in 1934.

Until the electric tram appeared, the horse gave employment to a large number of people in the town. The horse-drawn coach is seen here outside the Royal Hotel in 1909, when the era when the horse was supreme was at an end. The electric trams drawn up beside the Mallock clock are ushering in the beginning of a new century of promise. At the time of this picture the proprietor of the Royal Hotel was John Vivian Thomas who still provided good post horses and lock-up coach rooms. Within a few years, though, the smell of his stables and harness would disappear from the Strand, to be replaced by mechanical vehicles and petrol fumes.

A delightful picture taken on Coronation Day showing the line of horse-drawn wagons carrying schoolchildren in the parade.

Laying track at Hollicombe Gasworks after the landslip of 3 February 1903. The line was opened in July 1859 and the top picture was taken near Hollicombe Gas Works, looking west, with the bottom one looking east. It was on 3 February 1903 that a Mr Bonning, a railway employee, noticed the subsidence; he ran through the Livermead tunnel and stopped the 10.49 p.m. train from Torquay in time. The photographs show navvies at work. The nineteenth century was the railway age and yet most people tend to forget that the railway was made by navvies not by machines. It is easy to ignore the vastness of the Victorian railway system and that almost all the lines were built with picks and shovels. Early photographs of navvies are rare, and these are of great historical interest.

The heart of the town, May 1965. Frantic efforts were being made to complete the traffic changes before the start of the summer season. Opposite the old Town Hall in Union Street premises have been demolished and the site levelled for the roundabout on the right. Down traffic uses Union Street (centre) and up traffic Abbey Road on the left. The one exception is shown by the bus, which is trying to keep to its new route up Pimlico.

Nearly the same view in 1907 but a different perspective, with an electric tram for Beacon Quay approaching and ordinary mortals daring to walk on the road.

Torre station with staff, 1866. The engine shown here was South Devon Railway 4–4–0 Tank Locomotive, no. 2127 'Zebra'. This photograph was taken during the year this engine was built. The man in the light suit was William Farrant, who was the GWR agent. The signal on the left was rotated by the handle at its base to show a rectangle for danger and a disc for all clear.

This extraordinary photographic image is of an event which occurred on the Torquay railway at Hollacombe, 21 September 1866. The 9.53 a.m. up train from Dartmouth ran off the line and did much damage at the siding near the gas works. Workmen had been laying a switch and it was not completed when the train came up. Note that this was still a broad gauge railway, with 7 ft gauge.

Claude Grahame-White's bi-plane at Torquay, 27 July 1910. The previous day King George V and Queen Mary had arrived in the Royal Yacht to inspect the fleet, and the following day Grahame-White had flown over the fleet during this inspection. It was reported that this was the first time that their Majesties had seen an aeroplane in flight. Although primitive the Farman bi-plane was a fine machine, and with its rotary Gnome engine was stable and reliable.

The Strand, 1900. This photograph shows the lamppost erected to commemorate Queen Victoria's 1887 jubilee. In 1902 it was removed to make way for the Mallock Clock and was re-sited at the junction of East Street and South Street. It was originally lit by gas, and later altered to take electricity.

Traffic in Union Street, August 1965. The 1960s saw an increasing number of complaints about the effect of cars. Motorists and non-motorists alike complained about the clogging of the town centre by motor traffic. It was about this time that new regulations came into force making this a one-way street to down traffic only. The dreaded yellow 'no parking' lines also made their appearance, with most local authorities using gallons of warning paint on kerbs.

Torbay Road, November 1959. Note the Volkswagen Beetle followed by a Ford car, with a Mini in the rear. The Mini had only just burst on to the motoring scene. First named the Austin Seven, it quickly became the Mini Minor, the latter title finally capturing the public imagination. It was priced originally at £466 19s 2d and was an unprecedented success.

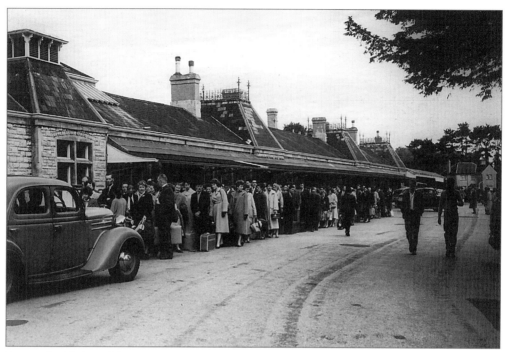

During the 1950s 6,000 to 7,000 visitors a week would arrive at Torquay station during the summer season. Here we can see some of them queueing outside the station during the summer of 1959.

Days when pedal power ruled in the social life of Torbay are recalled by this photograph, taken just after the First World War. Cycling was then a pastime for all classes. Note the variety of headgear worn by the riders.

The south line between Exeter and Newton Abbot was opened on 31 December 1846 and passengers between that town and Torquay were conveyed by coach. Within two years the line to Torre was open for traffic and the opening ceremony, which took place in December 1848, was observed as a holiday. As usual the poor were feasted, the inhabitants dined together and marched in procession to the railway station, flags were waved and a good time was had by all. The romance of steam disappeared in the 1950s and here you can see the first diesel engine on the Torbay Express in 1959.

DEDICATION TO THE MISSES HAMBLIN

This book is dedicated to the Misses Eleanor and Edith Hamblin. It was on 9 April 1953 that they were asked to accept the positions of Chairman and Hon. Secretary of the Pictorial Records, Torquay Natural History Society, in accordance with the decision of the then Executive Committee. They accepted these positions, Miss Edith Hamblin becoming the Chairman. For the following twenty-one years, until their resignation in September 1974, they devoted a great deal of their time to building up this collection of pictorial records. The pictures used in this book bear witness to their painstaking dedication. All the photographs in the collection were remounted and furnished by them with a hand-printed descriptive note, and as far as possible each picture had been dated.

ACKNOWLEDGEMENTS

The photographs in this book all come from the wonderful collection in the picture record department of the Torquay Natural History Society Museum.

I am indebted to Dr Michael Bishop, the curator, for allowing these pictures to be used and for the kindness and help shown to me by his staff, which made the task of putting together this book a pleasure.

Thanks must also go to John Pike, Edna Everitt and Roy Chapple for much appreciated help.

I am grateful to my wife Carol for her help and encouragement and to Simon Fletcher at Sutton Publishing for his assistance. The accuracy of the facts presented in this book has been checked as carefully as possible. However, original sources do contain errors and memories fade over the years. The dates presented are correct in my opinion and when accompanied by a 'circa' may be about ten years out.

These old photographs are truly fascinating. They bring back so vividly times past and how it was to live in them; this quality will never die, as long as these precious pictures continue to be preserved and looked after.

BRITAIN IN OLD PHOTOGRAPHS

Lincoln
Lincoln Cathedral
The Lincolnshire Coast
Liverpool
Around Llandudno
Around Lochaber
Theatrical London
Around Louth
The Lower Fal Estuary
Lowestoft
Luton
Lympne Airfield
Lytham St Annes
Maidenhead
Around Maidenhead
Around Malvern
Manchester
Manchester Road & Rail
Mansfield
Marlborough: A Second Selection
Marylebone & Paddington
Around Matlock
Melton Mowbray
Around Melksham
The Mendips
Merton & Morden
Middlesbrough
Midsomer Norton & Radstock
Around Mildenhall
Milton Keynes
Minehead
Monmouth & the River Wye
The Nadder Valley
Newark
Around Newark
Newbury
Newport, Isle of Wight
The Norfolk Broads
Norfolk at War
North Fylde
North Lambeth
North Walsham & District
Northallerton
Northampton
Around Norwich
Nottingham 1944–74
The Changing Face of Nottingham
Victorian Nottingham
Nottingham Yesterday & Today
Nuneaton
Around Oakham
Ormskirk & District
Otley & District
Oxford: The University
Oxford Yesterday & Today
Oxfordshire Railways: A Second
   Selection
Oxfordshire at School
Around Padstow
Pattingham & Wombourne

Penrith
Penzance & Newlyn
Around Pershore
Around Plymouth
Poole
Portsmouth
Poulton-le-Fylde
Preston
Prestwich
Pudsey
Radcliffe
RAF Chivenor
RAF Cosford
RAF Hawkinge
RAF Manston
RAF Manston: A Second Selection
RAF St Mawgan
RAF Tangmere
Ramsgate & Thanet Life
Reading
Reading: A Second Selection
Redditch & the Needle District
Redditch: A Second Selection
Richmond, Surrey
Rickmansworth
Around Ripley
The River Soar
Romney Marsh
Romney Marsh: A Second
   Selection
Rossendale
Around Rotherham
Rugby
Around Rugeley
Ruislip
Around Ryde
St Albans
St Andrews
Salford
Salisbury
Salisbury: A Second Selection
Salisbury: A Third Selection
Around Salisbury
Sandhurst & Crowthorne
Sandown & Shanklin
Sandwich
Scarborough
Scunthorpe
Seaton, Lyme Regis & Axminster
Around Seaton & Sidmouth
Sedgley & District
The Severn Vale
Sherwood Forest
Shrewsbury
Shrewsbury: A Second Selection
Shropshire Railways
Skegness
Around Skegness
Skipton & the Dales
Around Slough

Smethwick
Somerton & Langport
Southampton
Southend-on-Sea
Southport
Southwark
Southwell
Southwold to Aldeburgh
Stafford
Around Stafford
Staffordshire Railways
Around Staveley
Stepney
Stevenage
The History of Stilton Cheese
Stoke-on-Trent
Stoke Newington
Stonehouse to Painswick
Around Stony Stratford
Around Stony Stratford: A Second
   Selection
Stowmarket
Streatham
Stroud & the Five Valleys
Stroud & the Five Valleys: A
   Second Selection
Stroud's Golden Valley
The Stroudwater and Thames &
   Severn Canals
The Stroudwater and Thames &
   Severn Canals: A Second
   Selection
Suffolk at Work
Suffolk at Work: A Second
   Selection
The Heart of Suffolk
Sunderland
Sutton
Swansea
Swindon: A Third Selection
Swindon: A Fifth Selection
Around Tamworth
Taunton
Around Taunton
Teesdale
Teesdale: A Second Selection
Tenbury Wells
Around Tettenhall & Codshall
Tewkesbury & the Vale of
   Gloucester
Thame to Watlington
Around Thatcham
Around Thirsk
Thornbury to Berkeley
Tipton
Around Tonbridge
Trowbridge
Around Truro
TT Races
Tunbridge Wells

Tunbridge Wells: A Second
   Selection
Twickenham
Uley, Dursley & Cam
The Upper Fal
The Upper Tywi Valley
Uxbridge, Hillingdon & Cowley
The Vale of Belvoir
The Vale of Conway
Ventnor
Wakefield
Wallingford
Walsall
Waltham Abbey
Wandsworth at War
Wantage, Faringdon & the Vale
   Villages
Around Warwick
Weardale
Weardale: A Second Selection
Wednesbury
Wells
Welshpool
West Bromwich
West Wight
Weston-super-Mare
Around Weston-super-Mare
Weymouth & Portland
Around Wheatley
Around Whetstone
Whitchurch to Market Drayton
Around Whitstable
Wigton & the Solway Plain
Willesden
Around Wilton
Wimbledon
Around Windsor
Wingham, Addisham &
   Littlebourne
Wisbech
Witham & District
Witney
Around Witney
The Witney District
Wokingham
Around Woodbridge
Around Woodstock
Woolwich
Woolwich Royal Arsenal
Around Wootton Bassett,
   Cricklade & Purton
Worcester
Worcester in a Day
Around Worcester
Worcestershire at Work
Around Worthing
Wotton-under-Edge to Chipping
   Sodbury
Wymondham & Attleborough
The Yorkshire Wolds

To order any of these titles please telephone our distributor, Littlehampton Book Services on 01903 721596
For a catalogue of these and our other titles please ring Regina Schinner on 01453 731114

Land

BASQUE
COUNTRY
of Spain and France

a countryside guide
Fourth edition

Philip Cooper

SUNFLOWER BOOKS

Fourth edition
Copyright © 2023
Sunflower Books™
P O Box 36160
London SW7 3WS, UK

All rights reserved.
No part of this publication
may be reproduced, stored
in a retrieval system, or
transmitted by any form
or by any means, electronic,
mechanical, photocopying,
recording or otherwise,
without the prior written
permission of the publishers.

Sunflower Books and
'Landscapes' are
Registered Trademarks.

ISBN 978-1-85691-536-6

Donostia — Peine de los Vientos

Important note to the reader

We have tried to ensure that the descriptions and maps in this book are error-free at press date. The book will be updated, where necessary, in future editions. It will be very helpful for us to receive your comments (sent in care of the info@sunflowerbooks.co.uk, please) for the updating of future printings.

We also rely on those who use this book — especially walkers — to take along a good supply of common sense when they explore. Conditions can change fairly rapidly in the Basque Country, and *storm damage or bulldozing may make a route unsafe at any time*. If the route is not as we outline it here, and your way ahead is not secure, return to the point of departure. *Never attempt to complete a tour or walk under hazardous conditions!* Please read carefully the notes on pages 52 to 61, as well as the introductory comments at the beginning of each tour and walk (regarding road conditions, equipment, grade, distances and time, etc). Explore *safely*, while at the same time respecting the beauty of the countryside.

Cover photograph: St Jean-Pied-de-Port/Donibane Garazi
Title page: Laguardia (Car tour 5)

Photographs: pages 7 and 24 : istock-photo; page 23, 60-61 and cover: Shutter-stock; all other photographs by Philip Cooper and Nini Olaizola
Maps: Sunflower Books, based on maps from various sources: see page 52.
A CIP catalogue record for this book is available from the British Library.
Printed and bound in England by Short Run Press, Exeter

☀ Contents

3

❀ Preface

The Basque Country — Euskal Herria or Euskadi — can be defined in several ways. This book covers seven provinces forming a fairly homogeneous region in terms of language, culture and traditions. The Basque language — Euskera — is spoken to a greater or lesser extent in all these provinces, and is now widespread on road signs and maps, etc. For this reason Euskera names have been used in this book, together with their hitherto more common Spanish or French names as appropriate.

In Spain, the Basque Autonomous Community — la Comunidad Autónoma Vasca or C.A.V. for short — comprises the three provinces of Gipuzkoa (Guipúzcoa), Bizkaia (Vizcaya) and Araba (Alava). A fourth province, Nafarroa (Navarra) has separate autonomous status. The other three provinces, on the French side — Lapurdi (Labourd), Behe Nafarroa (Basse Navarre) and Xiberoa (Soule) collectively make up Iparralde ('the north side'). They do not have separate *département* status, since they form part of the Département des Pyrenées-Atlantiques, but nonetheless they share a common language, culture and tradition with the four provinces on the Spanish side. The total population of the seven provinces is around three million, about 260,000 of whom live in Iparralde.

Collectively the region presents a varied palette of landscapes and architectural styles, and this guide offers the chance to get to know some of the most beautiful corners of each province — areas which are only now starting to be discovered by non-locals as unspoilt travel destinations. The entire Basque coast from Biarritz to beyond Bilbao is mostly very rugged, with many thriving fishing towns and villages, plus the added attraction of some beautiful beach resorts, among which the most renowned is Donostia-San Sebastián, an excellent base for touring the region. All of Gipuzkoa and Bizkaia and northern Nafarroa, from the Baztán Valley eastwards towards the Pyrenees, are mountainous and have lush green countryside, in stark contrast to the drier plains of southern Nafarroa and Araba around and to the south of the provincial capitals of Iruña-Pamplona and Vitoria-Gasteiz respectively; these areas have more in common with parts of neighbouring Castile to the south, both geographically and to a certain extent culturally too. The main pilgrims' route to Santiago passes through here by way of an added attraction. The French side is characterized by unspoilt picture-postcard inland villages and the more abrupt, dramatic mountain scenery of the north side of the Pyrenees, most spectacularly so in the canyon area of Xiberoa.

Historically, the origins of the Basque race and language continue to be open to debate. Archaeological finds — above all skull fragments of late Cro-Magnon man, and the similarity to present-day skull shape — lend weight to the theory that the region may have been continuously inhabited since Palaeolithic times, pre-dating the Indo-European invasions. Another attraction on walks in the region is the huge number of bronze and iron age burial sites in the form of dolmens and cromlechs.

It is said that the Basque Country was one of the last places to become urbanized in Europe, and the traditional Basque farmhouse or *caserío* (*baserri* in Euskera) remains an important focal point of Basque rural life today. One of the classic images one sees when touring through the region is the pastoral green valley with half-timbered or sturdy stone *baserri* dotted over the limestone rock hillsides. The very strong family unit, based on a traditional matriarchal society, would be centred on these places, and at times in the past, most notably during the Franco era, when Euskera was banned, use of the language was mainly confined to them. Verse-improvisation in Euskera as practised by *bertsolariak* originally developed in *baserri* and would play a key role in the language's survival and evolution.

This guide, while by no means being exhaustive, provides a series of car tours which in general follow minor scenic roads, off the beaten track wherever possible, to include many of the region's finest landscapes. There are 32 walks which include ascents of some of the best known peaks such as Mounts Txindoki, Anboto and Aitzkorri. These do not always follow the classic route, but rather one which is perhaps more beautiful and varied. Other walks include some of the best stretches of the Basque coast of Gipuzkoa, Bizkaia and Lapurdi, and some of the region's most beautiful forested areas, together with rivers, caves and canyons. There are also 19 relatively short walks for motorists which may be combined with the different car tours and are of a maximum of around 2 hours' duration.

The Basques are keen walkers themselves, and some of the better known routes can be well trodden at weekends, although all provide wonderful opportunities to get to know this beautiful and as yet relatively unspoilt region.

— PHILIP COOPER

Acknowledgements

First and foremost I am indebted to my partner Nini Olaizola, who has provided me with the emotional support and encouragement to complete this project, accompanied me on most of the walks, taken many of the photographs and helped out enormously with the maps.

I would then like to thank the people from the relevant tourist offices throughout the region who gave me many ideas and suggestions.

A special thanks also to Iñaki Garmendia Barrena from the Departamento de Ordenación del Territorio Vasco y Medio Ambiente of the Basque Government in Vitoria-Gasteiz, Mark Wilson for providing good company on some of these and many other walks in the Basque Country over the years, and my daughter Sara for giving me constant inspiration in everything I do.

Rock strata west of Zumaia (Car tour 1)

Useful books

This book focuses on an exploration of the countryside in the Basque region, and is intended to be used in conjunction with a general guide such as the Rough Guides to the Pyrenees, Spain or France. For general background reading, the following are recommended:

Kurlansky, Mark (2000); *The Basque History of the World* (Vintage): an extremely informative book on all things Basque; very good background reading

Hooper, John (2006); *The New Spaniards* (Penguin Books Ltd.); contains an interesting section about Basques and the Basque Country

Crane, Nicholas (1997); *Clear Waters Rising* (Penguin Books Ltd.); a walk across Europe from Cape Finisterre to Istanbul, passing through the Basque Country

Woodworth, Paddy (2007); *The Basque Country: A Cultural History* (Signal); an informative read that offers a lot of interesting background information

Atxaga, Bernardo (1993); *Obakakoak* (Pantheon); the best-known novel by the Basque Country's best-known author, relates the mysterious goings-on among inhabitants of the fictional village of Obaba

Atxaga, Bernardo (2008); *The Accordionist's Son* (Vintage); a later novel by the same author following the life of an inhabitant of Obaba who goes to live in California

Hemingway, Ernest (1926); *Fiesta: The Sun also Rises;* Hemingway's classic novel that did much to popularize the running of the bulls during the St Fermin festivities in Pamplona

The Center for Basque Studies at the University of Nevada, Reno, USA (http://basque.unr.edu), publishes a wide range of books in English on different subjects relating to Basques and the Basque Country.

Finally, if you will be spending most of your time in the Pyrenees and travelling outside the Basque Country, another guide from the same series may be of interest:

Jenner, Paul, and Christine Smith (2016); *Landscapes of the Pyrenees* (Sunflower Books), which covers the entire range.

Short walks and picnic suggestions

Within the eight car tours described, there are 19 **short walks** of maximum 2h15min duration which are relatively easy, involving minimal climbing. These have been selected to provide a cross-section of different landscapes and are ideal for motorists who wish to explore some beautiful corners of the region without requiring any hiking experience. (Among the longer main walks described, there are also shorter options which follow part of the longer route; details are given in the introduction to each walk.)

Some of the short walks described in the car tours include well-known beauty spots and so may be quite busy in high season; others, for instance those visiting picnic sites, are simply some of my favourite spots — convenient stopping-off points on car tours, where it is worthwhile parking the car and setting off on foot.

There are unlimited options for **picnicking** throughout the Basque Country. The area is largely mountainous and forested, and many areas have been set aside for such a purpose. These may sometimes consist of just a couple of wooden benches beside a river, while others may have barbecue facilities and flush toilets.

I have called attention to some of my favourite picnic spots; these are mentioned in the introduction to each tour. There are also picnic spots along many of the main walks, and these are highlighted on the walking maps by the symbol (*P*) printed in green. Otherwise, to find picnic sites in general, look for signs indicating *merendero*, *pique-nique* or *atsedenlekua*.

When stocking up on supplies for picnics and walks, note that even small villages in the Spanish Basque Country usually have a bar where you can ask for substantial *bocadillos/bokatas* — ideal walkers' fare. Among the most common fillings for these sandwiches are different *tortillas* (omelettes), cheese, ham and chorizo. The Basque Country in general is renowned for its cuisine, and Basques take their eating very seriously indeed. The *sociedades gastronómicas* (gastronomic societies) constitute an important part of social life in the Spanish Basque provinces, where friends and family get together to prepare classic dishes to perfection, and the *tapas* tradition (always referred to as *pintxos* in the Basque Country) is one to be savoured, with the

8

best variety being available in coastal towns. Traditional markets are also excellent sources of fresh produce on both sides of the border. Another option is to look out for signs showing *baserriko produktoak* — farmhouse products — obtainable directly from farms along the way. In the French Basque Country, the best bet is to stock up on supplies either from supermarkets or village bakeries and small food shops, although many farms also sell their produce direct to the public. Look out in particular for signs indicating *ardi gasna* (sheep's cheese) throughout inland Iparralde.

Start of Walk 8 outside Etxalar

Touring

The Basque Country is an excellent centre for touring, as the landscapes are very varied and the distances relatively short. Roads are in the main in good condition, although often winding and narrow with much of the terrain being so mountainous.

The eight car tours described, while not covering every corner of the region, have been selected to offer a decent cross-section of different landscapes, as well as architectural and historical highlights, enabling the visitor to explore some of the most beautiful coastal and inland areas. All car tours give details of picnic sites, and also link up conveniently with the short walks for motorists and the longer walking routes.

The tours avoid main roads wherever possible, although some short stretches may be covered by dual carriageway or motorway if the alternative would entail driving through the centre of busy, congested towns. By and large, however, the tours follow the most scenic routes, at times quite off the beaten track. In fact, once away from the more popular coastal resorts, most of the Basque Country is waiting to be discovered!

Six of the car tours are circuits starting and finishing in the main provincial capitals of the region. Tours 1 and 2 start from Donostia-San Sebastián, justifiably the Spanish Basque Country's prime tourist destination with its fabulous beaches and very much the epicentre of all things Basque, culturally-speaking. Tour 3 is based around Bilbao, the region's largest and most dynamic city and former industrial giant which has been put on the map in recent years in particular by the Guggenheim Museum.

Tour 6 starts and finishes in Iruña-Pamplona, renowned for its *encierro* — the running of the bulls — during the fiestas of *San Fermines*. The city is steeped in history and is the capital of the immensely varied province of Nafarroa, the largest of the seven provinces covered in this book.

Tours 7 (from Bayonne/Baiona) and 8 (from St Jean-Pied-de-Port/Donibane Garazi) include many of the most beautiful corners of Iparralde, the French Basque Country. The French Basque coast makes another fine touring centre, with the famed resorts of Biarritz and St Jean-de-Luz/ Donibane Lohizun being ideal bases from which to explore both the coast itself and the unspoilt hinterland of the Pyrenean foothills and higher peaks of the canyon country of Xiberoa.

Tours 4 and 5 are somewhat different in that they have been designed as one-way routes between major centres, to enable the visitor to cover a larger area and link up with the other car tours. These tours converge in Vitoria-Gasteiz, the elegant yet relatively off-the-beaten-track administrative capital of the *Comunidad Autónoma Vasca* and the city in Spain with the most green spaces per inhabitant. Tour 4 follows some of the least-known yet most picturesque corners of southern Bizkaia and Western Araba, using Bilbao as a starting point. Tour 5 covers the Rioja Alavesa wine-growing country and the sierras of Toloño-Cantabria, Kodes, Urbasa and Aralar, terminating in Iruña-Pamplona.

Needless to say, all eight tours, although designed to be completed in the time estimated, can easily be extended over several days, especially taking into account the wide range of accommodation options available in even the most rural of areas. Note that driving times given do not make allowances for more than the briefest of stops!

Lack of space makes it impossible to include town/city plans, but precise directions are in any case given for leaving towns and cities.

The large touring map is designed to be held out opposite the touring notes and contains all the information you need to follow the tours suggested. **Symbols** for various amenities are printed in the text but only shown on the map for the more remote locations; any reasonably-sized town will have petrol, restaurants, and accommodation, etc.

Should you wish to buy **more detailed maps**, there are a couple of very useful ones covering the whole region. Two maps which cover all areas included in this book are the Firestone R-2 1:200 000 map of *Navarra, País Vasco and Rioja*, especially useful if travelling to neighbouring regions and on sale in local petrol stations, and the 1:250 000 *mapa turístico de Euskal Herria* which is available from bookshops and kiosks throughout the region. Also worth considering is the 1:200 000 Firestone T-33 map of the Pyrenees, incorporating Car tours 2, 6, 7 and 8.

Regarding **weather conditions**: the Pyrenean sections of Car tours 6 and 8 in Nafarroa and Xiberoa and, to a lesser extent, the routes through the sierras visited on Car tours 4 and 5 may well be snow-covered in mid-winter, meaning that some of the more minor roads might be temporarily closed until the snow plough can get through. In all other cases, roads would normally be open all year round.

Car tour 1: THE VERDANT VALLEYS, MOUNTAINS AND WILD COASTAL SCENERY OF GIPUZKOA

Donostia-San Sebastián • Tolosa • Larraitz • Ordizia • Errezil • Azpeitia • Loiola • Azkoitia • Madariaga • Lastur valley • Zumaia • Getaria • Zarautz • Orio • Donostia-San Sebastián

159km/98mi; about 4h driving time
En route: Short walks for motorists 1 and 2; Walks 1, 2, 3, 4 and 5
Picnic suggestions: in Donostia-San Sebastián itself, either near the top of **Mt Urgull** or on **Santa Clara**

island (0km), **Larraitz** (40km); **Beunde** near the start of Walk 5 to Aitzkorri (a 21km detour from Ordizia at the 49km-point); **Aittola** (101km); **Ratón de San Antón**, Getaria (131km)

This tour covers much of the best mountain and coastal scenery of Gipuzkoa. The province is extremely green and mountainous, and some of the classic hill walks in the region are on or near our route. The beautiful, tranquil valleys of Errezil and Lastur provide a marked contrast to the rugged coastline with its colourful fishing villages.

Donostia-San Sebastián★ (❋✝▲▲ ✕🐾🏛M) is an attractive seaside resort with a colourful harbour and a lively old town filled with bars offering the most succulent *pintxos*. Other focal points are the San Telmo Museum, the Aquarium and **Mt Urgull** (🏛P) and its fortifications. Many paths lead up this hill, from where there are great views over the city and out to sea; an excellent picnic spot is just below the Christ statue at the top. The city also boasts three good beaches. The main one — the perfect horseshoe bay of **La Concha** — looks out to **Santa Clara Island** (🏛P), another great place to picnic and spend the day in summer. Walk 1, to the Faro de la Plata (light-house), starts from Kursaal bridge.

From the Pio XII roundabout, follow motorway signs for VITORIA-GASTEIZ, heading down the fairly industrial **Oria Valley** via **Andoain**★ and **Tolosa** (23km ▲▲ ✕🐾), famous for its riotous week-long carnival held around the end of February each year. Soon after Tolosa, at JUNCTION 431, turn off the dual carriageway to **Alegia** (28km ✕🐾). Follow signs into the village and when you reach a small car park

beside the railway station, take an unmarked street to the left, down through the village proper and across the river bridge.

Immediately after the bridge, turn right along the river and up the hill on the GI3670, signposted towards ABALTZISKETA. This fairly narrow road climbs up through the forest until it reaches the ridge-top (35km) from where the spectacular views begin. Directly in front of you is the abrupt north face of the **Sierra de Aralar** and far below to the right the Oria Valley with the mountains of central Gipuzkoa beyond. Along the route there are numerous *baserri* and, on the ridge itself, a couple of wonderfully located hilltop villages. The main one is **Abaltzisketa** (39km ✝▲▲ 🏛), where the Church of John the Baptist contains one of the most interesting Romanesque-Gothic porticos in the province. From here on, the impressive 'Matterhorn' of **Mt Txindoki** looms directly ahead, at the far end of the Sierra de Aralar (photograph page 56). The sierra ends at **Larraitz** (40km ❋▲▲ ✕🏛🏛P), just a couple of houses and rustic bars, with a nice, shady picnic site. This is the

At the Txindoki summit (Walk 4)

starting point for Walk 4 to Txindoki.

Follow the winding road down through **Zaldibia** (46km 🏠 ✕), with great views of the south face of Txindoki to the left and its smaller neighbouring mountain, **Gaztelu**, slightly further to the right. On reaching the main road at the first roundabout in **Ordizia** (49km ✕ 🛒) — where the traditional Wednesday morning farmers' market in the main square is the best in the province — turn right towards *DONOSTIA-SAN SEBASTIÁN*, rejoining the N1 after 500m. (Or, to get to the start of Walk 5, turn *left* (south) on the N1 towards *VITORIA-GASTEIZ;* see access notes on page 72.)

The main tour now loops back past **Alegia** to the next junction, *JUNCTION 433* (61km), and onto the GI2634 towards *AZPEITIA*. Turn sharp left almost immediately on a narrow road beside the river, and turn right after 2km for **Albistur** (🏠 ✕), where there are a couple of small bars/restaurants renowned for their high quality red Tolosa beans, served with cabbage and chorizo — hearty walkers' fare. As the road climbs, the views of this valley become increasingly impressive, flanked by the limestone form of **Mt Ernio** to the right.

Continue over the **Bidania Pass** (510m) and through the village of **Bidegoian** (🏠), the highest in Gipuzkoa. At the main fork in the village (70km), veer right towards *ERREZIL* and *AZPEITIA*. Just after the **Iturburu Pass** (550m) the road passes under a bridge, and before us is the **Balcón de Gipuzkoa** (📷), high above the lush green **Errezil Valley** (✻). This is a classic Basque landscape — with sheep grazing on the hillsides, scattered *baserri* and the beautiful village of Errezil below.

Descend to **Errezil** (75km ♁🏠 ✕), dominated by the church of St Martin de Tours — dating from the early Middle Ages and worth a visit for its huge wood carving of St Martin on horseback.

From Errezil move on towards the important furniture-making town of Azpeitia on the valley floor, overlooked by the **Izarraitz Massif**; the highest peak in the range, **Erlo** (1026m), rises just above the town. Keep to the main GI2634 towards the centre, but follow signs for *AZKOITIA* along the ring road, to circle round **Azpeitia** (85km ♁🏠 ✕🛒) and follow a tree-lined avenue past the 17th-century **Basilica of San Ignacio de Loiola** (89km ♁⛰ ✕), the birthplace of the founder of the Jesuit movement. Continue on to the first roundabout just before **Azkoitia**, and follow the ring road around town and signs towards *ELGOIBAR* (still the GI2634). This main road flanks **Mt Xoxote** (906m), the lower peak of the Izarraitz Massif, crowned by a huge statue of San Ignacio de Loiola. At a junction, turn right towards *AZKARATE PASS* and *MADARIAGA*. From **Azkarate Pass** take the road which veers sharply to the right and narrows as it passes through the hamlet of **Madariaga** and winds through an extensive pine forest. The small Bar Otarre (99km ✕ 📷) on the left, with its ornate garden and benches, makes a very pleasant place to stop and view the valley and surrounding mountains. Alternatively, press on for another 2km

Short walk for motorists

🚗 **1 Lastur valley circuit**
5km/3mi; 1h40min. This circuit provides a good overview of the valley's charms, as you follow the remnants of an old water channel through the forest and back along the valley floor. At the start there is a fairly steep ascent of 300m up into the forest, from where the path is almost completely on the flat before descending to the valley floor and returning on a quiet road.

Opposite the village square in **Lastur**, take the yellow/white way-marked path (signposted DEBA) which climbs quite steeply to the left of the *fronton,* through a couple of turnstiles and up into the pines.

On reaching a white *baserri,* turn sharp left along the path, which now levels out, and some way further on go through a gate (**15min**). Continue along the old trail, built above a former water channel, with glimpses of the valley down through the trees. Pine gives way to oak and, after you go through another **turnstile** (**30min**), moss-covered limestone increasingly invades the somewhat narrow (but perfectly safe) trail.

Take the upper path (still way-marked), ignoring the overgrown path down left, soon leaving the forest and enjoying clear views of the valley's karst landscape. Just after passing a large beech tree to your left, ignore the gravel path up right to Mt. Arbil (**45 min**) *and* the waymarked path straight on (part of a longer PR circuit). Instead, head downhill, through two gates, to the **Arrasketa** *baserri.* This *agroturismo* is beautifully located above the valley and opposite is a huge, centuries-old holm oak. Descend an asphalted lane to the **valley floor** (**1h**) and follow the road back to **Lastur** (**1h40min**).

along this highly scenic road to a car park and the small **Aittola picnic site** (101km 🅿️P). This beautiful stretch of road meanders along the ridgetop for a while, with views down to a rocky gorge to the right.

(*Detour:* Just 1km further on, a road to the right leads to AITTOLA ZAR. The road drops steeply into the **Goltzibar Gorge** and **Aittola Zar** (❄️⚓️✕), a *baserri* perched just above it. This remote *venta* (inn) is several hundred years old and, although refurbished, retains its charm.)

On the main route, *take special care* on the sharp bends of this narrow mountain road as it descends into the **Lastur valley**. Once down in the valley, turn left to the hamlet of **Lastur** (109km ❄️⚓️✕🚗1). This is a beautiful valley, only marginally spoilt at the beginning by the eyesore of a fairly large quarry; otherwise, Lastur and its surroundings have a forgotten, edge-of-the-world feeling. The village itself consists of an old church, a fully operational water mill making corn flour for delicious *talo* bread (on sale in the shop by the bar), a couple of half-timbered houses, a cosy little bar serving food and the whole main square serving as a rustic bullring for centuries. Four or five young bulls (*novillos*) are still let loose at weekends. The karst scenery throughout this valley is well worth exploring, preferably on foot from the village square.

From Lastur, return to the cross-roads (110km) and turn left to **Itziar** (115km 🚉) on the main N634 Bilbao-San Sebastián road. Turn right at the crossroads and descend to the coast and the busy, attractive fishing town of **Zumaia** (125km ♨️⚓️⚓️✕🚉M) at the mouth of the **Urola River**. There are good beaches and interesting cliff formations just a few hundred

Water mill at Lastur

metres west of the town, which is very popular in summer with locals. The main road crosses the river once beyond the town and passes the house-museum of the Basque painter Zuloaga on the left (open Easter-15/09; Wed-Sun 16.00-20.00). The route hugs the coast as the Ratón de San Antón — the mouse-shaped hill jutting out to sea at Getaria — comes into view. This is one of the most dramatic stretches of road on the Basque coast, and the waves often crash over, occasionally breaking the sea wall and requiring a rather tortuous detour inland via Meagas. **Getaria** (131km ☀✝🏔🏕✕📷🚐2) is another colourful fishing village, dominated by the 15th-century Gothic church of San Salvador, curiously built right over the tunnel of the main street. There are many high-quality fish restaurants here. Juan Sebastián Elcano, the Basque seaman who captained Magellan's ship *Victoria* back to Spain after the latter's untimely death in the Philippines, was born here, and there is a large memorial to him on the main road. From the harbour, the **Ratón de**

San Antón makes a delightful picnic spot (🚐*P*), and there is a maze of paths snaking up to and around the lighthouse at the tip of the hill.

More wild coastal scenery accompanies us as we head into **Zarautz** (134km ⛴🏔🏕✕🚐), a popular surfing and seaside resort with a beautiful long sandy beach. Continue through the town centre, past the motorway entrance to the right. Our route proceeds up the hill, still on the N634, and on to the next village of **Orio** (141km 🏔△✕), built alongside the **Oria River** estuary, where there are more of those colourful Basque fishing boats moored by the quayside. Cross the long river bridge into town and take the first left turn, signposted HONDARTZA and UDAL-CAMPING. Keep to the one-way system, along the main street and out of town for barely 1 km, until you come to a roundabout, then follow the road with the estuary to your left and pass under the motorway bridge. Follow the sign for IGELDO immediately afterwards and then take the next left at the roundabout just before the motorway toll, still following the sign to IGELDO. This fairly narrow road soon reaches the ridgetop (146km), offering great views down to the sea. There are some rustic bars serving food along the top, and some picnic tables (150km 🚐*P*) to the left of the road. Pass the large Garoa camp site (△) and bypass Igeldo village (🏔), before descending towards the city via **Ondarreta Beach** and the **Antiguo** district. Following the one-way system, turn left towards CENTRO and drive around the famous **Concha Bay**. Turn right into CALLE URBIETA in the city centre, to return to our starting point at Pio XII in **Donostia-San Sebastián** (159km).

Getaria and the Ratón de San Antón from San Prudentzio's vineyards

Short walk for motorists

🚗 **2 Txakoli vineyards**

5km/3mi; 1h50min. This circuit partly follows an old cobbled path that originally formed part of a coastal branch of the Pilgrims' Route to Santiago known as the 'Calzada de la Costa.' Most of the route meanders through txakoli *vineyards — txakoli is a very dry, acidic sparkling white wine produced in just a few villages along this coast. It is served in any bar in the area. There is a short (50m) climb at the beginning of the path and about 250m of steady ascent up to the hamlet of Askizu, but overall this is a very easy circuit.*

From the roundabout at the entrance to **Getaria**, take the road up the hill (signposted to MEAGAS). After about 150m, turn right uphill on an attractive cobbled trail. Almost immediately to your right is the **first vineyard**. On reaching a roundabout (**5min**), the trail, signposted to ASKIZU and ZUMAIA and waymarked in yellow, continues beside a large house called **Akerregi-Txiki**. This is the best-preserved section of the *calzada*, meandering up and down through the vineyards. When you join a road, follow it past the turning for San Prudentzio and down the hill. Then take a small lane to the left, past a very **old green- and white-painted house** (**30min**).

The lane winds up to the hilltop hamlet of **Askizu** (**45min**), with its

16

imposing Gothic church. From the square, ignore the yellow waymarks on the road to the left; take the road to the right, out of the village. Soon you can see the breakwater of the port of Zumaia and its beach below.

Take the second asphalted lane to the left by a vineyard surrounded by a **high hedge** (**55min**), past some large **greenhouses** and a couple of houses. When the lane ends, descend on an initially muddy, then grassy path, keeping the sea directly in front of you. As you approach the sea, ignore the main path to the left; keep straight on down a narrow, slightly overgrown path, with the hedgerow to your right. Veer right and go through a gate (**1h05min**), along a scenic path parallel to the clifftops, with the vineyards now to your right. Just after passing through a small oak grove you reach the very old **Bizkarraga** farmhouse (**1h15min**) — and a fantastic view of the Ratón de San Antón (the 'mouse' of Getaria).

Go through the farm — there are unlocked gates on either side — and follow the lane to **San Prudentzio** (**1h25min**), with a Romanesque chapel and a bar with nice terrace — the ideal place to rest and sample *txakoli*. Keep straight on to the crossroads, then turn left back along the road towards Getaria, returning on the same cobbled trail to the **Getaria** roundabout (**1h50min**).

Car tour 2: THE BAZTAN VALLEY OF NORTHERN NAFARROA AND PYRENEAN FOOTHILLS

Donostia-San Sebastián • Aiako Harria Parke Naturala • Lesaka • Etxalar • Zugarramurdi • Señorío de Bertiz Gardens • Doneztebe/ Santesteban • Ituren • Zubieta • Goizueta • Donostia-San Sebastián

182km/113mi; about 4h30min driving time
En route: Short walk for motorists 3; Walks 6, 7, 8, 9, 10
Picnic suggestions: Collado de Uzpuru (a 12km detour from Oiartzun motorway turn-off at the 9km-point, on the way to the start of Walk 6); **Aritxulegi Tunnel** (21km); **Otsondo Pass** (78km); **Señorío de Bertiz Gardens** (105km); **Embalse de Mendaur** (a 5km detour from Aurtitz at the 116km-point); **Ugaldetxo,** beside the **Urumea River** (165km)

This tour offers the opportunity to visit some of the best-kept and most beautiful villages of Nafarroa in the picturesque Baztán Valley region. In olden times this was a land of nobles, evidence of which remains in the form of the many *casas-torre* (fortified houses) in the area. The tour also includes the fascinating area around Zugarramurdi (famous for its caves and the scene of many witch trials during the Inquisition) and the Aiako Harria Nature Reserve, the area around one of the Basque Country's most striking mountains bearing the same name.

For more details about **Donostia-San Sebastián**, see page 12 (Car tour 1). From Plaza Centenario, follow the motorway signs to FRANTZIA/FRANCIA and turn off at JUNCTION 3 for OIARTZUN (9km). Turn left at the roundabout (but go *right* here, to get to the start of Walk 6 or to picnic at the Collado de Uzpuru). The main tour takes the first right turn under the motorway

bridge, to Oiartzun. Just beyond the village, turn right (12km) on the GI3420 for LESAKA. Go through the village of **Ergoien** (14km 🏠 ✕), where there are several excellent rustic places to eat at very reasonable prices. The road heads straight towards the vertical rock face of **Aiako Harriak (Peñas de Aia)**, and starts climbing as it enters the **Aiako Harria Parke Naturala** (17km ☀),

Embalse de San Antón

Short walk for motorists

⚒ 3 The 'witches' trail'

6km/3.7mi; 2h. This mostly cobbled trail (well-waymarked green/white) runs through caves and connects the village of Zugarramurdi with the Sara Caves in the French Basque Country. (The walk may be done in reverse from the Sara Caves during Car tour 7, and a direct bus from St Jean-de-Luz is a good public transport option.) Allow an extra hour to visit the Zugarramurdi Caves themselves (€ 3.50 adults; € 2 children; daily 10.30-20.00 Jul-Sep, 11.00 till 18.00 Oct-Jun). The Sara Caves (€ 8.50 adults; € 4.50 children; daily 10.00-19.00 summer, 14.00-17.00 Nov-Mar) offer guided tours.

From the main square in **Zugarramurdi**, go down the lane opposite the church (sign: CUEVA/LEZEAK). Take the next left turn, past some beautiful old *baserri*, three of them converted into *landa etxeak*. Pass the entrance to the caves, on the left (**10min**), and continue to the end of the unsurfaced road. Then join the trail (sign: SARAKO LEZEAK). It plunges down into the verdant forest and crosses a rickety old wooden bridge beside **Infernuko Zubia** (Devil's Bridge; **15min**) over the **Infernuko Erreka** (Devil's Stream; the stream emerging from the cave). You then rise to a gravel road beside a stone house (**25min**). Rejoin the path, to the right, by some curious 'talking' stones (**30min**), and descend to another cave, inside which the nearby **Venta Halty** offers lunch in summer (**40min**). The trail now runs alongside a lane to a quarry just above the **Sarako Lezeak** (Sara Caves; **50min**). When the trail ends, take the road ahead to the caves (**55min**).

Retracing your steps to **Zugarramurdi** (**2h**) involves slightly more uphill walking.

a protected area around the mountain. The border with Nafarroa is reached at the **Aritxulegi Tunnel** (439m; 21km ✕☎🅿*P*), where there is a refuge with bar/restaurant and a pleasant picnic site above the tunnel — just where Walk 7 begins.

Descend to the **San Antón Reservoir** (25km) and go on to **Agina** (30km 🚻), where there are a couple of **dolmens** close to the road. From here a short, 10-minute walk to the right (following the waymarked track towards BIANDITZ) leads to the hilltop site of **Aita-Donostia** (☎), one of the best known works by the Basque sculptor Oteiza, a good vantage point from which to view Aiako Harriak.

An extremely winding descent brings us to our first main stop in Baztán, **Lesaka** (39km 🚻🛏🏨🏦 ✕🚍). Take the time to stroll along the river through the village; focal points are the Zabaleta *casa-torre*, one of the most impressive of its kind in the region, and the imposing 16th-century Gothic church of San Martín de Tours just above the village, accessed via a pretty cobbled alleyway. From Lesaka follow signs towards IRUÑA-PAMPLONA and turn right on the main N121-A (41km), following the **Bidasoa River** to the **Venta de Etxalar**. Then turn left for **Etxalar** (46km 🚻🏦 ✕), one of the most beautiful Baztán villages. The church graveyard has a fine collection of discoidal headstones and the village houses boast some of the most colourful wood-beamed façades in the area. Walk 8 starts from the church.

From Etxalar take the road to the right, past the church, signposted to ZUGARRAMURDI. Soon after leaving the village the road crosses the river and passes a collection of *baserri* (48km). Walk 8 continues to the right here. Then this rather potholed road narrows and winds its way

the right here would take you to the attractive village of Urdazubi/Urdax (🛉🏨✕∩) itself, site of the 11th-century Monastery of San Salvador and birthplace of Pedro Axular, who wrote the first texts in the Basque language.)

When you reach the main N121B road, turn right towards IRUÑA-PAMPLONA. The road climbs to the **Otsondo Pass** (602m; 78km 🚎*P*), where there is an excellent picnic site to the right, and then descends towards the heart of the Baztán Valley proper. (*Detour:* At 83km you might like to take another short detour to the left, to the one-street walled village of Amaiur (🏨), which is entered via a beautifully preserved gateway.)

The main tour keeps straight on, then takes the next left turn, the NA2600 towards ERRATZU (87km). Just before the hamlet of **Bozate** there is an interesting *casa-torre* to the left, once owned by the *conquistador* Pedro Uxua.*

Leave Bozate by heading south-west. Follow signs to **Arizkun** (90km 🏨✕), which boasts some beautiful rural architecture, as well as the Monastery of Our Lady of the Angels. Turn left for **Elizondo** (95km 🏘🏨△✕🚌), the largest town in the valley, with more traditional Baztán architecture, especially around the old bridge over the river. From the town centre, return to the main N121B road (103km) and continue to **Oronoz-Mugarri** (✕🚌). Just after the crossroads, the **Señorío de Bertiz Gardens** (105km ❀🚎*P*) are to the right — another pleasant shady stop. Apart from the gardens themselves

through an especially verdant section of hill country to the **Ibañeta Pass**. Take special care on the bends along this stretch. A large stone monolith marks the top of pass and a short, steep descent brings us to the village square of **Zugarramurdi** (64km ❋🏨✕∩🚌3). This was a major centre of witch trials during the Inquisition. In the immediate vicinity are three sets of **caves**. The caves at Zugarramurdi itself are the most impressive — their centrepiece is a huge natural arch through which a stream flows — purportedly the site of many an *akelerre* (witches' coven) in the past.

From the village square by the **church**, turn right, following signs towards DANTXARINEA and then a minor lane (66km) signed CUEVAS DE URDAX. Continue past the **Urdax Caves** (67km ∩) and take the next left turn. (*Detour:* A 1km detour to

*A short detour straight on from Bozate leads to the beautiful old village of Erratzu (🏨✕) and Walk 9.

19

Left: house in Zugarramurdi;
above: houses at Etxalar

(entry fee), there is a picnic site to the left of the entrance and various waymarked paths in the woods around the gardens (details available from the tourist office by the picnic site).

Continuing on the N121A towards IRÚN, turn left on the NA170 to **Doneztebe/Santesteban** (110km ▲ ✕ ☎), on the **Bidasoa River**. Follow signs towards LEITZA through more attractive villages, **Elgorriaga** (♨) and **Ituren**. Just after the latter is the tiny hamlet of **Aurtitz** (116km), directly below the sheer south face of **Mt Mendaur** (you can spot its summit chapel from the road). Walk 10 begins at Aurtitz. (*Detour*: A 5km-long, somewhat-potholed track leads from here to the Embalse de Mendaur (⌂P) and a beautiful shady picnic site. You could also start Walk 10 at this reservoir, reducing the time to only 2h.)

The main tour continues ahead, passing a restored watermill, and turning left into **Zubieta** (118km), the most traditional and perhaps best preserved village of the area, with its wonderful collection of houses around the square. The fascinating *zanpan-zar* procession takes place between here and Ituren on the last

Monday and Tuesday in January, when locals from both villages don sheepskins and carry huge cowbells on their backs.

From here continue climbing, go through the hilltop village of **Ezkurra** (128km), and at **Arkiskil** turn right (134km) towards GOIZUETA, following the **Urumea River**. Exercise caution on the bends of this fairly narrow road, which follows the river's winding course. Beyond the delightful riverside village of **Goizueta** (149km ♨ ✕) there are several shady spots beside the river for a picnic, but it is best to continue on to **Ugaldetxo** (165km), where there are tables and other facilities to the left of the river bridge (⌂P).

Reaching the industrial area before Hernani (☎), turn right on the GI131 dual carriageway* following signs for DONOSTIA-SAN SEBASTIAN, turning right at the Anoeta football stadium to return to our starting point (182km).

*About 2km along this dual carriageway a detour can be made to **Astigarraga** (174km ♨ ✕), centre of Basque cider production. Look for the 'blue barrel' signs with the name *sagar-dotegia* (cider house); there are many around the town, and although traditionally the season is from January to April, many now serve food and cider throughout the year. This is recommended for a raucous and traditional Basque experience, and further details can be obtained from the main tourist office in the Boulevard in Donosti-San Sebastián.

Car tour 3: The RUGGED COAST AND MOUNTAINS OF CENTRAL BIZKAIA

Bilbao • Durango • Bolibar • Lekeitio • Elantxobe • Gernika • Urdaibai Estuary • Bermeo • San Juan de Gaztelugatxe Island • Armintza • Castillo de Butrón • Bilbao

213km/132mi; about 5h driving time
En route: Short walks 4, 5, 6; Walks 11, 12, 13
Picnic suggestions: Urkiola, where Walk 12 begins (a 13km detour from Durango, the 28km-point in the tour); **Karraspio Beach, Lekeitio**

(82km); near the entrance to the **Santimamiñe Caves** (a 2km detour from Kortezubi at 122km); **San Juan de Gaztelugatxe,** on the clifftops and on the island itself (149-150km); grounds of the **Castillo de Butrón** (188km)

This tour covers most of the extremely beautiful Bizkaia coast-line, passing through the best-known fishing villages and exploring the dramatic seascapes of the island monastery of San Juan de Gaztelugatxe and the cliffs of Ogoño and Ermua. Other highlights include the Urdaibai Estuary Biosphere Reserve and the ancestral home of Simón Bolivar. Don't miss the detour to the Santimamiñe Cave, with its well-preserved prehistoric paint-ings, and the 'painted' forest of Oma, both visited on Walk 13.

Bilbao★ (🏨✖🚇M), the starting point for Walk 11, is the Basque Country's largest city. Among the 'sights' are the bustling 'seven streets' of the old town, the Guggenheim Museum, and many examples of award-winning modern architecture.

Leave the city from Plaza Moyua: follow signs to PLAZA ZABALBURU and TODAS DIRECCIONES, climbing out of the city and onto the **motor-way** (2km) towards DONOSTIA-SAN SEBASTIÁN. Exit at JUNCTION 17 for **Durango** (28km 🏨✖🚇)*, then follow the signs beyond the motor-way toll gate onto the N634 back towards Bilbao. Take the next right turn (30km) onto the BI3332 and then fork right again (35km) for MUNITIBAR. At the village of **Urru-txua** (41km) turn right onto the BI3231. The **Bizkaiko Begiratokia/ Balcón de Bizkaia** (44km 📷) is a

fine viewpoint at the highest point on the road, above the forest. From here your views stretch over the green rolling hills of inland Bizkaia and to the distant Urdaibai Estuary.

Continue to **Munitibar** (48km ✝🏨), with its Andra Mari church, then turn right in the direction of MARKINA on the BI2224. This winding road descends through the forest to the pretty village of **Bolibar** (54km ✝✖M), the ancestral home of

Bridge at Ondarroa

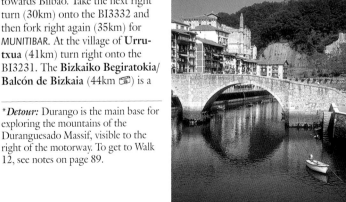

★Detour: Durango is the main base for exploring the mountains of the Duranguesado Massif, visible to the right of the motorway. To get to Walk 12, see notes on page 89.

the South American liberator, Simón Bolivar. The small Casa-Museo Simón Bolivar, housed in the building originally owned by the family, traces the history of his exploits (check https://simonbolivar museoa.com or call 946 164114 for opening times/details).

I highly recommend a short walk from the village (35min return) up to the **Colegiata de Zenarruza**, the 15th-century former collegiate church shown above and only medieval abbey in Bizkaia. Start from the lane beside the Errota Taberna bar and follow the old paving of a coastal branch of the Pilgrims' Route to Santiago up through the forest. The cloisters beside the main church are particularly attractive, and a couple of the original stations of the cross which lined the trail ascending from the village are still standing.

Leaving Bolibar, continue down the hill to the next main crossroads (56km), turning left on the BI633 to **Markina-Xemein** (✕🍴) and on to **Ondarroa** (69km 🏔△✕🍴). At the second roundabout, turn left to drive beside the river, cross the harbour bridge to the colourful port area and old town, and at a further round-about, turn left onto the BI3428 signposted LEKEITIO, to head uphill

22

and out of town. Since the completion of the new BI2405 road from Ondarroa to Lekeitio inland via Berriatua, this narrow road is now largely traffic-free. It meanders high above the sea through eucalyptus plantations, providing us with our first real taste of the dramatic coastline.

Just before Lekeitio, a sign to the right points to **Karraspio Beach** (82km), the best of several in the area, at the end of which are a couple of small bars and a lovely little picnic site (🚏P). Cross the river bridge to enter **Lekeitio** (83km ✳️✝🏔🏘△ ✕P), probably the most beautiful fishing town on the entire coast — the harbour lined with bars and restaurants, the waterfront Gothic church of Santa María de la Asunción and bay dominated by San Nicolás island (which may be accessed at low tide and where goats still roam).

After passing this church on your right, keep straight on at a cross-roads towards GERNIKA, leaving town on the BI2238. Then turn right (87km) towards ISPASTER/EA on the BI3238. Take the next right through the small hilltop village of **Bedarona** (92km ✕) and, now on the BI3481, return to the main road and on to **Ea** (94km 🏘✕), with its attractive old riverside houses and stone footbridge. At the next junction (97km), just after **Natxitua**, follow signs via **Ibarrangelua** (🏘✕) to the next fishing village, **Elantxobe** (100km ✳️✕🍴🚗4). Ignore signs here to 'PORTUA'; instead, fork left and park just before the entrance to the village. From here there is a great view down to the port itself, which may be reached by walking down the incredibly steep main street from the square; driving is *not* recommended!

Urdaibai Estuary from the hilltop chapel on Short walk 5

Short walks for motorists

🚌 4 Ogoño

3km/1.8mi; 1h20min. Ogoño is the highest point on the vertical cliff face above Laga Beach. It provides magnificent views both west along the Bizkaia coast and back towards Elantxobe. The route is well signposted and waymarked in yellow and is easy, apart from an initially steep ascent of 140m. Park just before the entrance to Elantxobe.

From the village square in **Elantxobe**, with its curious turntable for buses, head left up the steep cobbled **Kale Nagusia**. Emerging by the **cemetery** (**10min**), turn right along the lane signposted to OGOÑO until you reach the last houses, from where there are great views back down to Elantxobe (**15min**).

Fork left along the track into a small wood, past a secluded picnic spot. Reaching a gravel road, turn right almost immediately (**20min**), to re-enter the forest along a pretty path. Ignore a couple of signposted paths to the right, then climb over limestone rocks — to a clearing from where there are fantastic views down to Laga Beach directly below (**35min**). Now continue following the yellow marking over the rocks to the highest point (**40min**), with fine panoramic views.

Return the same way (**1h20min**).

🚌 5 San Pedro de Atxarre

3.5km/2.2 mi; 1h15min. San Pedro de Atxarre, a small hilltop chapel, provides the best vantage point for views over the Urdaibai Estuary (declared a World Heritage Site and Biosphere Reserve by UNESCO in 1984). This fairly short walk involves a gradual ascent of just over 100m from Akorda up through the forest. Once out of Akorda on the main route, the path and signposting are clear. Park in Akorda's square, just before the Bar/Restaurante Akorda.

From **Akorda**'s village square, walk a short way back along the road, to a large white **cross**. Now follow the track to the right; it enters a field for a few metres, then climbs straight ahead as a narrow path. You rise through a higher field, to a white house at the far end (**5min**), where a signpost (GR98 to SAN PEDRO ATXARRE) directs you to the right along a path. Gradually climbing through holm oaks, turn right on a second path (**15min**) which levels out. At the next junction (**25min**), continue right on the GR98, gradually climbing on a rockier path to **San Pedro de Atxarre** (**40min**).

Enjoy the awesome views down to the Urdaibai Estuary and east to the sheer cliff face of Ogoño. Then return the same way (**1h15min**).

23

Return to Ibarrangelua and turn right just beyond the village towards LAGA BEACH. (**Detour:** At 104km a turn-off to the left on the BI4236 leads to the small village of Akorda (✕🚻5) and the short walk on the previous page; allow 2.5km for this detour.)

From the junction on the main road, continue on to **Playa de Laga** (106km ✳). the beautiful stretch of sand directly below Ogoño. Follow the road hugging the coast around to the mouth of the **Urdaibai Estuary** and the second, much larger **Playa de Laida**, set back from the sea on the estuary itself. Passing the large **Arketa** campsite (110km △), continue on the main BI2238 towards GERNIKA. Just before **Korte-zubi** (122km 🏛✕) a detour leads to the Urdaibai Bird Center (March-Oct 11.00-19.00 Sat/Sun, every day in July and August; slightly shorter hours weekends Nov-Mar; admission €5) and just after this village is the turn-off to the Santimamiñe Cave and the Painted Forest of Oma (Walk 13). Some 3km beyond Kortezubi, enter **Gernika** (125km ⛰✕🍴M), made famous by the nightmare portrayed in Picasso's famous painting. Of interest here are the Casa de las Juntas, the Arbol de Gernika (the tree considered the emblem of Basque nationalism) and the attractive Parque de Europa, with several works by renowned sculptors such as Henry Moore. Following signs to BERMEO, drive along the left bank of the Urdaibai to **Mundaka**

(137km ✳⛰△✕🚠), a haven for surfers, with a pretty waterfront *atalaya* (📷) affording fine views out to sea and the estuary. Continue through the large fishing port of **Bermeo** (⛰🏛✕🍴) and turn right towards BAKIO on the BI3101.

The road climbs high above the sea, past a pleasant cliff-top **picnic site** (149km 🍴P). Just 1km further on, a right turn leads to the parking area, tourist office and start of the steep walk down to the old stone causeway and chapel now famous as a setting in *Game of Thrones*. 221 steps lead from here up to the chapel of **San Juan de Gaztelugatxe** (✳⛪🍴P), perched atop a tiny island. The chapel, much venerated by fishermen, has been rebuilt several times after being attacked over the centuries, including infamously by Sir Francis Drake. (Free) tickets with a time slot must be obtained in advance if visiting in summer, at Easter and weekends March to October (details at https://www.euskoguide.com/places-basque-country/spain/san-juan-de-gaztelugatxe). There is another lovely, partially covered picnic site beside the chapel.

Continuing on the main road, just beyond the small seaside resort of **Bakio** (157km ⛰✕🍴), turn right on the BI3151, briefly heading inland before returning to the coast and on to the pretty village of **Armintza** (173km ⛪✕). From here

The island chapel of San Juan de Gaztelugatxe rises above sea caves.

Short walk for motorists

🚗 **6 Ermua sea cliffs**

6km/3.8mi; 2h15min. This well-waymarked and signposted circuit highlights the contrast between the green hillsides above Gorliz Bay and the fascinating cliff formations below Ermua, the highest point on this part of the Bizkaia coast. Apart from fairly steep ascents up the cliffs from the beach and also before the lighthouse, the walk is not especially strenuous (overall height gain: 330m). By the roundabout at the entrance to Gorliz village, follow signs downhill to 'Playa/Hondartza'. Park at the end of the road at Atsondo Beach, by Hospital de Gorliz and a Nordic Walking information panel.

From the **information panel** go down to the beach and follow the promenade to the right. Turn right up steps (black/red/blue waymarks) to the coastal path and climb steadily through woods until you reach the clifftops by another **information panel** (**15min**) with great views back to the bay of Gorliz and along the coast. The path winds through woodland before descending for a detour to the **Azkorriagan promontory** (**30min**) and then climbing steeply once more. Reaching a road (**45min**), turn left

towards FARO, to reach the **lighthouse** (**55min**) and some benches.

From here the coastal path, sign-posted to ERMUAMENDI/ARMINTZA, climbs up through ferns with fantastic views of the coast and towards the (allegedly) dragon-shaped islet known as Isla de Villano. When you come to some **meadowland** (**1h15min**), fork left across it (black waymarking), to a stile. Continue up to the summit of **Ermua** (290m, **1h30min**). Just beyond is a curious old stone shelter topped by another marker, where we turn right and head through a holm oak grove to another path junction (**1h35min**). Turn right for FANO, to descend inland through the forest. Emerging on a road just before the large **Fanos** *baserri* (**1h50min**), pass this farm and walk down the next lane to the right (signed to ASTONDO). Now just follow red waymarks, along the lane itself or on a parallel path, to pass a white farmhouse on the left (**2h**) and reach the edge of a built-up area. Where the lane describes an 'L', descend steeply to the Astondo Beach road and turn right, back to the **information panel** (**2h15min**).

turn right again, on to your last port of call on the Bizkaia coast, **Gorliz** (178km 🏖️ △✕🅿️📷🚗6).

From Gorliz, turn left just beyond the town on the BI2120 towards MUNGIA. Then turn right (185km) towards GATIKA ON THE BI3111 and right again on the BI634 to the **Castillo de Butrón/Butroiko Gaztelua** (188km ▌✕). A sharp turn to the right descends to a parking area with a couple of bars. Cross the footbridge to enter the grounds of this impressive 13th-century castle, albeit much restored (only the exterior can now be visited, free, at any time). The

grounds themselves, beside the river, are very pleasant to stroll around and make a nice place to picnic (**P**).

Return through the village of **Butrón** on the BI634 towards MUNGIA and join the BI631 dual carriageway (194km). Head south, following signs to BILBAO past the airport turn-off, to pick up the N637 dual carriageway (207km). From here follow the blue motorway signs marked ARTXANDA, to pass through the **tunnel** (toll) and descend to **Bilbao**, crossing the bridge beside the Guggenheim Museum to return to Plaza Moyua (213km).

Car tour 4: BILBAO TO VITORIA-GASTEIZ VIA THE MOUNTAINS AND WATERFALLS OF SOUTHERN BIZKAIA AND WESTERN ARABA

Bilbao • (Baltzola Caves) • Artea • Itxina • Orozko • Gujuli • Orduña • (Salto del Nervión) • Puerto de Orduña • Parque Natural de Valderejo • Salinas de Añana • Mendoza • Vitoria-Gasteiz

156km/97mi; about 3h30min driving time

En route: Short walks 7, 8, 9; Walks 14, 15, 16, 17

Picnic suggestions: San Lorenzo chapel, near the **Baltzola Caves** (an 8km detour from Igorre, the 23km-point); **Urigoiti** (at the start of Walk 14, a 3km detour from Ibarra at the 34km-point); **Bikotz Gene** viewpoint (32km); **Delika** (81km); **Monte Santiago**, a 3km detour from the Orduña Pass at the 94km-point; **Lalastra,** the main village in the Valderejo Nature Reserve, a 20km detour from the junction with the A2622 at the 111km-point); **Villados**, beside the medieval bridge (137km)

This tour is an interesting and scenic route between Bilbao and Vitoria-Gasteiz on mainly minor roads through delightful countryside. Highlights include the landscapes of the Gorbeia and Valderejo *parques naturales* and the spectacular Sierra Salbada escarpment around the Orduña area — this is the Cantabrian-Mediterranean watershed, with the two highest waterfalls in the Basque Country. The tour is also designed to link up with Car tour 5 to Iruña-Pamplona.

From Plaza Moyua in central **Bilbao** (see Car tour 3 for further details of the city), follow signs to PLAZA ZABALBURU and TODAS DIRECCIONES, driving just to the right of the Hotel Carlton and then onto the **motorway** (2km) in the direction of DONOSTIA-SAN SEBASTIÁN. Exit at JUNCTION 105 onto the N240 towards VITORIA-GASTEIZ (12km). (*Detour:* From the industrial town of **Igorre** (23km ☻), you can take an 8km detour via Dima (🏠 ✕) to visit the Baltzola Caves; 🚗7.)

Four kilometres beyond the Dima turn-off, turn right off the N240 to enter **Artea** (27km 🏠✕M). Turn right at the main crossroads in Artea, on the BI3524 towards OROZKO. Then take the next left turn, on a road which climbs steadily to the **Bikotzgane** (32km ☎🚗P) viewpoint and small picnic site, affording excellent views over the valleys to the north. We now

skirt the edge of the **Gorbeia Nature Reserve** and the vertical limestone wall of **Itxina** (Walk 14) comes into view ahead. To reach the start of Walk 14, turn left on the BI4514 to pass through the hamlet of **Ibarra** and follow a winding road to **Urigoiti** (34km 🏠; Walk 14), nestling on a hillside directly below the highest part of the rockface. Both hamlets boast some of the finest examples of traditional rural architecture in Bizkaia.

From Ibarra continue to **Orozko** (45km 🏔🏠✕), a small town with an attractive cobbled main street and old houses overlooking the river. Crossing over the river bridge, turn left towards VITORIA-GASTEIZ on the BI2522, to head up the **Altube Valley**. When you come to a motorway entrance (57km), ignore it; instead continue on to the **Altube Pass** (638m; 63km) and, just beyond it, turn right (65km) on the

26

Entrance to the second cave, Aburo, after heavy rain

Short walk for motorists

🚗 7 Baltzola Caves

3.8km/2.4m; 1h30 min. This easy walk leads via a beautiful natural stone arch to caves steeped in Basque mythology. Both are entered from an extraordinary natural hollow through which a stream flows. The first of the two caves can be entered, but the second, Aburo, is now closed to the public. A torch is recommended to explore the further reaches of the larger cave to the left (but not to just visit the main chamber). From Igorre turn left on the BI2543 to Dima (4km). Continue past the tourist office along the main road towards Puerto de Dima for a further 3km and turn left by a bus stop down the lane signposted to Indusi and Cueva de Baltzola. Park after 100m by the chapel of San Francisco.

From the chapel of **San Francisco** cross the bridge over the stream and turn left at the first crossroads (signposted BALTZOLA). Proceed along this lane until you come to another bridge just before some large farmhouses that make up **Indusi**. Cross the bridge (signposted GIBELTAR and BALTZOLA) and head up to the **farm** at the end of the lane (**10min**).

Turn right along the path above the stream, take the first fork to the left to cross the stream, and come to the **Puente de los Gentiles** (**20min**), a beautiful natural stone arch built, according to legend, by a *gentile* (a mythical giant from Basque folklore). Pass under the bridge and follow the stony path as it veers sharply to the right up through the pine forest and emerges on the open mountain, until you reach the **hollow** from where both of the **Baltzola Caves** are accessed.

Descend to the entrance of the larger cave, on the left (**30min**). You can walk straight through this, although towards the end things get a bit slippery beyond the main chamber. To the left of the chamber is an opening from where you can also exit the cave and scramble down the hillside back to the Puente de los Gentiles.

Return to the **hollow** (**45min**) and follow the path to the left of the yellow/white-waymarked rock to the entrance of Aboro, the second cave. As it is now no longer possible to follow the stream through this cave, take the gravel path to the right to some delightful pastureland and descend to a small **waterfall** just beyond the far end of the cave (**55min**).

From here simply retrace steps to your car (**1h30min**). (Alternatively, if continuing along the gravel path, this leads up a lane past a couple of houses in 20 minutes to the chapel of **San Lorenzo** (🏠*P*), where there is a pleasant picnic site with tables.)

Source of the Nervión from the Salto de Nervión (recommended detour at 94km); this photograph was taken in high summer, when the falls are only a trickle — or non-existent. Below: Ribera's abandoned church (Walk 16)

A2521 towards ORDUÑA. At the **Goiuri/Gujuli** crossroads (72km ✻⛪), turn right to enter this tiny village and on reaching the church, follow the sign indicating CASCADA. Park on the right just before the railway bridge and walk through a stile and over the railway line *(careful! there is no level crossing here!)*, then over another stile. From this point you get a good view of the Basque Country's highest **waterfall**, although it often has no more than a trickle of water in the summer months. Whether the river is dry or not, the view down to the valley far below is awesome, and a path may be followed for some way beside the fence. Watch your step, however, as it is very narrow and at times stays a bit too close to the edge for comfort.

Proceeding a little further along the road towards Orduña affords first views of the **Sierra Salbada**, the escarpment forming the Cantabrian-Mediterranean watershed — views which are increasingly spectacular as we descend to the valley bottom and re-enter Bizkaia.

Turn left along the BI4097 to enter the village of **Artomaña** and from the square, take the unmarked lane directly opposite to continue to **Delika** (✕). Turn left before the church, to pass under the railway bridge, and park at the end of the lane by the Restaurante El Infierno, beside the river (84km ⊼*P*⊜8) — open every day, with inexpensive lunchtime specials. The grassy area beside the river just beyond the bar is a nice picnic spot.

Return under the railway bridge, this time veering left through the village, keeping the church on your left. You reach the main road and enter **Orduña** (87km ✝▲✕; ⛽ in Amurrio 8km to the north). Orduña has an attractive main square dominated by the former *aduana* (customs house); this is one of the very few places in the Basque Country where storks nest on the rooftops. A detour from here leads via the A3618 to the start of Walk 15.

Follow SALIDA CIUDAD/HIRI IRTEERA from the town centre to return to the main road towards BURGOS. This road snakes up to the top of the escarpment, briefly leaving Euskadi and entering the province of Burgos just before the **Puerto de Orduña** (900m; 96km 📷). (***Detour:*** 1km beyond the pass — just before a large white obelisk — a gravel road to the left (94km) leads in 3km to the large picnic area of Monte Santiago (*P*). From there a track signposted SALTO DEL NERVIÓN runs 1.8km to a platform beside the Nervión Waterfall (📷) — a fantastic viewpoint hanging out over the edge of the escarpment, more than 300m above the valley and visible from the short walk described at the right. This may be a better option at times of heavy rain than Short walk 8.)

The main tour continues through **Berberena** (101km ⛽); we re-enter Araba (on a noticeably better road surface!) and reach the turn-off right (111km) for the **Parque Natural de Valderejo/Valderejo Parke Naturala** (Walk 16). Follow this road for 1km to **Villañane** (📷) and the **Torre-Palacio de los Varonas** (■), the best-preserved fortified building in the province, which has been continuously inhabited for 500 years by the Varona family.

Return to the A2625 towards BURGOS and, just beyond **Espejo** (⛪), turn left onto the A2622 for **Salinas de Añana** (119km ✕📷🚗9). This is the only place in the Basque Country where there are extensive salt marshes; salt extraction was the major source of employment in the area until sea salt extraction became a cheaper option by the early 20th century. The split-level terraces

Short walk for motorists

🚗 8 Desfiladero del Nervión

6.5km/4mi; 2h15min. This is a fairly level walk (total height gain 100m) which follows the course of the Nervión upstream to the immense cliff face of the escarpment (shown opposite), close to its source. After periods of heavy rain, especially between November and April, a waterfall plunges over 300m at the start of the river's journey to the Bilbao estuary. Note that the last part of the walk crosses the river several times, meaning that the detour and short walk to the viewing platform at Monte Santiago referred at the 94km-point in the tour may then be a better option. The first part of the walk from Delika is muddy at any time of the year. However, when the river bed is dry it is possible to get practically to the base of the escarpment. Regardless of the time of year, this is an extremely beautiful walk.

From the Restaurante El Infierno at **Delika**, go through the gate and follow the rather overgrown and narrow path to the right of the stream, crossing a stile (**5min**) and continuing along a farm track to an old **stone bridge** (**10min**). Turn right after crossing the bridge and take the first left-hand track (ie, *not* the one that continues beside the stream). The track ascends gradually and then levels out (**20min**) as the escarpment comes into view directly ahead. Go right at the next fork (**25min**) and right again at the following one (**40min**). Pass an animal trough and reach the river and the **end of the track** (**45min**). From this point follow a path close to the river, going over a stile and crossing the river

Continues overleaf

several times as you enter a narrow gorge, the **Desfiladero del Nervión**. A viewing platform at the Salto del Nervión (a detour from the Orduña Pass) is visible at the top of the escarpment to the right as you turn the final bend towards the base of the cliff and the waterfall. (The path ends here (**1h10min**), and of course the amount of water in the falls depends on the time of year.

Retrace your steps to where you last crossed the river; re-cross it (**1h35min**) and, at the first junction after the path widens, take the left-hand fork to cross the river again (**1h40min**). Then follow the track downstream on the opposite bank through gall oak and beech forest. This track maintains a reasonable height above the river, but descends to cross it one more time (**2h05min**), to return to the old stone bridge and **Delika** (**2h15min**).

Short walk for motorists

🚗 **9 Salinas de Añana**
2km/1.2mi; 40min. A short but interesting circuit around the terraces used for salt collection, now being restored after years of neglect. Park by the church on the main road in Salinas de Añana.
Walk up the main road through **Salinas de Añana** and turn right to the **Convento de San Juán de Acre** (**15min**). Follow the path beside the convent wall to a *mirador* (**20min**), the best viewpoint over the terraces. Take the next right-hand fork, down to the head of the valley, and return on the far side. Cross the stream at the lower end (taste the salt in it!) and return to **Salinas de Añana** (**40min**).

Right: bales of hay just south of Puerto de Orduña

30

Orduña: church in the main square

make a unique landscape for a short walk (see Short walk 9 overleaf).

Continue on the A2622 towards VITORIA, going under the motorway and turning right just after a petrol station (129km 🚉). Then turn left to pass through **Nanclares de Oca** (136km). (*Detours:* Beyond this town, short detours to the left of 1km and 3km respectively lead to the beautiful medieval bridges of Villados (140km 🚐P) and Trespuentes crossing the river Zadorra.)

Turn left on the A3302 for **Mendoza** (**M**), dominated by a fortified tower which formerly housed the Heraldry Museum of Araba. From here the A3302 winds through this fertile countryside, with fine views of hilltop villages, to the outskirts of **Vitoria-Gasteiz** (154km). At the first roundabout after crossing the Zadorra River, keep straight on Avenida de los Huetos, following signs to CENTRO/ ERDIALDEA, and on to the Cathedral of Maria Inmaculada, around which there are good car parks from where the CASCO MEDIEVAL (old quarter) and the mostly pedestrianised city centre can be explored (156km).

Car tour 5: The WINE-GROWING AREA OF RIOJA ALAVESA, THE MONTAÑA ALAVESA, AND THE SIERRAS OF TOLOÑO-CANTABRIA, URBASA AND ARALAR

Vitoria-Gasteiz • Faido • Peñacerrada • Laguardia • Kripan • La Población • Kanpezu • Contrasta • Sierra de Urbasa • San Miguel de Aralar • Sierra de Aralar • Lekunberri • Iruña-Pamplona

211km/131mi; about 5h driving time
En route: Short walks 10, 11, 12; Walks 17, 18, 19, 20, 21, 22
Picnic suggestions: Balcón de Rioja (39km); **source of the Kripan River** (a 2km detour from Kripan at the 63km-point); **Nuesta Señora de Okón** (start of Walk 18; a 6km detour from La Población at the 69km-point); **Santuario de Kodes** (an 11km detour from the 74km-point, not far past La Población); **Sierra de Urbasa** (122km); **San Miguel de Aralar** (166km); **Albia** (170km)

T his tour can be enjoyed in its own right or can be combined with Car tour 4. It is a linear route from Vitoria-Gasteiz to Iruña-Pamplona along scenic minor roads. It covers the little-known Montaña Alavesa, the wine-growing area of Rioja Alavesa and the Sierras of Toloño-Cantabria, Urbasa and Aralar, all with their unique landscapes. Much of the terrain lies in areas protected by three different nature reserves, so there are plenty of opportunities to get out of the car and do some fine walking.

Vitoria-Gasteiz (♥▲△✕☕M) has more green spaces per inhabitant than any other city in Spain. Also notable are the recently-restored Gothic Cathedral of Santa María (don't miss the fascinating guided tour of the ongoing restoration work), the Fournier Museum of Playing Cards, the beautiful *casco medieval* (old quarter) and many cycle tracks leading from the city centre right out into the countryside (free bicycle hire from the tourist office, with collection points around the city). Walk 17 is easily reached from the centre.

Starting in the centre near the **tourist office**/bottom of San Frantzisko Aldapa, drive along **Calle Olagüibel** and turn right into **Calle de la Paz**, past the Corte Inglés department store. From here follow signs to PEÑACERRADA and LOGROÑO, crossing the railway line and leaving the built-up area (2km). At the **roundabout** on Calle Iturritxu, turn left and then take the first right turn, on the A2124 to PEÑACERRADA, crossing the **Puerto de Vitoria** (758m; 9km). Turn left (11km) to the tiny village of **San Vicentejo**, to see the interesting **Ermita de la Inmaculada**, then continue south on the A2124/BU750. At the crossroads just before the Venta de Armentia (a large bar and restaurant; ✕ 14km), turn left on the CL127 towards OBECURI, and then take the next right on the A4148 signposted CUEVAS ARTIFICIALES. You can visit these caves on a short walk from the pretty village of **Faido** (22km ▲∩☕10).

Go back along the road out of the village and, just after a small walled cemetery, turn left up a fairly potholed road (the A4129) to the church in the hamlet of **Baroja**. From there rejoin the A2124/BU750 and turn left to continue to **Peñacerrada** (31km ♥▲✕☼). The village itself is largely walled, with the gateway at the southern end

Short walks for motorists

🚶 **10 Cuevas artificiales de Faido — 'little Cappadoccia'**
3.5km/2.2mi; 1h. An interesting, easy walk to two of the hundred or so man-made caves first lived in by hermits in this part of Araba and the Condado de Treviño (Burgos province) as early as the 6th century, and the 13th-century cave chapel of Nuestra Señora de la Peña. To arrange a 30-minute tour inside the chapel, check with the main tourist office in Vitoria-Gasteiz.
From the information board in **Faido** which details the route and history of the caves, head down c/Virgen de la Peña beside the church and turn right at the end along a lane, signposted SAN MIGUEL, forking left up the path to the first **cave chapel**. Climb up on the rocks above it, to visit a second small **cave** beside the belfry (**15min**). Return to the lane and follow it round to the other side of the field, where a fairly overgrown path through the woods leads to the **caves of San Miguel**, the larger one of which contains a small **shrine** (**35min**).
Retrace steps to **Faido** (**1h**).

🚶 **11 La Población**
3.6km/2.2mi; 1h15min. A short and safe walk, but with a steep climb of 300m to the pointed peak of La Población (photo overleaf), an incredible viewpoint over Rioja and neighbouring mountains.
From the **church** at **La Población**, follow the track (behind some houses) signposted MICRORESERVA — a protected area for butterflies. Turn sharp left (**10min**) to join the start of the summit path; this zigzags up to a fine viewpoint towards the long Sierra Tolona-Cantabria to the west and Ioar to the east (**30min**). Continue to the top of **La Población** (**40min**).
Return the same way (**1h15min**).

being particularly impressive.

Keeping to the A2124, the next point of interest along the route is the **Balcón de La Rioja/Errioxako Ikkuspegia** (39km 📷🍴P), an extraordinary viewpoint (with picnic site) over the plains of Rioja at the point where the road cuts through the Sierra de Toloño-Cantabria.

Descend to the plain to enter Rioja Alavesa, the northern part of the wine-growing area still within the *Comunidad Autónoma Vasca*. Turn left along the A124 to reach the beautiful walled town of **Laguardia**★ (50km 🚻🏔🏨🍴🚌), backed by the jagged peaks of the Sierra de Toloño-Cantabria. Visit the *centro histórico*, whose focal point is the church of Santa María de los Reyes with its extraordinarily ornate portico (key from the local tourist office on the main road). The tourist office can also organise a visit to one of the many wine *bodegas* in the area.

From Laguardia take the A3228 towards ELVILLAR but, just before the village, turn left to **la Chabola de la Hechicera** (55km 🏛), one of the best-preserved dolmens in the Basque Country. From **Elvillar** go straight on to **Kripan** (63km). (***Detour:*** Just before Kripan, by the km 74 marker, a partially-asphalted lane to the left leads in 2km to a shady picnic site (🍴P) by the source (*nacedero*) of the Kripan River.

Just beyond Kripan, follow signs towards BERNEDO on the A3220/NA730 to the hilltop village of **La Población** (69km 📷🚶11), from where you can take an unforgettable walk to the top of the mountain of the same name. (Or, if you prefer, just walk *round* the mountain on the new SL.NA195 signposted footpath.) To reach the start of Walk 18, from La Población follow the NA7210 (later A2126) for 6km to Bernedo on the northern side of the mountain range.

Contrasta (top) and gateway at the southern end of Peñacerrada (right)

To continue the car tour, turn right through the village along a scenic hilltop road past a large wind farm, and turn left on the NA7211 (74km) towards GENEVILLA. (A right turn at this point leads to Aguilar and the start of Walk 19; ⇌*P*.) The road cuts back through a gap in the sierra to re-enter the Montaña Alavesa. At the main crossroads in **Kanpezu** (82km ✕🍽), turn right towards ESTELLA. (A left turn here leads towards Vitoria-Gasteiz and Antoñana, and the start of Walk 20.)

Follow CENTRO URBANO signs to enter Kanpezu's old town. From here take the A2128 towards CONTRASTA; this winds through the rolling farmland of the Arana Valley via some idyllic villages, most notably **San Vicente de Arana** (92km ✕; the only village in the valley with a place to eat). Go through the pretty walled village of **Contrasta** (97km 🏰) and take the next right turn (99km) on the A4160. This road becomes the NA7130 and runs through **Larraona** and **Eulate**, then you turn left on the NA718 (113km) towards

OLAZTI. (A right turn leads to Zudaire (🔺✕🍽), Estella, and Walk 21.)

We now enter the Sierra de Urbasa as we approach the immense cliff face of the **Balcón de Pilatos**. Stop at the viewpoint (117km 📷) and, just after entering the **Parque Natural de Urbasa** (✳), park at the right-hand side of the road (marked 'Balcón de Pilatos'; 119km). From here the top of the cliff face can be reached on foot: walk straight ahead from the end of the car park for five minutes, then follow the fence for 10 minutes, around to the projecting rock visible from the head of the Urederra Valley (see Walk 21). During the Spanish Civil War, Franco's troops allegedly pushed Republican prisoners off this rock in order to save bullets.

From here the road crosses the plateau of the **Sierra de Urbasa**,

33

Above: La Población from the north, near Kanpezu. The eponymous village is on the south side of the mountain.

where there are many fine picnic spots, the best being close to a small roadside shepherd's hut — Venta Mendinagusi — which has been converted into an information centre and where there is an interesting restored *txondorra* (charcoal kiln; 122km ⼝*P*). Urbasa sheep's cheese *(ardi gasna)* is famous and on sale here and at other places along the road. Just after the **main park office** (129km), where maps may be obtained detailing several walks in the Sierra, the road descends dramatically through a gap in the rocks to **Olazti** (136km) on the **Plain of Araba**.

Turn right on the main road and follow signs onto the A10 towards IRUÑA-PAMPLONA. Soon after passing the long ridge of **San Donato** to the right, turn off the dual carriageway at JUNCTION 12 for UHARTE-ARAKIL (154km). Cross over the A10 and take the first left, signposted MONASTERIO DE ZAMARTZA, to go round the back of

Uharte-Arakil and pass an old stone bridge to the right and some picnic tables by the river. About 400m further on, turn left up a narrow potholed road signposted to SAN MIGUEL DE ARALAR (156km). The road rises steeply through beautiful forest. On reaching the top of the ridge, turn right to park beside **San Miguel de Aralar** (166km (✳♦☞), with its Romanesque church. The views from here are awesome — especially across the valley towards the long ridge of San Donato. It is possible to eat your own food at the tables inside the *hospedaría* beside the church; otherwise, simple meals and drinks are served, and the hilltop area around the sanctuary makes an excellent **picnic site** (⼝*P*).

From the sanctuary continue downhill to the large car park at the site of the former **Guardetxe/ Casa Forestal de Aralar** (169km ✳🜚), the main base for walks in the **Sierra de Aralar** and the starting point for Walk 22. The road continues

34

Short walk for motorists

🚗 12 Nacederos de Iribas)
5km/3.1mi; 1h30min. This route explores the curious geological phenomenon of the two sources of the Ertzilla River — the first source emerging from the cliff face of Aitzarrateta, the second source being where the river re-emerges after its underground journey, just below the village of Iribas. The walk is waymarked throughout in green and white. Overall ascent of about 100m. Park just beyond the entrance to the village, beside a map providing details of the route.

Follow the sign AITZARRATETA SL-NA302 and the green/white waymarking through **Iribas**, past the *frontón* and onto an unsurfaced road (**5min**). At the first fork (**10min**), keep straight on and at the second (signposted; **15min**) head right. At the next junction (**20min**) turn left, to descend along a clear gravel path past a *borda* and down to the river (**30min**).

Turn right here, to follow the crystal-clear **Ertzilla River** beside moss-covered rocks and thick vegetation — a magical place! You pass the remains of an **old mill** just before reaching the cliff face of

Aitzarrateta (**35min**), from where the **river emerges for the first time**.

Retrace your steps along the river, but this time keep straight on beside it, still in the forest, until the river carves a U-shape and then disappears underground. Take the time to descend to the right here, beside a small **information panel** marked ERTZILLA (**55min**), to make a small loop to the point where the river actually disappears.

Return to the path and continue along it, and when you come to a farm track, follow it to the right uphill; then, after 100m, take the next fork to the left to reach an **electricity substation** and, just beyond it, a circular walled area, within which is the huge **Lezegalde Chasm** (**1h10min**). Walk round the top of the chasm and follow the path down a dry valley. Where the **GR20** cuts across the path, keep straight on downhill and, at a second fork, continue a further few metres on to the **second source of the Ertzilla**, known as **Basakoitz** (**1h20min**).

Return to this last fork and follow the path that climbs steeply up above the left bank of the river, back to **Iribas** (**1h30min**).

---

through karst rock formations and dense forest in the heart of the sierra, making for a delightful drive. The parking area for **Albia** (170km 🚻*P*) is another good base from which to explore or picnic.

(*Detour:* At 181km, just before Lekunberri, a detour of 3km to the right leads to the tiny village of Iribas (🚗12).)

The main tour continues straight on to the crossroads at **Lekunberri** (182km ▲▲△✕🚗), where you turn right on the NA1300, to join the A15 dual carriageway to IRUÑA-PAMPLONA at JUNCTION 123. The road passes through a gorge flanked

by one of Nafarroa's best-known natural landmarks — **Biaizpe/Dos Hermanas**, rocks known as the 'Two Sisters' (192km), then enters the flat, fertile plain of the Pamplona basin at Irurtzun.

Join the motorway here, then leave it at JUNCTION 97 (206km), to enter **Iruña-Pamplona**. Follow the long Avenida de Pio XII towards ZONA CENTRO, and turn right just after the main park. You pass the old ramparts and reach Plaza de La Paz by the bus station (211km).

Car tour 6: THE PYRENEAN VALLEYS AND HISTORIC TOWNS OF NORTH/CENTRAL NAFARROA

Iruña-Pamplona • Olite • Sangüesa • Castillo de Javier • Lumbier • Foz de Arbaiun • Ochagavia • Orreaga/Roncesvalles • Auritz/Burguete • Iruña-Pamplona

259km/160.5miles; about 5h driving
En route: Short walks 13, 14, 15, 16; Walks 23, 24, 25
Picnic suggestions: Foz de Lumbier (133km); Ochagavia (165km) — either 1km beyond the village, **beside the river** or at the

Santuario de Muskilda (a 4km detour, also on the route of Short walk 16); **Casas de Irati**, at the start of Walk 24 in the Forest of Irati (a 23km detour from Ochagavia); **Col d'Ibañeta** (208km); **Zandueta** (223km)

Nafarroa is by far the largest of the seven provinces covered in this book, and the most varied. This tour covers many of the most scenic corners of the more arid, central part of the province. Highlights include the *foces* (gorges), towns and villages steeped in history going back to Roman times, the verdant Pyrenean valleys of Salazar and Aezkoa, Irati (one of Europe's largest forested areas) and finally the collegiate church of Orreaga/Roncesvalles, one of the major starting points in Spain for the Pilgrims' Route to Santiago.

Iruña-Pamplona★ (♣♨▲△✕🍴) is famous for its week-long San Fermines festival during the second week in July, with the running of the bulls *(encierro)*. There is also an historic old town with ramparts to be seen.

From the Plaza de la Paz by the bus station in the city centre, go along **Avenida del Ejército**, then turn left, following signs to the ZONA HOSPITALARIA along **Avenida de Pio XII**. Keep straight on out of the city, joining the AP15 motorway at JUNCTION 88 in the direction of ZARAGOZA (5km). Pass the impressive 18th-century **Noain Aqueduct** (12km) and continue south. At 42km turn off at JUNCTION 50 for OLITE and follow the N121 into the centre of **Olite** (47km ♣♨▲△✕🍴). Park to the left of the entrance gate to the beautifully preserved historic old town, dominated by the 14th-century former Royal Palace. Built by Carlos II, part of the palace has now been converted into a *parador* (go to

https://tickets.palaciorealolite.com. en/909-the-royal-palace-of-olite to book guided/unguided visits).

Continue left around the town, onto the NA5300, and drive through vineyards to **San Martín de**

Right: Olite; below: cutting grass near Pamplona

Unx (57km ✕). (*Detour:* A right turn just beyond San Martín de Unx leads to the picture-postcard medieval hilltop village of Ujúe (✳✝🏠✕🖼🚌13), dominated by the large 12th/13th- century church-fortress of Santa María, overlooking terraced hillsides. The village streets form a winding maze — much too narrow and steep for cars.

The main tour continues on the NA132 through vineyards, with wind farms lining the long ridges on both sides of the road. (*Detour:* A turn-off right on the NA5320 (72km) leads to Gallipienzo (🖼), another medieval hilltop village affording fantastic views above the Aragón River.)

The main tour goes straight on, crosses the Aragón, and enters the historic city of **Sangüesa/Zangoza** (87km ✝🏔△✕🚤). The church of Santa María La Real, with its famed portico, is just to the left after the bridge (guided tours arranged by the tourist office directly opposite). Proceed along Calle Mayor, following signs for JAVIER on the NA5410. There is a well-known castle at **Javier** (95km 🏔✕), the birthplace of the patron saint of Nafarroa, San Francisco Javier.

Cross the **Irati River** (100km) and carry on to **Yesa** (🏔✕), then turn left on the A21 highway towards IRUÑA-PAMPLONA. (*Detour:*Cross the A21 here for the Monasterio de Leire (✝🖼) and the

Short walk for motorists
🚗 **13 El Camino de las Pilas**
5.8km/3.6mi; 1h45min. This circuit explores some of the terraced hillsides surrounding Ujúe, passing some abandoned farmsteads and the pilas de agua *(places for washing clothes) used up until 1952, when piped water reached the village. Parts of the route are quite overgrown and there is a fairly steep ascent from the* pilas *back to the village. Overall ascent: 250m. The walk is partially waymarked green/white and signposted SL.NA177A, but pay extra attention on the ascent to the drovers' road. Park at the entrance to Ujúe, an 8km detour from San Martín de Unx.*
Starting from the ruined church of **San Miguel** at the bottom end of **Ujúe**, where there is a weather-worn board detailing the route, follow the track downhill, turning left almost immediately. You descend to the valley floor and join another track (**15min**): follow this to the left, to pass the ruins of the **Corral de**

Porta. From here the remains of an old **watermill** may be seen by the stream, to the right (**25min**). Cross the stream, then take the first track to the left and continue beside the stream to the remains of a second farmstead, the **Corral del Fausto** (**45min**). Vines cover the narrow valley floor, and from here the path, although reasonably well way-marked, becomes very overgrown, as you make your way to the ruins of the old *pilas* (**55min**).

Continue through the long grass past the *pilas,* cross the stream (**1h**) and follow the old *cañada real* (drover's road) which zigzags up the terraced hillside to the highest point at a small pass, **El Portillo de las Pilas** (**1h20min**). From here Ujúe comes into view again, and it is a simple walk back to the road (**1h30min**). Follow the lower road, to the left of **Ujúe**, back down to the church of **San Miguel** (**1h45min**).

start of Walk 23 to Arangoiti — the long ridge parallel to the road.)

Beyond **Liedena** (107km 🚗) pause at the archaeological remains of the old Roman villa bearing the same name (free entry), where there is a fine viewpoint over the sheer walls of the Foz de Lumbier (109km). At the next junction, turn right on the NA150, towards LUMBIER (113km). (*Detour:* At the round-about just before the town centre, turn right along a narrow

lane to the Foz de Lumbier (🚗14). The lane ends after 1.5km, at a car park a short way before the entrance to the Foz.)

From the centre of **Lumbier** (116km ✳△✕🚗) go straight on towards NAVASCUES (NA178). Turn right at the **Iso Pass** (129km ✳📷), the main viewpoint over the **Foz de Arbaiun**, an immense canyon through which the Salazar flows. The canyon is 6km long, and the far end may be clearly seen from the

Short walk for motorists

🚗 14 Foz de Lumbier

5.8km/3.6mi; 1h45min. This is an excellently waymarked circuit (green and white, signposted SL.NA113) above and through the Foz de Lumbier, an impressive gorge through which the Irati River flows. The return route through the gorge follows the old Pamplona-Sangüesa railway line through two tunnels (a torch is highly recommended, although plenty of people manage without). Total height gain: 200m. Alternatively, simply walk out to the end of the gorge and back (1h-1h15min). Look out for the many griffon vultures and other birds of prey which nest in the gorge — binoculars essential! Park in the car park before the entrance to the gorge.

From the **Foz de Lumbier car park** carry on along the lane beyond (closed to vehicles) to a small picnic site (**5min**; 🌲**P**) with a spring. Then turn left to follow the waymarked path as it climbs up to the plateau, where you join a wide track (**20min**). The chapel of Trinidad is visible to the left on the top of the ridge.

At the point where the track levels out (**30min**), turn right and, later, turn right again, to descend to within sight of the **Irati River**. Join a path which emerges on the old railway line beside the river (**45min**). Follow this to the entrance to the **first tunnel** (**1h**). Just *before* going through this tunnel, turn left on an extremely narrow path — which is also very slippery after rain — to see the ruins of a bridge, the **Puente del Infierno**, which crosses the entrance to the gorge.

Return to the tunnel (**1h15min**) and walk through it to enter the **Foz de Lumbier** proper, passing through a **second tunnel**. At the far end you emerge by the path you ascended at the start of the walk. Retrace your steps to the **car park** (**1h45min**).

Arangoiti ridge in the course of Walk 23. Many birds of prey are also easily spotted here, perching on rocks on the higher part of the canyon, so have the binoculars ready again.

Continuing up the valley, we pass a turn-off left, the NA2112 (134km). (*Detour:* This leads towards Aspurz and 🚗15.) Continue past the sleepy town of **Navascues** (139km) and up the Salazar Valley via **Oronoz** (160km 🚰) to the riverside village of **Escaróz** (162km 🏨🍴), with its

delightful main cobbled street and square.

Fork right to enter **Ochagavía** (165km 🛐🏚🏨🍴🚗16), one of Pyrenean Nafarroa's most attractive villages, at the confluence of two rivers which flow into the Salazar. The Anduña River runs through the centre of the village, flanked on both sides by the typical old stone houses of the region. Cobbled streets lead off up towards the fortress-like church of San Juan Evangelista. This

39

Short walks for motorists

🚗 **15 Foz de Santa Colomba**
3.1km/2mi; 1h15min. This circuit (green/white waymarking, signposted SL.NA111) follows the course of the little-known Foz de Santa Colomba, not as spectacular as the two previous *foces* visited on this tour, but well off the beaten track. Prickly bushes invade the path, so shorts are not recommended. The walk crosses the gorge, involving a bit of seasonal wading, and the final ascent is quite steep (total height gain: 120m). Turn left over the bridge towards Aspurz (NA2112); a car park is on the left about 200m further on.

From the **car park** follow the path behind the map detailing the route, through quite thick vegetation. Take the first left-hand fork (**5min**) to walk above the **Salazar River** along a narrow stony path, then descend to the right, to an old **stone bridge** at the entrance to the **Foz de Santa Colomba** (**20min**).

Cross the bridge and follow the path through even thicker vegetation, quite close to the **Egúrzanos River** (which is practically dry in summer). The path ends at the point where the valley narrows to the **gorge proper** (**40min**). Look for waymarking on the opposite bank and handrails in the rock — to cross the gorge, which may involve a little seasonal wading. Then continue up the ravine on the far side, climbing to a fine **viewpoint** (**50min**) over the scenic, uninhabited valley beyond the gorge.

From here continue climbing quite steeply, to a clearing above the forest (**1h**), from where a track descends abruptly back to the **car park** (**1h15min**).

Foz de Santa Colomba

The 12th-century Santuario de Muskilda, restored in the 17th century

🚗 **16 Santuario de Muskilda**
6.2km/3.8mi; 2h. Another SL green and white circuit (SL.NA65), also coinciding with the GR11 Trans-Pyrenean route at the start. We visit the 12th-century Romanesque chapel of Muskilda perched on top of the heavily-forested hill of the same name above Ochagavía. This is a splendid viewpoint over the valley and the forest is wonderfully shady. Total height gain: 295m. Park in the centre of Ochagavía.

From **Ochagavía** walk up the cobbled street behind the **church** until you reach the last houses in the village (**5min**). Follow the GR11 markings to the right, on an attractive cobbled trail which climbs fairly steeply up though the forest, past **stations of the cross**, to the **Santuario de Muskilda** (**35min**). Walk right, through the entrance gate and courtyard, passing a small picnic site (🚻**P**). Join the road and turn right almost immediately, to re-enter the forest on the SL.NA65. After passing a rather incongruous **water tank** at the top of the hill, descend to cross the road (**55min**) and continue along a track which emerges on the open mountain just before the **Borda Xubri** (**1h10min**). From here the GR11 continues over the long ridge of Abodi ahead, but we turn sharp left, to begin our return route through the forest, past a **spring** to the right (**1h20min**). The path widens to a track and bends sharply down to the right (**1h35min**). At this point we carry straight on along a narrow forest path, back to the top end of **Ochagavía** (**2h**).

is an extremely popular touring centre, and the many *casas rurales* fill up quickly in high season and at weekends; either book in advance or be prepared to stay at other nearby villages (Escaróz, Jaurrieta, Izalzu or the villages in the neighbouring Roncal Valley all have similar accommodation). There is a nice riverside picnic site and natural swimming pools (⊓*P*) about 1km beyond the village towards Isaba. Walk 24 in the Irati Forest begins 23km north of Ochagavía.

Returning to **Escaróz** (168km), turn right over the bridge on the NA140 towards JAURRIETA and AURITZ/BURGUETE. This mountain road passes through **Abaurre-gaina/Abaurrea Alta** (181km), the highest village in Nafarroa at 1035m, with great views towards the Pyrenees. From here the road descends, with continually fine views of the mountains, to **Aribe** (192km ⛪⛲), with its triple-arched medieval bridge over the Irati River. Aribe is the base for a detour to Orbaitzeta and the start of Walk 25.

Continue on the main road (NA140). (Just beyond Aribe, about 100m to the left along the road towards OROZ BETELU, is an impressive crag which may be climbed in a few minutes, up to the **Ariztokia** viewpoint, from where there are excellent views of the Irati River and Gorge.) On reaching the main N135 road, turn right to enter **Auritz/Burguete** (201km ⛪⛪△✕⛲), one of the prettiest villages in the region, with lovely old houses and water channels lining its main street. It is worth stopping here, as there are several fine accommodation and eating possibilities.

From here a tree-lined avenue soon brings us to **Orreaga/Ronces-valles** (206km ☨✕). This important sanctuary and hospital is the most popular starting point in Spain for the Pilgrims' Route to Santiago. It is also the site of the legendary battle of Roncesvalles in 778, when the Basques defeated Charlemagne's army, as immortalised in the *Chanson de Roland*, which spread the word of Christianity. Carry on up to the **Col d'Ibañeta** (1057m; 208km 📷), where a monolith commemorates the battle and there is an interesting bird migration centre. During September and October, the centre sets up several telescopes on the col which may be used by the public for observing the thousands of migrating birds as they cross this relatively low part of the Pyrenees. The col also makes a fine picnic area (⊓*P*). (See *Landscapes of the Pyrenees* for details of walks in this area.) From here it is also possible to descend into France to St Jean-Pied-de-Port/Donibane Garazi and link up with Car tour 8.

Return along the main road *past* the NA140 from Aribe, and take the next left turn, the NA1720 towards AOIZ/AGOITZ. This scenic road follows the course of the **Urrobi River**, passing several small hamlets with old stone cottages. One of them, **Zandueta** (223km ⊓*P*), has a nice little picnic site to the left by the river. Leaving the forested area, the valley widens out to rolling farmland. We cross the **Canal de Navarra** (237km) just before Aoiz/Agoitz and go around this town, to join the NA150 to IRUÑA-PAMPLONA. On the outskirts of the city (252km), turn left on the PA30, initially following signposting to ZARAGOZA, and then right at the next roundabout onto the NA2303 to PAMPLONA. Keep straight on to enter the city, following signs to CENTRO URBANO/ERDI ALDEA, to return to the bus station in **Iruña-Pamplona** (259km).

Car tour 7: THE FRENCH BASQUE COAST AND PICTURESQUE INLAND VILLAGES OF LAPURDI

Bayonne/Baiona • Biarritz • (Guethary) • St Jean-de-Luz/Donibane Lohizun • La Corniche • Ascain • Ainhoa • Espelette • Pas de Roland • Bidarrai • Cambo-les-Bains • Route des Cimes • Mougerre • Bayonne/Baiona

151km/94mi; about 4h30min driving time
En route: Short walks 3, 17; Walks 26, 27, 28, 29
Picnic suggestions: St Jean-de-Luz/Donibane Lohizun, on the **Sainte Barbe** headland at far of the

beach (31km); **Domaine d'Abbadie**, Hendaia (40km); **Pas de Roland**, beside the river (92km); **Baztán Gorge** (a 2km detour from Bidarrai at the 101km-point, on the way to the start of Walk 28)

This tour covers the rugged French Basque coast and its attractive resorts, combined with the beautiful villages of inland Lapurdi and undulating countryside of the Pyrenean foothills.

Bayonne/Baiona (✝🏔△✕🛒M) has a Gothic cathedral, the Musée Bonat and an interesting old town (Petit Bayonne). Start the tour from the roundabout on the D810 by the river, just north of the tourist office: proceed along Allées Marines towards ANGLET-PLAGES. This road keeps parallel to the **Adour River** at the start of the estuary. When you reach the mouth of the river (6km), turn right at a roundabout to **la Barre**, the lighthouse and break-water — a good point from which to observe the shipping activity and sea. Return to the roundabout and follow signs towards BIARRITZ; from here on, lanes lead off to the right, to a string of pleasant beaches.

At another roundabout (10km), make a short detour for GROTTE DE LA CHAMBRE D'AMOUR, where there is a particularly fine beach. Return to the roundabout, following the road up to the clifftops that becomes Bld de la Mer. You are now entering the stylish resort of **Biarritz★** (🏔△✕🛒) proper. On arriving in the town centre, turn right at the first traffic lights (a little beyond the Hotel du Palais; 13.5km) towards PORT VIEUX. In this way you avoid

the often-congested town centre and can drive along the most spectacular stretch of coast around Biarritz. The old port itself, on the right opposite the church of Saint-Eugenie, is well worth exploring. Continuing through a tunnel under the cliff, you arrive at the **Rocher de la Vierge** (15km ✳🖼), the French Basque coast's best-known landmark. A walk across the footbridge to the rock topped by a statue of the Virgin Mary, provides an exhilarating short stroll, especially when the sea is high and the waves come crashing in around the rock and spew out through a natural arch jutting out from the cliffs.

Continue around the small **Plage du Port Vieux** and follow signs on the D911 towards ST JEAN-DE-LUZ. Turn right on the main D810 (21km) and proceed through **Bidart** (24km), where the road again reaches the sea by the village's main beach, and above Guethary (25km). (*Detour:* It's worth turning right from the traffic lights at the top of the hill to divert 1km to this pretty village (🏔△✕) with its tiny fishing port.)

On reaching **St Jean-de-Luz/**

Donibane Lohizun (⛺△✕🍴
⛺M), follow the bypass road round
the town towards *DONOSTIA-SAN
SEBASTIAN* at the roundabout by the
main railway station; turn right to
park at one of the car parks on either
side of the roundabout on Bld du
Commandant Passicot (31km) to
explore the fishing port and very
attractive old town centre. Of special
interest is the Maison Louis XIV,
where the young king was married
(on the main square of the same
name) and a nice picnic site (🍴P) at
the far end of the beach on the
Sainte Barbe headland.

Leaving St Jean, cross the bridge
over the river Nivelle and take the
first right turn, to enter **Ziburu-
Ciboure**, returning to the road
which hugs the bay. At **Sokoa** you
cross a small bridge over the river
and head along the D912 towards
HENDAYE-PLAGE — to the start of **La
Corniche** (34km ✳🖼), the
beautiful cliff-top drive towards the
Spanish border. A turning to the
right just before a roundabout on
the outskirts of the border town of
Hendaye/Hendaia (⛺△✕) leads
to the **Château d'Abbadie** (40km
✳*MP*🚗17). The estate — especially

Short walk for motorists

🚗 **17 Chateau d'Abbadie**
*4km/2.5mi; 1h40min. A leisurely
stroll, but with a steep descent of 80m
to Loya Bay, this takes in some of the
most dramatic cliff formations on the
coast. From the roundabout just past
the entrance to Domaine d'Abbadie,
take the steep lane down to the right
and park at the bottom of the hill.*
Start by the **'Sentier Littoral'
panel** showing the 25km coastal
walk from here to Bidart: enter
the **Abbadie estate** on a paved
path. Turn left at the **Larretxea
information centre** and cross the
field to the cliff path. Once up on
the cliffs, two paths lead to **viewpoints** over Hendaye's fine sandy
beach (**10min**). *For the best views,
always follow the path closest to the
cliff-edge.* Les Deux Jumeaux,
where many cormorants nest, are
best viewed from the far side of
the first cove (**25min**). According
to legend, these twin off-shore
rocks were thrown from the top
of Aiako Harriak (Peñas de Aia;
Walk 7) by the angry *basojaun*
(giant) guarding the mountain.

Beyond some large derelict
WW2 bunkers, the main headland (**Pointe Ste Anne; 35min**),
offers fine views to some of the
best sandstone cliff formations
and back to the château on the
highest part of the estate. As you
emerge from woodland, turn left
(the château now directly ahead).
At a T-junction (**50min**), turn left
again on a wide path (the *sentier
littoral* to Bidart). After 150m
look for a narrow *unmarked* path
to the left and descend steeply to
the **Baie de Loya** (**1h05min**).
Return to the T-junction at the
50min-point (**1h25min**) and pass
a farmhouse (the château now
just to your left). At **Larretxea**
(**1h 35min**), return on the paved
path to the **car park** (**1h40min**).

43

the Pointe Ste Anne headland —
makes a good spot for a picnic with
sea views. The château was originally
built in the mid-19th century by a
half-Irish, half-Basque adventurer
and explorer, Antoine d'Abbadie,
best remembered for his research
work close to the sources of the Nile
in Ethiopia and his correspondence
with the poet Rimbaud.

Continuing to the roundabout
mentioned above, turn right along a
lane marked DOMAINE D'ABBADIE
for the start of Short walk 17 or, to
continue the main tour, turn left on
the D658 signposted CHATEAU
D'URTUBIE, to pass under a railway
bridge and join the D810 again
(44km). Turn left again in the
direction of BAYONNE.

On reaching a roundabout just
beyond **Urrugne** (49km ▲ △ ✕),
turn right under the motorway
bridge on the D4 towards ASCAIN
and SARA/SARE. The road now heads
inland towards the Pyrenean
foothills as they fall away into the
Atlantic. Continue on this road
towards SARA, taking the left fork
(52km) towards OLHETTE. Opposite
the Trabenia Hotel/Restaurant in
Olhette (55km), turn right onto the
lane marked CHEMIN DU XURIEN
BORDA to reach the car park for the
start of Walk 26 to Larrun.

From Olhette the road follows
the flanks of Larrun and soon
reaches the pretty village of **Ascain**
(61km ▲ △✕). At the clock tower
by the main square, turn left towards
SARE. The road climbs to the
funicular station of **Le Petit Train
de la Rhune★** (65km). An easy
alternative to Walk 26 is to take the
train up and return back down the
mountain on a waymarked path
which ends at the funicular station.

The road meanders downhill. At
the first roundabout, head straight
up the hill to the square in the centre

of **Sara** (68 km ▲ △✕), another
picture-postcard traditional Basque
village. A beautiful tamarisk-lined
street leads off this square. Park and
take the time to look around. There
is normally a kiosk near the square
selling freshly-made *gateau basque*
(with cream or sour cherry filling).

Leaving Sara, take the road
heading uphill from the square by
Hotel Arraza, signposted GROTTES-
LEZEA, and descend to a **mini-
roundabout** just before the river
(69km). (*Detour:* A 5km detour
from this roundabout leads to the
Caves of Sara, signposted 'Grottes
Prehistoriques' (∩🚌3). On the way,
there are many beautiful farmhouses,
several of which are *chambres d'hôtes*.
Short walk 3 for motorists,
described on page 18, may be done
in the reverse direction from here,
and the caves are also accessible by
bus from St Jean-de-Luz.)

From the mini-roundabout the
main tour heads over the river
bridge, still on the D4, towards
AINHOA. Some 3km further on, turn
right over the Nivelle River and then
left on the D305, a narrow country
lane which meanders through a thick
forest alongside a stream. When you
reach the main D20 road, turn right
and immediately you will find your-
self on the main street of **Ainhoa**
(77km ✝▲✕), lined with extremely
colourful houses with wood-beamed
façades. This is perhaps the most
beautiful village of all in Lapurdi.
The border is just 2km further
south, at Dantxarinea (from where
Zugarramurdi, described in Car tour
2, may be reached in 4km from the
first roundabout after the former
customs post).

From Ainhoa this tour heads
back along the D20, then turns right
on the D918 to **Espelette** (83km
▲ △✕). From the first roundabout,
at the entrance to the village, head

Top: Pas de Roland; above: red peppers drying on a butcher's shop in Espelette

right uphill to a second one and park just to the left of it to explore the main, winding street, with more colourful half-timbered houses. This is another pretty place, famous for its red peppers, which may be seen drying outside the houses. From the car park/roundabout follow signs towards *ITXASSOU-ITSASU* on the D249.

Continue through **Itxassou** (89km 🔺△✕), past the main square, and turn right down a lane opposite an incongruous-looking indoor *frontón* called Trinquet Balaki. Pass the church and the Hotel Restaurant du Chene, and go on towards the **Pas de Roland** (✳). Having driven through rolling hills for a while on this tour, this narrow gorge now gives you the sensation of really being in the Pyrenees. For Walk 27 and/or to allow plenty of time for exploration, park in the small car park on the right just before the gorge (91km). Otherwise, continue on the narrow road (with passing places) beside the fast-flowing Nive River, a popular rafting spot. For a short stop, park by the quaint little Hotel Restaurant Pas de Roland (92km 🔺✕⊓P) and enjoy the glorious scenery by the river, which makes an ideal place to picnic and view the circular rock arch associated with the Roland legend. Walk 27 begins here.

To continue the tour, turn left over the bridge at Pas de Roland and go uphill past another attractive hotel/restaurant, following the narrow lane beside the Nive. You pass a pretty collection of farmhouses scattered over the valley on the outskirts of Bidarrai. On reaching the valley floor about 300m further on (101km), the lane to the right leads to the starting point for

Walk 28, as well as picnic sites (⊓P) along the Baztán River.

The main tour heads left here: cross the metal bridge, and turn left again to reach the old **Pont d'Enfer** over the Nive (102km). Continue past the hotel of the same name and up the hill to the pretty village of **Bidarrai** (✝🔺✕), with its church and *frontón*. The famous **Iparla Ridge** may be climbed from behind the Aunamendi refuge in the corner of the square (see *Landscapes of the Pyrenees*).

Return to the **Pont d'Enfer** (104km), cross the new bridge and turn left on the main D918. Shortly after passing the turn-off left to Itxassou, turn right (signposted to *CAMBO* and *HASPARREN*) to enter **Cambo-les-Bains** (117km 🔺△✕)

Pont d'Enfer at Bidarrai

— where *Cyrano de Bergerac* was written. In the town centre, turn right at the first roundabout, on the D10 towards HASPARREN. Just outside the town there is an impressive **spa** with ornate, Moorish-style gardens off to the right. The road continues through **Urcuray/Urkoi** (124km 🚶) with its quaint little church and cemetery. Walk 29 starts here.

Beyond the village, take a sharp left (126km) up the hill before Hasparren, heading for BAYONNE/ BAIONA. This is the start of the D22, the **Route des Cîmes** (✳), a pleasant route over the hilltops, with panoramic views all around. Turn right on the D257 (140km) towards MOUGERRE, to stay up on the ridge. After crossing the A64 motorway, at the next main crossroads, turn left uphill on the D712, to enter **Mougerre** (143km 🚶), a collection of more wonderfully colourful half-timbered houses along two cobbled streets separated by a beautiful church. This village is perched on

46

top of the highest hill for miles around.

From here continue on to the **Croix de Mougerre** (📷), a large war memorial dedicated to victims of the 1813-14 Napoleonic War. From the car park on the right, walk up to the memorial and admire the view of the river Adour and Bayonne/Baiona, with its twin-spired cathedral clearly visible. The G8 Adour-Pyrenées long-distance footpath from Sara to Urt (on the banks of the Adour to the north) passes by here, and there is an explanatory map in the car park. Continue downhill on the D712 to the main road, turn right and almost immediately you are on the banks of the **Adour** (147km). From the roundabout by the river, drive under the A63 motorway bridge to edge the river. Once in the old town (**Petit Bayonne**), cross the bridge over the Nive and return to the tourist office in **Bayonne/Baiona** (151km).

Car tour 8: THE MOUNTAINS, FORESTS AND CANYONS OF XIBEROA/ZUBEROA

St Jean-Pied-de-Port/Donibane Garazi • Selva de Irati • Larrau • Logibar • Holtzarte Gorge • Kakueta Gorge • Santa Grazi/Ste-Engrâce • Arette • Tardets • Gotein • Mauléon • Bidouze River • St Jean-Pied-de-Port/Donibane Garazi

162km/101mi; about 4h15min driving time
En route: Short walks for motorists 18, 19; Walks 30, 31, 32
This route includes some mountain roads which may be snow-covered in winter — the road via the Chalets of Irati reaches 1327m, and the road above the small ski resort of Arette-la-Pierre-St Martin 1765m, although the latter road at least is usually kept open all year round. The detour to the start of Short walk 19 at the Source de

Bidouze involves a 3km drive on an unsurfaced, fairly potholed road, but it can be negotiated by normal vehicles.
Picnic suggestions: Lacs d'Iraty (28km); **Kakueta Gorge**, just before the waterfall (60km); **Arette River** (90km); at the end of lane leading to Short walk 19 to the **Source de la Bidouze** and also at the start of the walk itself, by the river (detours of 3.5km and 6.5km respectively from Donaixti Ibarre-St Just, the 140km-point)

This tour covers some of the most intriguing landscapes of the Western Pyrenees, in particular the extraordinary canyon country around Santa Grazi/Ste-Engrâce. The province of Xiberoa also provides perhaps the best chance to observe rural Basque life in and around its small villages. Until fairly recently these pastoral settings were still a fairly isolated part of the French Basque Country. The tour starts in beautiful St Jean-Pied-de-Port/Donibane Garazi, a not-to-be-missed town.

St Jean-Pied-de-Port/Donibane Garazi (✝🏔⛺✕⌕) is a major departure point for the Pilgrims' Route to Santiago and a wonderfully preserved, colourful old town of cobbled streets full of character. Turn right from the **office de tourisme** along the main road heading out of town and follow signs towards the D933 and *PAU* at the first round-about. At **St Jean-le-Vieux** (4km), turn right on the D18 towards *IRATY*. The road initially winds through farmland and a series of hamlets with great views ahead to the pointed summit of **Mt Behorlegy**. It then starts its steep climb (14km) up towards the Irati plateau, until it runs roughly parallel with the long, crescent shaped-ridge of Behorlegy, now on the far side of the valley. (*Detour:* After 19km, a narrow lane

descends to the right, to a beautiful, isolated valley below Mt Irau, a detour of 4km.)
The main tour keeps ahead to the **Col de Burdinkurutz** (23km 🍽), where the long ridge of Mendibeltza and Arthonatze meets the road. Descend to the **Chalet de Cize** (or **Etxola**; 25km ✕) on the plateau. The **Selva de Irati** (✳) forms part of one of the largest forested areas in the Pyrenees. This chalet provides meals and refreshments, as do Le Kaiolar, a delightful converted sheep hut a detour of about 500m from the main road and, a further 1km, past some ponds on the plateau, Chalet Pedro (✕), with some nice tables beside the river. From here, the GR10 ascends to the cromlech-topped site of Okabe (⛩), and a narrow road continues for a further

47

Santa Grazi/Ste-Engrâce under a sprinkling of snow

2.5km almost to the Spanish border in the heart of the forest.

From the Chalet de Cize, continue along the D18 to the **Lacs d'Iraty** (28km △⊟*P*). The second and smaller of the two lakes makes an especially pleasant picnic setting. From here the road climbs up higher into the Forest of Iraty, to a flat area where there is a collection of wooden chalets known as the **Chalets d'Iraty** (32km ✕⌂). They are available to rent throughout the year and a cross-country skiing centre in winter. Continue a further 500m to Col d'Orgambidesca, a top spot for bird watchers with fantastic views to Mt Ori, the first Pyrenean peak over 2000m when travelling westwards from the Atlantic.

Continue on down the mountain to the pretty village of **Larrau** (44km ▲✕△⌂), perched on the hillside overlooking some impressive rocky crags. The road from here over the Pyrenees to Ochagavía in Nafarroa via the **Col de Larrau** is only reliably snow-free from May to October, but during these months it makes a good way to link up with Car tour 6. Descend through the village on the D26 to the bar/refuge

of **Logibar** (46km) tucked into the bottom of the valley. The GR10 passes through here, and Walk 30 to the hanging bridge of Holtzarte and its gorge starts from the car park behind the refuge.

Continue down the Larrau Valley and turn right (53km) towards *SAINTE-ENGRÂCE*. This is probably the most isolated valley remaining in the French Basque Country and one of its most beautiful. The road is narrow and winding as it follows the river past a small reservoir and a riverside campsite (△) to the entrance to the **Kakueta Gorge** (60km ✳⌂18).

After passing through some pretty hamlets you come to the car park/information centre for **La Verna** (63km), one of the largest caves in the world open to the public. It can be visited from mid-April to mid-November; there are several tours of varying degrees of difficulty from one hour to a full day, all of which must be booked online in advance via www.laverna.fr. The cave entrance is 8km up the mountain and tours include transport from the car park (although it is possible to walk there as well, on the nearby

In the Kakueta Gorge

GR10 (see map on page 130).

Just beyond is the charming hamlet of **Santa Grazi/Ste-Engrâce** (630m; 64km ♦📷). Its 11th-century Romanesque church (where Walk 31 to the amazing Ehüjarre Canyon starts) has some extremely old discoidal steles in the graveyard.

The tour continues from here on the D113 and after 700m passes Auberge Berriex, which makes an excellent food/refreshment stop from where there are fine views over the entire valley, church and the immense walls of the Ehüjarre Canyon. You enter the **Forêt Comunal de Lanne** and climb to the **Col de Suscousse** (1216m; 71km 📷). (*Detour:* From this pass a narrow road to the left leads to the cross country ski resort of Issarbe.) The main tour continues to a cross-roads at the **Col de Soudet** (1540m; 75km), just before the fairly small ski resort of Arette-la-Pierre- St Martin. (*Detour:* A right turn here leads to the top of the pass on the Spanish border at 1765m, for Walk 32. The road continues to the attractive Navarran villages of Isaba and Roncal on the far side of the pass.)

Short walk for motorists
🚗 **18 Kakueta Gorge**
4.5km/2.8mi; 2h. This is the most famous gorge in the French Basque Pyrenees, 2km long and over 350m deep in places. At its narrowest, the walls are only 5m apart. Although this is a very popular tourist attraction, it's a beautiful walk. The lush vegetation is more reminiscent of tropical climes than the Pyrenees. There is a waterfall towards the end of the gorge, with pleasant picnic spots nearby, and beyond it is a cave. Take care negotiating the rocks and the plank boardwalks, which can be slippery. NB: as of September 2022, the gorge was closed to the public; check www.sainte-engrace.fr to see when it will reopen.

From the **Bar Cascade** descend to the emerald-green waters of the small **Bentia Reservoir** and cross a second gorge on a footbridge. As you ascend on the far side of the lake, the vegetation thickens and info boards provide details of the wide variety of lichens and other plant life on view. Descend to the river on the other side of the hill and pass through a **tunnel** (**15min**) — into the narrowest part of the gorge, known as the **Grand Etroit**, with its huge limestone walls covered in moss. An elevated boardwalk with railings helps on slippery sections.

Cross the river just before some **rapids** (**30min**) and rise gradually as the gorge widens out. You come to a **waterfall** (**45min**); it pours out of an underground river emerging from the rock face — a beautiful spot to rest (⊟P) in view of the falls. It is possible to walk right up behind the falls. The path continues a further 200m, up to a small grotto, which may be entered (**1h**).

From here retrace your steps to the **Bar cascade** (**2h**).

St Jean-Pied-de-Port/ Donibane Garazi

The main tour heads left from the crossroads on the D132 towards ARETTE. Once on the valley floor, there are several nice picnic sites (90km 🚐P) beside the road by the **Arette River**. Continue on to **Arette** (96km 🏔️△✖️🛏️) and turn left by the church. Drive through the village on the D918 towards LANNE and MAULEON. Another mountain road leads back up to Issarbe (101km), but we continue through the pretty village of **Montory** to **Tardets** (110km 🏔️✖️🛏️), with its attractive main square. (***Detour:*** A highly recommended 7km detour leads from the street on the right of this square, by the *office de tourisme*, to the hilltop chapel of La Madeleine (795m ✳️✝️📷) via the extremely narrow and steep D347. It is a good idea to leave the car at the col about 1km before the chapel and walk up. There are twice-yearly pilgrimages to this site (on the Sunday before Easter and on July 22nd), and this is one of the best vantage points from which to view the high Pyrenees and the valleys of Xiberoa.)

50

The main tour continues from the square at Tardets on the main road towards MAULEON. It is worth stopping at **Gotein** (118km ✝️△), to view the 16th-century church of **Saint André**, probably the best example of the style of church typical of this region, with its *clocher trinitaire* and curious outside wooden staircase granting access to the upstairs pews (where the women traditionally sit — a custom still maintained today in these parts).

Carry on to the centre of **Mauléon** (121km 🏨🏔️✖️🛏️), the sleepy provincial capital of Xiberoa and the only town of any size in the province. Cross the river bridge and park in the large main square, to do a walking tour of **Vieux Mauléon** and the old hilltop castle. There is a helpful tourist office in the square, with details of walks in the area and information about the *maskaradak* and *pastoralak*, plays and pageants performed and sung in Euskera which are unique to this area and are held in summer. For the annual *pastoralak* (usually at the end of July

or early August), each village takes it in turn to go on tour around Xiberoa with up to 70 participants.

Turn left at the end of the main square and follow the *TOUTES DIRECTIONS* sign to a roundabout and then head towards *ST JEAN-PIED-DE-PORT* on the D918. There are more great views over the valley from the **Col d'Osquich** (392m; 133km 📷), from where a 1km detour to the hilltop chapel of St Antoine is signposted.

(*Detour:* At 140km, just before Donaixti Ibarre-St Just, a lane to the left signposted *SOURCE DE LA BIDOUZE* descends to the Bidouze River. The asphalt ends after 3.5km by a farm and small picnic site (⊼P). From here it's another 3km on a track to park by the footbridge where 🚗19 starts.)

The main tour continues on the main road from **Donaixti Ibarre-St Just** to the junction with the D933 (146km). Turn left here, back via **St Jean-le-Vieux**, to **St Jean-Pied-de-Port/Donibane Garazi** (162km).

Short walk for motorists

🚗 **19 Source de la Bidouze**
*4km/2.5mi; 1h40min. This is a fairly short walk through the lower part of the Forêt d'Arbailles (Arbailleta), a beautiful and remote, unspoilt region of dense forest, to the extraordinary cave out of which the River Bidouze flows. The path involves crossing a couple of small streams, and the rocks on the approach to the cave are usually quite slippery, but this is otherwise an easy walk, with a total height gain of 350m. **NB:** If you decide to leave your car at the farm where the asphalt ends, allow an extra 6km/ 1h30min for this walk. Otherwise follow the fairly potholed unsurfaced road for a further 3km from the farm, to a small footbridge and another small riverside picnic site (350m; ⊼P), still inside the forest.*
Cross the **footbridge** and follow yellow and scarlet marks on the rock, going uphill and further into the forest, gaining height above the river. Carry straight on where another path comes up from the river (**15min**). As you climb steadily, the route becomes more spectacular, as the path is carved out of the rock face and the river descends in a series of waterfalls (**25min**).

Cross a first stream and continue to follow yellow way-marking, ignoring a path to the left (**35min**). Go straight on at the next junction (**40min**) and *carefully* cross a second stream, strewn with large, moss-covered rocks (**45min**). When you come to a **cave** (650m; **50min**), go inside, to see the Bidouze emerging from its underground source and enjoy the view looking out at the dense forest in this magical place.

Then retrace your steps to the **footbridge** (**1h40min**).

51

Walking

The walks in this book have been carefully selected to offer as much variety as possible in terms of landscapes and level of difficulty. The Basque Country is blessed with many areas of outstanding natural beauty. Access details are given for those travelling by car or public transport; for more public transport details, see the reverse of the touring map inside the back cover.

GRADING, WAYMARKING, MAPS, GPS

There is a quick overview of each walk's **grade** in the Contents. But we've only had space to show the grade of a *main* walk: for full details, including easier versions, see the walk itself. Here is a brief overview of the two gradings under which all these walks fall:

● easy — ascents/descents of no more than about 300-500m/1000-1800ft; good surfaces underfoot; easily followed. *The short walks for motorists all fall into this category.*

● moderate-strenuous to strenuous — ascents/descents may be over 500m/1800ft; variable surfaces underfoot — you must be sure-footed and agile; possible route-finding problems in poor visibility. *Most of the main walks in this book fall into this category.*

Either of these grades may be followed by the symbol ❣: danger of vertigo — you must have a good head for heights.

All 32 main walks are manageable by any reasonably fit person who is used to hill walking, and many involve relatively little gradient. Sections of walks which might demand a head for heights have been kept to an absolute minimum, and where possible an alternative route is given.

The longer, more strenuous walks featured may be shortened in most cases; if so, shorter alternatives are mentioned in the 'logistics' section at the start of the walk. But of course you could just start out on a walk and retrace your steps.

The Basques themselves are keen walkers, and **waymarking** is in general of an extremely high standard. Firstly, there are the various GR routes crossing the region — long-distance footpaths on both sides of the Pyrenees, way-marked in red and white. These include the Trans-Pyrenean GR10 and GR11 crossing the entire Pyrenees from coast to coast (on the French and Spanish sides respectively) and the GR12 Sendero de Euskal Herria across the whole Spanish Basque Country. There are also relatively short GR routes, such as the three-day GR20 Vuelta de la Sierra de Aralar and the week-long GR121 Vuelta de Gipuzkoa.

There are also short-distance PR and SL routes, which are waymarked in yellow and white and green and white respectively, which cover local areas.

Thirdly, there are many short trails waymarked in other colour combinations, details of which are usually given on information boards at the start of trailheads.

Many of the walking routes in this book follow sections of *all* the aforementioned types of footpath. In any case, all the walks described provide precise instructions, regardless of whether waymarking is adequate or not.

Our **maps** have been adapted from different sources, depending on the area covered. All are at scale of 1:50 000, and should provide sufficient detail for the walker. Maps of the **Iparralde**/French Basque Country walks have been adapted from the French IGN 'Top 25' series, those of the three provinces of the **Comunidad Autónoma Vasca** are adapted from the Gobierno Vasco's 1:25 000 series, and those of **Nafarroa** from the Instituto Geográfico Nacional maps covering the whole of Spain (also at a scale of 1:25 000).

While there are five fold-out sheets which cover the whole of Iparralde (1245 ET, 1245 OT, 1345 ET, 1346 ET and 1346 OT), the Gobierno Vasco and Spanish IGN maps are sold as very small sheets, and over 200 maps are needed to cover the four provinces! A better bet is to obtain specific maps in the 'Cuadernos Pirenaícos' series, published by Sua Edizioak. These are very detailed, high quality, reasonably priced maps, on sale in local bookshops in the main towns. They also include booklets (in Spanish) outlining many walking routes.

Free **GPS track** downloads are available for all these walks: see the Basque Country page on the Sunflower website. Please bear in mind, however, that GPS readings should *never* be relied upon as your sole reference point, as conditions can change overnight. *But even if you don't use GPS on the ground,* it's great fun opening our GPX files in Google Earth to preview the walks in advance!

WHERE TO STAY

The Basque Country has an extensive network of reasonably priced accommodation in rural areas. In the **Comunidad Autónoma Vasca**, the *agroturismo/nekazalturismoa* (rural accommodation programme) extends to every corner of the region, and all local tourist offices stock a booklet containing a comprehensive list. You can also book such accommodation on the internet (www. nekatur.net). In **Nafarroa**, these are called *casas rurales/ landa etxeak* and, as the name implies, it is often necessary to rent a whole house rather than just a room. The Gobierno Foral de Navarra publishes a comprehensive booklet detailing all accommodation in the province, again available through tourist offices or on the internet (www.cfnavarra.es/ turismonavarra). In **Iparralde**, there is an excellent choice of rural accommodation in the form of *gîtes* (www.gites-de-france.fr) and

many small country hotels — the best source of information for the latter in the French Basque Country, many of which are grouped together as 'Logis de France', is via www.logishotels.com. All the types of accommodation mentioned above are easily recognised by distinctive signs (the photograph above illustrates signposting in the Comunidad Autónoma Vasca).

Most towns of any size in the Spanish Basque Country, especially those on the coast, also have an inexpensive, albeit at times fairly basic *casa de huésped, hostal* or *pensión*, recognisable by the signs CH, H and P respectively, and in the major tourist resorts such as Donostia-San Sebastián and Biarritz there is a variety of accommodation across the spectrum.

Further into the mountains, other options for walkers are: **on the French side**, *gîtes d'étapes* (www.gite-etape.com), usually located conveniently along the GR long-distance walking routes, notably the GR10 Trans-Pyrenean walk as it passes through the French Basque provinces. **On the Spanish side**, most mountain areas covered in this book (not just those in the Pyrenees) have a *refugio/aterpe*. These, and the *gîtes de'étapes* in France, are shown on the relevant walking maps and mentioned in the descriptions. It is always advisable, however, to phone in advance to check opening times if travelling out of season, even if the refuge concerned is supposed to be open year round. Finally, there are campsites in most areas of natural beauty in the region, details again being available through local tourist offices.

WEATHER

There is a **marked contrast in weather between the three distinct areas** comprising the Basque Country — those close to the coast, the high mountains, and the plains. The coastal region and immediate hinterland (and indeed the entire Atlantic coast of northern Spain and southwest France) is extremely green for good reason. It can rain at any time of year, and when it does, you can be in for a soaking. On the other hand, the region also enjoys a generally mild climate without extremes of temperature either in high summer or mid-winter. The plains (central and southern Nafarroa and Araba) are both physically and climatically an extension of Castile — in other words dry, with hot summers and harsh winters when the temperature drops below zero. The high mountains (including the Pyrenees and the interior of Gipuzkoa, Bizkaia, Iparralde and northern Nafarroa) may be snow-bound from November to April.

Essentially, **most of the walks in this book can be done at any time of year**, although mountain ranges like the Sierra de Aralar or Sierra de Urbasa may be covered with snow for some part of the winter. However, Walks 24, 25, 30, 31 and 32 may be out of bounds from November to April because of the risk of snow. Conversely, temperatures do not necessarily soar so high in mid-summer as to make walking really uncomfortable (except possibly in the more southern corners of the region, where Walks 16, 18, 19 and 23 are located). The Basques, who are renowned hearty eaters, tend to do their walking before lunchtime. Thus they avoid the hottest part of the day, and they descend or return to the nearest bar or restaurant in time for a huge lunch!

CLOTHING AND EQUIPMENT

The general rule is always to carry the minimum possible, without leaving any essentials behind. Decent walking boots, provided they have already been broken in, are required for many of the walks and indeed advisable for all of them, although sturdy shoes or good trainers may be enough for some of the more gentle coastal and forest walks. Where this is the case, mention is made in the introduction to the walks concerned. Raingear is also *essential*, as even on the sunniest of days, the weather can easily change, albeit in the form of a brief passing shower.

If you need to buy any equipment, there are excellent sports and camping shops in all major towns in the region, a good place to start being one of the branches of the Decathlon hypermarket chain, in Anglet (near Bayonne/Baiona), Donostia-San Sebastián, Bilbao or Iruña-Pamplona.

A basic checklist for day walks could be as follows:
   small backpack
   water bottle
   small first aid kit
   torch (for exploring caves)
   walking boots (broken in)
   smartphone/emergency numbers
   telescopic walking stick (also handy for shooing away barking dogs)
   insect repellent
   fleece
   detachable trousers
   sunhat, sunglasses, suncream
   compass/gps
   waterproof/windproof (preferably Goretex) jacket
   lightweight waterproof trousers
   gloves
   penknife
   food
   binoculars

DOGS AND OTHER ANIMALS
The walker will invariably come in contact with **farm dogs**, as practically all Basque *baserri* have one tied up to warn their owners in good time of possible intruders. These will usually bark incessantly, but rarely do more than bark!

Sheepdogs need to be given a wide berth wherever possible, as they can be quite intimidating as they go about their duty looking after the flock. A decent stick is recommended to ward them off, and is an extremely useful piece of equipment for any walk. If dogs really worry you, ultrasonic 'Dog Dazers' are available on the web.

Bulls fortunately do not tend to roam loose on mountainsides, and cows in the main are pretty docile. Nonetheless, I generally *avoid making direct eye contact* with **cows**, **horses** or even **billy goats**, and will always try to respect their space if they happen to be on or near the path — certainly *it is important not to get between a young calf or foal and its mother.*

In 20 years of walking in the Basque Country I have never seen a **snake**, although vipers do exist. The biggest nuisances you will doubtless encounter are **flies**, **mosquitoes** and **midges**, especially in heavily forested areas, so it is important to carry an adequate supply of insect repellent.

SAFETY AND RESPONSIBLE BEHAVIOUR
For your own protection, please heed the following advice. Until you get used to the terrain, you can always start off by doing a couple of the short walks for motorists or a shorter section of one of the main walks.
•   **Do not overestimate your ability**. Much of the Basque terrain is mountainous, and many of the walks described involve varying degrees of ascent/descent, sometimes on narrow paths. Read through the introduction to the walk, to get a general overview of its degree of difficulty. (In fact,it is always a good idea to read through the *whole* walk in advance!)
•   Try to **avoid walking alone** if possible and/or inform a responsible person beforehand of your intended route.
•   **Always keep an eye on the weather.** Local people who are familiar with the terrain, such as farmers and shepherds, are the best sources of information. A compass or gps can be a life-saver if a

Mt Txindoki (Walk 4), seen from the N1 on Car tour 1

mountain should suddenly become enveloped in mist.
• Make sure you have enough **warm clothing** for higher altitudes.
• If a route is different from that described or has become **unsafe** due, for instance to storm damage, be prepared to turn back.
• Ensure that you have **sufficient water** (1-2 litres per person) before the start of the walk — natural springs with drinking water are noted in the text, providing the chance for a refill, but it's best to set off with enough for the entire walk anyway.
• **Do not light fires.** Use camping stoves.
• **Do not frighten animals.** Keep dogs on a lead.
• **Walk quietly** through all farms, hamlets and villages, **leaving gates just as you found them**.
• **Stay on the path** wherever it exists, to minimise damage to surrounding vegetation. Don't take short cuts on zigzag paths; this hastens ground erosion.
• **Protect all wild and cultivated plants.**
• **Take all your litter away with you**.
• **Respect local bye-laws**, especially with reference to 'wild camping'. Always choose an unobtrusive site.

• **Keep well away from streams** when attending to 'calls of nature'. Do not use detergents for washing/washing-up.

LANGUAGE HINTS
Castilian Spanish and French are universally spoken on their respective sides of the Pyrenees, but the Basque language (**Euskera**) is what most bonds the Basque people together, and any effort on the part of foreigners to learn a few phrases is much appreciated. Euskera has a standardised form known as *batua*, which is increasing in use and is taught in the schools, but there are still many discrepancies in terms of spelling (in particular between the Spanish Basque provinces and those of Iparralde). As a general rule, the further away you are from urban or tourist areas, the more Euskera you will hear spoken. Below are a few phrases to try out:

English	Euskera, followed by approximate pronunciation
Hello	Kaixo/**kai**-show
Goodbye	Agur/ah-**gore**
Good morning	Egun on/eh-goon-**on**
Good afternoon	Arratsalde on/ah-rats-**al**-deh-on
Good evening/ goodnight	Gabon/gab-**on**
How are you?	Zer moduz?/**sair**-mod-oos?
Fine, and you?	Ondo, eta zu?/**on**-doh, eh-tah-**soo**?
Please	Mesedez/meh-**seh**-dess
Thank you	Eskerrik asko/ess-keh-ree-**kas**-koh
very much	mil esker/mil-es-**keh**
Not at all	Ez horregatik/ess-or-**reh**-gah-tik

How much is it?	Zenbat da?/**sen**-bat-da?
Yes	Bai/buy
No	Ez/ess
Where is...?	Non dago....?, **noon**-dah-goh?
Is this the way?	Hau da bidea?/**ow**-dah-bee-day-ah?
To the right	Eskubira/ess-**koo**-bee-rah
To the left	Eskerrera/ess-**keh**-reh-rah
Straight on	Aurrera/ow-**reh**-ra
Up	Goian/**goy**-an
Down	Behean/**bay**-an
I'm lost	Galduta nago/gal-**doo**-tah nah-goh

GLOSSARY

Road signs tend to be in Spanish/Euskera or French/ Euskera (on the Spanish side, there is an ever-increasing tendency to use only Euskera on signposts, while on the French side, Euskera signposting and waymarking is less developed and many signs remain in French only).

Place names depend on the policy of individual town halls. In some cases, the official names of towns or cities may be double-barrelled (such as Donostia-San Sebastián), only in Euskera (such as Errezil) or most commonly referred to in Spanish or French (as is the case with Bilbao and Biarritz). *This book uses the most widely-used term in each case first*, followed by its equivalent in one of the two other relevant languages where necessary: for instance, St Jean-de-Luz/Donibane Lohizun.

As regards names of provinces, Euskera has been used. Note, however, the case of Xiberoa, which is the name that appears on road signs and maps most commonly on the French Basque side but is also referred to by Euskera speakers as Zuberoa, meaning that on maps of

the area published in Spain, it will appear as the latter.

The walker will come across many signs in Euskera on the routes described and on maps, particularly in the Spanish Basque Country, where the language is strongly promoted, so a basic vocabulary is useful. The letter *a* is added to nouns in order to form the definite article, unless the noun already ends in *a* (eg: *etxe* = house; *etxea* = the house); *k* is added to form the plural (*etxeak* = houses). Oft-recurring sounds are *tx* (pronounced like the *ch* in chat), *ts* (similar to *tx* but slightly softer), *tz* (pronounced like the *zz* in pizza) and *x* (pronounced like *sh* as in sheep).

Euskera, followed by approximate pronunciation	*English translation*
Aparkaleku/ah-**par**-ker-leh-koo	car park
Aran/ah-**ran**	valley
Aterpe/a-**tair**-peh	refuge
Atsedenleku/ah-**che**-den-leh-koo	picnic site
Baserri/**bah**-seh-ree	farmhouse
Berri/**beh**-ree	new
Bide/**bee**-deh	path
Borda/**bor**-der	(shepherd's) hut
Eliza/eh-**lees**-er	church
Enparantza/en-per-**antz**-er	square
Erdialdeair-dee-al-deh	town/city centre
Errota/eh-**roh**-ter	mill
Etorbide/eh-**tor**-bee-deh	avenue
Erreka/eh-**reh**-ker	stream
Errepide/eh-reh-**pee**-deh	(asphalted) road
Etxe/**eh**-cheh	house
Gailur/**guy**-loo-er	peak; summit
Gaztelu/**gas**-teh-loo	castle
Gurutz/**goo**-roots	cross
Haitz/aitz	rock; crag
Harri/**ah**-ree	rock; crag
Haritz/ah-**ritz**	oak/oak grove
Hariztitee/ah-**ris**-tee	oak/oak grove

Harrespila/ah-res-**peel**-yah — cromlech

Herri/**eh**-ree — village; small town

Hilerri/ill-**yeh**-ree — cemetery

Hondartza/on-**darts**-er — beach

Ibai/ee-buy — river

Ikurriña/ee-koo-**ree**-nee-er — (the Basque) flag

Iparralde/ee-pah-**rahl**-deh — the French Basque Country

Iturri/ee-**too**-ree — spring

Jauregi/how-**reh**-gee — palace

Kale/**kah**-leh — street

Laku/**lah**-koo — lake

Landa etxe/**lan**-der **eh**-cheh — casa rural

Lauburu/lau-**boo**-roo — (the Basque) cross (a symbol symbol seen everywhere)

Lepo/**leh**-poh — pass; col

Leze/**leh**-seh — cave

Mendi/**men**-dee — mountain

Mugarrimoo-gah-ree — boundary stone

Nekazalturismo/neh-kah-**sal**-tour-is-moh — agroturismo

Oihan/**oi**-ann — forest

Ostatu/oss-**tah**-too — inn

Pagaldi/pag-**al**-dee — beech/beech forest

Pago/**pag**-oh — beech/beech forest

Udal etxe/**oo**-dal **eh**-cheh — town hall

Uharte/oo-**ah**-teh — island

Sagardotegi/sag-**ar**-doh-tay-gee — cider house

Trikuharri/tree-koo-**ah**-ree — dolmen

Turismo bulegoa tour-**is**-moh boo-**leg**-oh-ah — tourist office

Urjauzi/or-**how**-see — waterfall

Urtegi/or-**tay**-gee — reservoir

Zahar/**sah**-ar — old

Zubi/**soo**-bee — bridge

GETTING ABOUT

The **Spanish Basque provinces** have a fairly extensive public transport system, enabling the walker to reach the start and end of many of the walks in this book, although sometimes a taxi is also required. The Spanish state rail system, *Renfe* (www.renfe.es) operates services in the provinces of the Comunidad Autónoma Vasca and Nafarroa on the main routes through the region, Irún to Donostia-San Sebastián and Bilbao to Vitoria-Gasteiz and Iruña-Pamplona. The most useful services for the walks included are the *trenes de cercanía,* local trains which stop at most stations, including request stops at minor halts.

A second rail system is operated by Euskotren (www. euskotren.es), which runs the routes primarily along the coast between Hendaye/Hendaia on the French side of the border and Donostia-San Sebastián, and from the latter via Zarautz, Zumaia and Durango to Bilbao, as well as routes serving the Bilbao conurbation and to Gernika and Bermeo. It also runs connecting bus services to certain points in Gipuzkoa.

Bus companies running routes in the Spanish Basque Country (and to other parts of Spain) are Pesa (www. pesa.es) and Alsa (www.alsa.es). In Gipuzkoa, Bizkaia and Araba, most local routes have now been grouped together by just one operator in each province, while in Nafarroa the most useful services are generally run by small companies covering the more rural areas. Names, telephone numbers and relevant timetables are shown on the back of the fold-out map at the end of this book.

In the **French Basque Country**, the French state railway SNCF (www.ter-sncf.com) operates the main coastal route from

Bayonne/Baiona to the border at Hendaye/Hendaia and also a useful, picturesque branch line from Bayonne/Baiona inland to St Jean-Pied-de-Port/Donibane Garazi, stopping at points fairly close to the start of Walks 27 and 28.

There are plenty of buses serving the relatively densely-populated French Basque coast between Bayonne/Baiona and Hendaye/Hendaia, but services to the more rural areas inland are limited, either being provided by Hegobus (from St Jean-de-Luz) or Le Basque Bondissant (from Bayonne/Baiona). But further into the mountains in the province of Xiberoa (Walks 30, 31 and 32), there is no public transport at all.

It is important to **check all timetables** shown for buses and trains, even though they were accurate at press date. It's a good idea to ask the relevant local tourist offices for up-to-date details, or to call the bus/train companies directly.

Another option is of course to **hire a car**, and this is easily done in all major towns in the Basque Country. In France, you will find rental firms at tourist centres such as Bayonne/Baiona, Biarritz and St Jean-de-Luz/Donibane Lohizun and in the provincial capitals of St Jean-Pied-de-Port/Donibane Garazi and Mauléon. In Spain, car hire is best arranged in one of the four provincial capitals: Bilbao, Donostia-San Sebastián, Vitoria-Gasteiz or Iruña-Pamplona.

ORGANISATION OF THE WALKS

The 32 main walks in this book have been designed to link up with the eight car tours as follows:

Walks 1-5: Car tour 1
Walks 6-10: Car tour 2
Walks 11-13: Car tour 3
Walks 14-17: Car tour 4

Larrun summit (Walk 26)

Walks 18-22: Car tour 5
Walks 23-25: Car tour 6
Walks 26-29: Car tour 7
Walks 30-32: Car tour 8

When planning a walk, begin by looking over the fold-out map at the back of the book and noting which walk are closest to the part of the region you are touring, and then check the details of the relevant car tour. Detailed maps, as well as descriptions are given for each walk, and there is at least one photograph showing a section of each walk, to give you an idea of the landscape.

Each walk has been carefully selected to include the most variety in terms of scenery. Where possible, routes are described so that most of the ascent is at the start of the walk. Many of the walks are circuits, but in the case of some mountain ascents, it is simply more practical to return along the same route. An effort has been made to ensure that starting points are as close as possible to public transport access, but often there will be a distance of a few kilometres to the nearest bus stop or train station. In the remote mountainous areas, however, and in particular in inland Iparralde (the French Basque Country), public transport is simply non-existent!

Each walk begins 'logistics': distance in kilometres and miles, approximate walking time, grade (including the quality of waymarking), and access. Where walks are accessible by bus or train, the relevant timetables are provided on the back of the large fold-out map, together with phone numbers and/or websites of the bus/railway companies (timetables should nonetheless always be re-checked beforehand, as changes inevitably occur). Below the 'logistics' is a brief summary of the attractions to be seen along the way.

Walking times given are those I calculated walking at a slow to average pace, and *do not allow for stops at the points of interest described*, even mountain summits. Be sure to increase walking times by *at least* a third. Invariably, most walks will last a full day if weather

conditions are optimum and you stop to picnic, swim, or take photos!

The following symbols are used on the walking maps:

═══	motorway	●▶	spring, waterfall, etc	⚑	prehistoric site
▬▬	dual carriageway	⚲	church, monastery	∩∩	cave.aqueduct
▬▬	main/trunk road	⚲	chapel	△	campsite
───	secondary road	†	cross	■	specified building
░░░	motorable track	▲	summit marker	⛫	refuge
───	other track	⊣	cemetery	🏠	agroturismo
– – –	cart track, path, trail	🖼	picnic site	☼ 3	mill.waypoint
2→	main walk	📷	viewpoint	◇	rock formation.cairn
2→	alternative walk	🚌	bus stop	⚔	monument, tower
🚌8	walk for motorists	🚉	railway station	*i*	tourist office
—400—	height in metres	🚗	car parking	⩛	electricity substation
		◼◻	castle, fort.ruins	⋀	communications mast

Below: the high meadows of Arraba (near Walk 14) with a view towards Gorbeia, Bizkaia's highest mountain

Walk 1: FARO DE LA PLATA

Distance: 7.5km/4.7mi; 2h35min
Grade: ● moderate, with a fairly steep 250m ascent from Gros Beach to Ulia at the start. The route then undulates along the cliff tops. The descent to the harbour of Pasai San Pedro is also fairly steep. The route is very well waymarked in red and white, forming part of the GR121 vuelta de Gipuzkoa.
Equipment: see page 55; decent trainers are fine.
Access: the walk starts in the city centre of Donostia-Sebastián, returning to the city by 🚐 from Pasai San Pedro.

This walk provides an excellent chance to gain access to one of the best stretches of rugged coast, with the advantage of being right on the city's doorstep. The path hugs the clifftops for much of the route, meandering around the side of the heavily forested Mt Ulia. The approach to the lighthouse and the descent to the narrow channel granting access to the harbour of Pasaia are further highlights.

To start the walk, cross the **Kursaal Bridge** over the **Urumea River** (**1**), pass the Kursaal building and walk along the promenade of **Gros Beach**. At the far end of the beach, in the part of town directly below Mt Ulia known as **Sagüés**, follow the main road past the **church** and, just before the **petrol station**, turn left up **Zemoria Kalea**. Steps provide a shortcut up the hill, to where the road ends in a cul-de-sac (**2**; **15min**). From here it's a short but steep climb of 250m up more steps to a lane on the hillside, from where you have a panorama of the whole city and its three beaches.

Turn left along the lane, passing a great viewpoint over the whole city and its three beaches. After about 100m it becomes a path between the hedgerows that veers right. After a further 100m, take the red/white-waymarked path to the left (**3**; **25min**). After briefly ascending through a pine forest, you emerge on the **clifftops** (**4**; **35min**). The path takes a sharp turn to the left just after the small spring of **Fuente Kutraia** (**5**; **45min**) and enters a narrow ravine; at the bottom of this pretty cobbled section of path, detour a few metres to the left, to a **viewpoint** (**6**; **50min**) overlooking the cliffs, before continuing along the main path up to the highest point on this part of the cliffs (**7**; **1h**). From here the Plata Lighthouse may be seen in the distance, and the view extends well beyond — to Cape Higuer on the French border.

The path crosses a road (**8**; **1h15min**) and then drops towards the attractive cove of **Illurgita**,

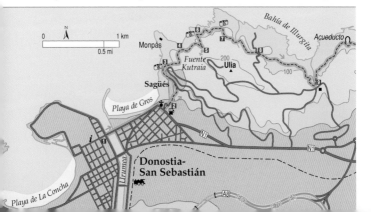

View over to Pasai Donibane from Pasai San Pedro

backed by lush vegetation. Sporadic yellow waymarking indicates the way through bushes towards the shore, but we continue on the main path which climbs steadily up the hillside towards **Mt Ulia** and then veers left (**9**; **1h35min**) towards the lighthouse, past the remains of an old **aqueduct** and another spring, the **Fuente del Inglés** (**10**; **1h55min**), which supplied water to the city in the 19th century.

The road is reached at the **Faro de la Plata** ('Silver Lighthouse'; **11**; **2h**), perched high above the narrow, treacherous channel granting access to the port of Pasaia. Around it and across the channel on the Mt Jaizkibel side, the sandstone cliffs form fascinating honeycomb shapes.

Turn right along the road (*normally* closed to traffic). Pass some roadside picnic tables and take the path to the left (**12**; **2h10min**) leading to a nicer, small **picnic site** (**⊼P**) with superb views of the channel, the whole port and the crags of Aiako Harriak in the distance. Some steps take you down to a second, smaller **lighthouse** about 50m above sea level (**13**; **2h15min**), guarding the entrance to the channel, and from there down to the water's edge. From here a pleasant promenade leads past the fascinating **Albaola Museum** (www.albaola. com), where a 16th century Basque whaling ship is being reconstructed and on to the beginning of the built-up area and the landing place for the shuttle ferry across to the attractive fishing village of Pasai Donibane, directly opposite.

To end the walk, follow the narrow street to the right, by a small **shrine** (**14**; **2h30min**), into the old town of **Pasai San Pedro**. Just after the **church**, turn left and then first right, to reach the **bus stop** (**15**; **2h35min**) — just past the round-about. Buses leave every 15 minutes for Calle Oquendo, beside the María Cristina Hotel in Donostia-San Sebastián — just two minutes' walk from our starting point.

63

Walk 2: ADARRA

Distance: 7km/4.4 mi; 2h45min
Grade: ● moderate; fairly gradual ascent of 500m to Mt Adarra, returning down a steeper, more direct route. Some waymarking, but the route is mostly clear anyway.
Equipment: see page 55
Access: 🚗 Follow Car tour 1 on the N1 to JUNCTION 447B, take the GI3722 towards URNIETA and after a further 3.5km, when the road reaches the top of the hill at the **Alto de Irurain**, turn right at the roundabout signposted GI-3721

BESABI. Continue 4km to the car park at **Bar/Restaurant Besabi** (19.5km; 43° 13.326'N, 1° 58.446'W).
🚌 G2 (Andoain-Urnieta bus, from Calle Oquendo, beside the María Cristina Hotel in Donostia-San Sebastián). Get off at **Alto de Irurain** just after the petrol station and walk 4km left up the road mentioned above to Besabi. Or alight in the main street in Urnieta (1km before the petrol station), from where a taxi can take you to the **Bar Besabi**.

Adarra is the closest mountain to the city of Donostia-San Sebastián and a popular walk — not only because it is so easily accessible but for the variety of landscapes it offers. The circuit described here combines a beautiful forest walk, Neolithic remains and fantastic views of the surrounding mountains and coast from the twin crags of Adarra's summit.

Start out from **Bar/Restaurant Besabi** (**1**), a very popular place with locals, especially on Sundays when it quickly fills up and walkers sit outside eating *bocadillos*. Take the asphalted lane to the left signposted ADARRAMENDI and then the first left steeply up the hill to the **Montefrio** farm (**2**; **5min**). Go through the gate opposite the farm — this first section is often quite muddy, due to its being a thoroughfare for walkers and farm animals alike. Follow yellow/white waymarking, passing a spring bearing the Basque *lauburu* (four head) symbol, to go through another **gate** (**3**; **10min**) and enter a pine forest. Pines soon give way to twisted beech trees as the forest becomes denser, and the path starts to level out, veers to the right and crosses a small stream.

On reaching the **Arroyo de Sorotxota** (**4**; **30min**), the main stream descending from Adarra, cross by making your way over the rocks, still following the yellow/white towards ADARRAMENDI, and

then take the path diagonally opposite. This zigzags further up above the beech forest, to a **clearing** (**5**; **35min**). From here the most direct approach to Adarra is up to the left. But instead, follow the PR-GI203 signposted to ETENETA. The path gradually gains height, with the rocky outcrops of Adarra to your left all the way and the tree line just to your right. After circling Adarra, the path flattens out as it reaches some **pastureland** (**6**; **55min**). From this point, with the forest still to your right, follow the path as it dips down to another small stream and then rises to the ridge and the **Menhir de Eteneta** (**7**; **1h05min**). This is one of the most striking Iron Age relics in the Basque Country, beside which is also a well-preserved **cromlech**, one of several in this area.

To ascend Adarra, go back along the ridge towards ADARRAMENDI, now on the GR285. The path is clear, and when you get to the base of the mountain, simply follow the path straight up towards the rocky

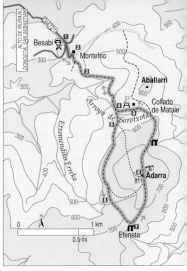

outcrop to the right, sporadically marked in red and white. When you reach the rocks, a small path veers up to the right to the clump of large granite rocks strewn over the summit of **Adarra** (**8**; 811m;

1h30min) affording great views in all directions.

Look for a path just to the north of the summit, to rejoin the GR285, descending a steep grassy spur towards a pass between Adarra and the smaller outcrop of **Aballarri**, with views ahead to the bay of Donostia-San Sebastián. This is an exhilarating part of the hike. When you reach another signpost by a fence at **Collado de Matale**, turn left for BESABI and make for a *borda* in the shady area of beech trees shown above, where some picnic **tables** and a **spring** (**9**; ⊼P; 2h05min) make a nice spot for a rest. Now the path descends further into the forest, rejoins the Arroyo de Sorotxota, and brings us to our earlier stream crossing (**4**; 2h15min). From here follow the yellow/white waymarks back to **Bar Besabi (2h45min)**.

Above, left: rustic picnic table on the woodland descent from Adarra.
Left: curiosities on the Adarra (top) and Ernio (bottom) summits. Many of the summits in the Spanish Basque Country are decorated with 'dolls' houses'. These are used as mailboxes, primarily by members of mountaineering clubs. People leave their names, and the name of their club, to prove that they've been to the top.

65

Walk 3: ERNIO

Distance: 13km/8mi; 4h45min
Grade: ●❢ fairly strenuous, with an
ascent of 700m from Alkiza to the
summit of Ernio and some quite
steep sections; otherwise fairly level
walking. A **longer alternative**
circuit returning along the Ernio
ridge (see page 69) involves a similar
700m steep descent to **Ernialde**,
although the path is at all times clear
and safe. A **shorter option** is to go
as far as the refuge at Zelatun (about
500m ascent and around 3h30min
return). Waymarked in yellow and
white from Alkiza to Zelatun
(PR-GI78).
Equipment: see page 55

Access: 🚌 Follow Car tour 1 on the
N1 to JUNCTION 439, then take the
GI3650 signposted to IRURA and
ANOETA. Go through Irura and on to
Anoeta and turn right (21km) over
the railway bridge. Then turn right
again on the GI3630 to the small
hilltop village of **Alkiza** and park in
the village square (43° 10.365'N,
2° 6.523'W; 26km). 🚋 and 🚐 There
are frequent trains from Donostia-
San Sebastián main station to
Anoeta (one stop before Tolosa).
Walk up into the village and turn
right about 100m along, on the road
to Alkiza. The bus stop for **Alkiza** is
beside the bridge.

Ernio is one of the most visited mountains in the Basque
Country and with great justification. It's easily accessible
from the coast, involves a very pleasant walk up through
beautiful forest interspersed with open views over coast and
mountains, a cosy refuge serving food, a spectacular final ascent
along a beautiful stone path, a summit covered with giant
crosses and the possibility of extending the walk along the entire
ridge. This itinerary from Alkiza is one of the lesser known
routes up Ernio — not the shortest, but the most varied.

First take the time to look over the
beautiful valley below from the main
square in **Alkiza** (**1**; 340m), then
start the walk: head back a few
metres along the road to Anoeta,
then take the first lane on the right
(signposted 'HERNIO'). Pass **Lete**
baserri on the right (now an
agroturismo) and then take the first
right turn beyond the village, along
an asphalted lane also signposted to
HERNIO (**5min**). After the large
Areta *baserri* (**2**; **10min**), the lane
veers steeply to the left and becomes
a farm track, gaining altitude as it
climbs above the wooded **gorge** to
your left. At the next crossroads (**3**;
25min), leave the track and take the
path to the right — we will return to
this track after making an interesting
loop.

Gaining further height, the path

emerges on a grassy mountain spur
from where there are splendid views
of the gorge and valley to the right
as well as the one to your left. Go
through a **gate** (**4**; **35min**) marked
itxi mesedez ('please close') and enter
a pine forest.

After a period of flat walking, the
path climbs fairly steeply again
through mixed woodland and
emerges up on the hillside at the
Collado de Itxurain (**5**; 680m;
55min). Just to your left are the
remains of a **tumulus**. Continue
straight ahead. The long ridge of
Ernio now looms closer as we
re-enter the forest. At the next
signpost (**6**; **1h10min**), keep
straight on (left is the return loop to
Alkiza). A few metres further on,
fork left uphill, following the yellow
and white waymarking, heading

deeper into the forest, as the path runs alongside the base of Ernio. Encircle a large **hollow** with some interesting limestone rocks and beautiful beech trees (**1h20min**). At the next, signposted, path junction (**7**; **1h25min**), keep straight on to **Irumugarrieta** (**8**; 770m; **1h40min**), a clearing above the tree line, where there is a large animal trough marking the border between four parishes.

From here take the path signposted EZKURRETAKO LEPOA that heads steeply uphill, soon re-entering the forest. When you come to a second signpost (**9**; 821m; **1h45min**), leave the PRGI78 and keep straight on beside the fence (look out for more sporadic

View to the Ernio summit from the Collado de Zelatun

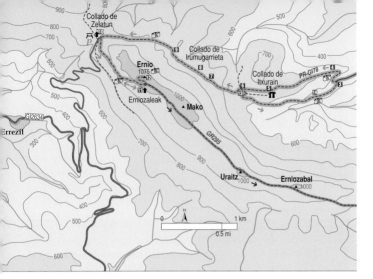

waymarking), to eventually emerge on the open mountainside and go on to the **Collado de Zelatun** (⑩; **850m; 2h**), where there is a rustic **refuge** (open weekends throughout the year and every day from May to September; serves food but no accommodation; tel: 943 8149816) and **picnic site** (⊼P). Overlooked by the steepest, most abrupt face of Ernio, this pass is a major junction for walking routes over the mountains in the area. It is possible to drive up to the refuge on a very narrow and steep, rough road from **Errezil** (see Car tour 1), but this is not encouraged or advised.

Some of the crosses and memorials on the summit of Ernio; see also the bottom photograph on page 65

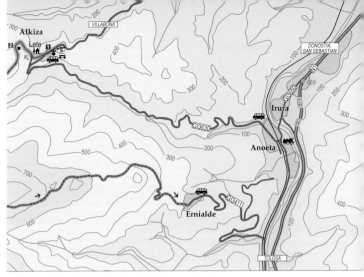

Our trail to the summit of Ernio continues beyond the refuge and climbs around the southern side of the mountain. In some places steps have been carved into the rock. As you ascend, the views of the valley far below and the village of Errezil become increasingly dramatic. The trail, hugging the mountain all the way, ascends to a small refuge called **Erniozaleak** (⑪; 'Friends of Ernio'; **2h30min**), a very welcome place to shelter if the weather changes. In front of this refuge is the first of the **many crosses**.

Turn left and make your way up to the summit of **Ernio** (⑫; 1075m; **2h35min**), the top of which is covered with crosses of all different sizes, the oldest dating back to 1855. The inscriptions are all in Euskera. This is an important pilgrimage site for Basques and the *romerías* (religious *fiestas*) held every Sunday in September attract many people from the surrounding area.

Enjoy the impressive views on all sides before descending again to **Erniozaleak** and retracing your steps via **Zelatun** and Itxurain to the **signpost** at ⑥ (**3h50min**), where you turn right towards ALKIZA LETEKO BORDATIK and descend

through the forest to an old *borda* (⑬; 623m; **3h55min**), where there is an info panel about forest birds and animals. From here continue descending through forest on the clearly waymarked path. About 300m after a path marked *'lotura'* (which you ignore), you start to round the hillside to reach a **viewpoint** over a gorge with another panel about griffon vultures, often visible on the crags opposite (⑭; 473m; **4h25min**). A little further on, rejoin the outward path at ⑧ (**4h30min**) and retrace steps to **Alkiza** (**4h50min**).

Alternative return: From Erniozaleak you have the option of continuing along a path close to the top of the ridge, following the red/white waymarks of the GR285 via the peaks of **Mako, Uraitz** and **Erniozabal**, all at around a height of 1000m, before dropping steeply to the village of **Ernialde**, where you could catch the Alkiza bus in the afternoon or walk a further 3km downhill to Anoeta. Allow 3h from the summit of Ernio to Ernialde, and another hour to descend to Tolosa on the valley floor.

Walk 4: TXINDOKI

See photos on pages 13, 56
Distance: 10.4km/6.5mi; 5h
Grade: ● strenuous, with an ascent of 946m. But whole families do this walk! The entire upward route — fairly gradual until the Oria Spring — is along a very well-used path. The final 200m of ascent from Collado Egurral to the summit is steep. Take care on the descent back to this pass, as the rocks can be slippery, although no scrambling is involved and the path is not overtly exposed. **Shorter alternative**: a shorter out-and-back ascends

Gaztelu, the rocky crag overlooking Txindoki; ●, less strenuous than the main walk (8.6km/ 5.3mi, 3h; overall ascent of 480m).
Equipment: see page 55
Access: 🚗 Follow Car tour 1 to **Larraitz** (40km). Park in the large car park for the **Zamaoko Atsedenlekua picnic site** (43° 2.102'N, 2° 5.795'W). 🚌 frequent buses and trains from Donostia-San Sebastián to **Tolosa**. From Tolosa take a bus to **Abaltzisketa**, then walk 1km along the road to Larraitz.

Txindoki is perhaps the most striking mountain in the Basque Country, with its classic Matterhorn-like shape. The summit, which is the end point of the Sierra de Aralar, offers incredible views over the entire region. A shorter alternative is to climb the 'mini-Txindoki' rocky crag known as Gaztelu, just to the south — the views are nearly as spectacular, and the route is considerably less frequented than the classic Txindoki hike.

Larraitz (400m), nestling below the north face of Txindoki, has a very popular picnic site and the Larraitz Gain Bar/Restaurante (tel: 943 653572) — a good places to procure substantial *bocadillos* for the walk up to the summit. **Start out** from the far end of the **Zamaoko Atsedenlekua** car park (**1**; 🚗P; 420m): go through a gate and follow the wide track waymarked in red, white and yellow. A short-cut **path** on the left

(waymarked) cuts off a bend and brings you to a signpost in the meadow above (**2**; 522m). This is where you head right for the Shorter alternative walk (see below). Keep ahead on the path marked 'TXINDOKI' and 'IGARATZA'. After 50m cross the track to proceed on a yellow/white-marked path, crossing another track a little further uphill. As the path levels out and rounds a bend (**3**; 682m; **35min**), there are wonderful

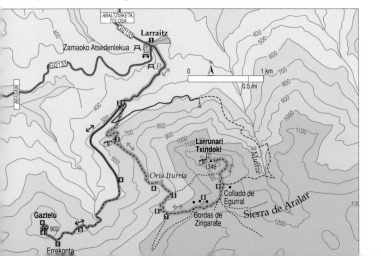

views through the adjacent pine forest towards Gaztelu in front of you, the long ridge of Aitzkorri beyond and the sheer rock face of Txindoki to the left.

After passing through a gate and still keeping the **pine forest** to your right, ascend around the mountain to **Oria Iturria** (◪; 837m; **1h05min**), a spring where you can refill your water bottle. Once the path reaches the head of the valley, you pass by an info panel about *'Tximista Bidea'* — the 'lightning' or extremely steep direct route to the summit (not recommended at all for the ascent and, if it's at all wet, then not advised for the descent either!). Then you go through another gate (◳; 834m; **1h10min**) and the path zigzags more steeply up to the edge of the **Sierra de Aralar** plateau, a beautiful unspoilt range of undulating green pastureland and limestone peaks lying between 1000m and 1400m.

Veer left and go through another gate (◳; 951m; **1h30min**). Now on the edge of the plateau, keep straight ahead at a *'LARRUNARRI'* signpost (◰; 984m; **1h30min**). The path traverses an area of limestone rocks and hollows, passing a group of *bordas* known as **Zirigarate** (◱; 1083m; **1h50min**), where it is sometimes possible to buy sheep's cheese (the sign *'ardi gasni salgai'* means 'sheep's cheese for sale'). From here go on to some large rocky outcrops (**1h55min**), just before the grassy spur of **Collado de Egurral** (◲; 1160m; **2h**). Now you have a steep climb to the summit. The path is clear (marked with yellow arrows throughout), although in some places quite eroded. The last 100m or so are over rocks, but no scrambling is required. From the summit of **Txindoki** (◴; 1348m;

2h35min), you can peer down to Larraitz almost 1000m directly below you, and on a clear day the view stretches to the sea and towards the Pyrenees.

Retrace steps via the **Collado de Egurral** (**3h05min**) to Larraitz (**5h**).

Shorter alternative (or detour) to Gaztelu: Follow the main walk to ◪. Then continue on the track to the right marked *'ATAUN GR20'*. Most of the route is clearly waymarked red/white/yellow. This fairly level track meanders around the southern lower flanks of Txindoki just above a pine forest and, a little further on, enters a nice shady beech wood. When another track joins from the left (◿; 574m; **30min**), the route continues as a mostly rocky path. The summit of Gaztelu is clearly visible through the trees at all times. On reaching a stream (◺; 659m; **50min**), the path starts to climb increasingly steeply beside it, to eventually pass through a gate and emerge on the **Errekonta** pass (◣; 765m; **1h**). Leaving the waymarking here, follow a vague *unmarked* path to the right steeply up to the rocks below the summit, by a memorial plaque to a local climber (◼; 846m; **1h10min**). Of the two ways of reaching the summit from here, I recommend the path to the right, up through rocks to the large circular rock 'turret' of **Gaztelu** (◣; 902m; **1h20min**), with amazing views in all directions on a clear day. *'Gaztelu'* means 'castle' in Euskara, and the remains now visible date from a 12th-century strategic lookout. To descend, look for a path just to the south of the summit that offers a slightly less steep, less exposed way back down to the memorial plaque and thence back to **Errekonta** at ◣. From here retrace steps back to **Larraitz** (**2h30min**).

Walk 5: AITZKORRI

Distance: 16km/10mi; 7h
Grade: ●‼ strenuous, with a steep climb of 500m from the San Adrián Tunnel to the summit of Aitzkorri (which at least is done early on in the walk), and a short scramble to the top of the highest peak, Aitxuri. The return involves a slight gain in altitude from the Urbia Refuge but in general is a fairly gradual descent. All paths used are well defined and clearly waymarked. Allow a whole day for the complete circuit, especially if walking the additional 5km each way from Zegama-Otzaurte Halt or descending to Arantzazu.
Shorter options are: a return hike up to the **San Adrián Tunnel**, the loop to the viewpoint above it called **Sandratiko Begiratokia** and/or beyond the tunnel along the **Calzada Romana** (1h30min-2h). An out-and-back return walk to **Aitzkorri**, the first and most-visited peak (4h), is another, strenuous option.

Equipment: see page 55
Access: 🚌 From Ordizia (the 49km-point on Car tour 1, head south along the N1 to JUNCTION 416, then turn right on the GI2637, signposted to SEGURA and ZEGAMA. *Do* stop in the historic village of **Segura**, to see the old mansions on its main street and the pretty square. Follow signs through **Zegama** towards ALTSASU. When the road reaches the top of the pass, turn right opposite the **Venta de Otzaurte** along a narrow lane signposted to ALTZANIKO ATSEDENLEKUA. After a further 2km, you pass the attractive **Beunde picnic site** (🌳P), with great views towards Mt Aratz ahead and the ridge of Aitzkorri to the right. Continue for a further 2.6km, to a large car park where the road ends at **Aldaola** (42° 56.108'N, 2° 18.199'W). There is an explanatory map here (as well as several information panels along the route). *No public transport.*

T his is a fairly long but extremely beautiful circuit. It visits the fascinating San Adrián Tunnel and takes in the well-preserved Calzada Romana (Roman Road; historically used as a link on the Pilgrims' Route to Santiago). You ascend through extensive beech woods to Mt Aitzkorri and walk along its ridge to Mt Aitxuri, the highest peak in the Basque Country outside the Pyrenees. At the Urbia Refuge you're surrounded by a typically verdant, high-meadow landscape.

Start the walk at Aldaola (**1**): from the car park, follow the path with many signs: 'URBIA, SANDRATIKO KOBA', GR282 (the **Senda del Pastoreo**). It descends to a stream and then climbs through woodland onto the open mountain — to the abandoned **San Adrián Refuge** (**2**; 900m; **10min**). Fill up your water bottle from the spring beside the building and continue following the same signposting along a clear trail, rising gradually to the **San Adrián**

Tunnel (**3**; 1010m; **30min**). The **Chapel of Sancti Spiritus** (*Sandratiko* in Euskera) inside this natural tunnel was originally used as a hospital for pilgrims. After passing through the tunnel you come upon the first stretch of the old **Calzada Romana**, with well preserved paving — this section actually dating from the 13th century. Just beyond the tunnel, the best preserved section of paving veers left (**4**; our return route), signposted to URBIA and

ARANTZAZU. Follow this for a shorter walk along the *calzada*, and/or take the green/white waymarked SL-GI3003 *SANDRATIKO BEGIRATOKIA*, a short but spectacular loop signposted at the same point. This leads up over some small ravines cut into the karst landscape and some magical forest to

On the ascent to Aitzkorri

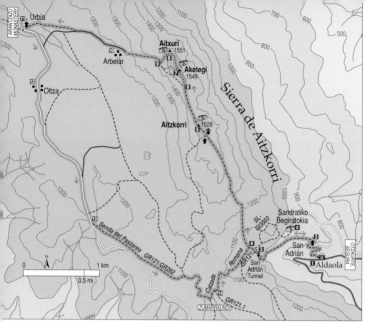

a **viewpoint** overlooking the tunnel (**2**; 1082m). To continue with the main route and climb Aitzkorri, turn right at the first bend on the Calzada Romana immediately after the above-mentioned signpost (**35min**), following some fairly faint yellow marking on the rocks.

The path climbs steeply up through dense beech forest, to emerge high on the mountainside at the start of a narrow but safe path cut into the limestone (**1h30min**; see photograph opposite). This path ascends steeply to the first of many **crosses** (**1h40min**), from where the village of Zegama is clearly visible below. Rounding the bend, the chapel and refuge of Aitzkorri come into view. From here an exhilarating short ridge walk and final climb bring us to the summit of **Aitzkorri** (**5**; 1528m; **2h05min**). The chapel is built just at the edge of the abyss, separated by a railing protecting walkers from a sheer 1200m drop to the valley below.

From the summit, descend to the **chapel** (the interior of which is accessed by a dark passageway), and

74

follow the path round to the right. Still waymarked in yellow, the path then contours slightly below the ridge itself. At a bend in the path (**6**; **2h35min**), just before it starts to descend towards the meadows of Urbia, some fairly faded markings show the way up the hillside on a small path to the second peak, **Aketegi** (**7**; 1549m; **2h45min**). From here descend slightly to a gully, following first yellow markings (**2h55min**) and then red markings up over the rocks to **Aitxuri** (**8**; 1551m; **3h**), the highest point. This last peak involves a slight scramble over the rocks, but the vestiges of a path will guide you. Return to the gully and follow the red markings steeply and directly down the hillside to rejoin the main path (**9**; **3h20min**).

Descend to the collection of red-roofed *bordas* called **Arbelar** (**10**; **3h55min**; simple meals usually available here in summer), and proceed along the track. Then veer right, away from the track: follow a line of trees which forms a natural avenue, leading you to the **Urbia**

*Right: visit historic Segura village
when you are driving to this walk.
Below (right): on the approach to the San
Adrián Tunnel; (left): woodland path
to the Aitzkorri summit.*

Refuge (**11**; Fonda de Urbia;
1136m; **4h30min**; open weekends
throughout the year and every day
May to October; food and beds;
tel: 943 781316), surrounded by the
verdant high meadows bearing the
same name. Another spring provides
a chance to refill water bottles.
(Option for those using public
transport: from here a well-trodden
path descends to the Arantzazu
Monastery in 1h15min.)
To begin the return journey to
Aldaola, follow the gravel road in
front of the refuge, keeping the
Aitzkorri Ridge to your left. Pass the
bordas of **Oltza** (**12**; **4h55min**),
descend to a stream and, just after a
curious **natural hollow** where a
stream disappears into a cave under
the road, fork right uphill
(**5h05min**). Continue until you see
more red and white markings (**13**;
5h25min), then follow the
waymarked path to the left. This
meanders in and out of the beech
forest, eventually rejoining the
Calzada Romana.
    Turn left and almost immediately

reach a junction with **signposts** (**14**;
6h10min), where the GR121.1
goes off to the right. Take the main
route (GR121) here, signposted to
SAN ADRIAN. Now you descend the
best-preserved section of the *calzada*
through the forest, back to the
junction with the Aitzkorri path and
the **San Adrián Tunnel** (**3**;
6h30min). Go through the tunnel
and retrace your steps past the **San
Adrián Refuge** (**2**; **6h45min**), to
the cattle grid. Turn right here, back
to **Aldaola** (**7h**).

Walk 6: ARTIKUTZA VILLAGE AND RESERVOIR

Distance: 9.5km/5.9mi; 3h30min
Grade: ● moderate. The walk descends gradually through the forest to Artikutza and, after a fairly steep climb of about 1km back up through the forest, follows the route of the former forest railway line. Waymarked throughout in yellow and white, following the PR-NA124 to Artikutza and returning on the PR-NA125. Overall ascents of 300m.
Equipment: See page 55
Access: 🚗 Follow Car tour 2 to the roundabout just beyond the Oiartzun motorway exit, where you turn right initially towards UGALDETXO. Then take the GI3631 towards ARTIKUTZA. This winding

scenic road ascends via **Collado de Uzpuru**, a small picnic site with fine views (12km 🚗*P*) and **Bianditz** (710m) to **Eskas**, the entry gate and guard's house for the **Artikutza Forest Reserve** (16km from the motorway exit). Park just before the gate (43° 14.363'N, 1° 48.218'W). (To continue beyond the gate by car to Artikutza, special permission must be obtained from the town hall in Donostia-San Sebastián.) 🚌 from Plaza de Gipuzkoa in Donostia-San Sebastián to the main square in **Oiartzun**, from where a taxi can be taken to **Eskas** (13km).
NB: There is a detailed map/info panel at Eskas.

T his walk offers the chance to see some of the densest forests of wild pine, oak and beech in the Basque Country, just forty minutes' drive from one of its major cities. Added attractions are the beautiful Erroiarri Waterfall deep in the forest, the unspoilt village of Artikutza and its neighbouring reservoir, and an interesting return walk along an old railway line through one of the higher parts of the forest — affording open views over the Artikutza basin.

Start the walk at Eskas (**1**; 650m): go through the **gate** and follow the sign down the road towards ARTIKUTZA. Take the first path to the left (**2**; **5min**; signposted to ARTIKUTZA), beside an explanatory board about forest wildlife. This path, called '**Elizmendi**', plunges deep into a beautiful forest, mainly oak and beech. Beyond a couple of **twisted beech trees** (**20min**) the path descends to a first stream, crosses it by a rickety old **wooden bridge** (**3**; **35min**), follows the stream and then crosses a **second bridge** (**4**; **40min**).

Soon after, take a path to the right (signpost: URJAUZIA-CASCADA). This leads to a viewpoint above the **Erroiarri Waterfall** (**5**; **45min**). A path to the right of the viewpoint

descends to a point just above the waterfall, where the crystal-clear water makes a wonderfully refreshing rest stop in the heart of the forest.

Returning to the main path, continue through the forest; the path narrows and gains height above the river, before beginning its descent towards the reservoir. On reaching a gravel road and **signposts** (**6**; **1h30min**), a left turn marks the start of the SL-NA121 circuit of 6km around the **Enubieta Reservoir** (add an extra 1h30min, if you do this).

The main walk turns right, through a gate. Fork right again along the asphalted lane, to pass the **church** and enter the village of **Artikutza** (**7**; 315m; **1h40min**).

Artikutza: the oak and beech wood (left) and the village (below)

The village itself consists of a few colourful, ramshackle old *baserri* and a *frontón*; there are plenty of picnic tables (⊼*P*), and spring water beside the river. The handful of residents in this idyllic village are involved in forestry and livestock farming, and the reservoir constitutes the main water supply for Donostia-San Sebastián.

Cross the main bridge opposite the *frontón*, following the sign 'ESKAS TRENBIDITIK', and proceed along the road past the **Ostatu Zahar** (a small refuge). Take the first path to the right, signposted to ESKAS (**8**; **1h50min**). This climbs fairly steeply, initially parallel to the road, and then runs deeper into the forest. Continue following signs to ESKAS at the next junction, which marks the start of the **old railway line** (**9**; BURNBIDE ZAHARRAREN BIDEA/CAMINO DEL ANTIGUO FERROCARRIL; **2h15min**). There are few traces left now of the railway itself, which originally carried timber and coal from the Artikutza basin to the port of Pasaia. This stretch of the walk affords good views through the trees across the Artikutza basin to the hills beyond. A sign indicates some old **millstones** to the right (**10**; ERROTARRIAK/ MUELAS; **2h35min**) and, further along to the right, a signposted promontory forms a magnificent **natural balcony** overlooking the entire basin (**11**; BALKOI NATURAL/ BALCÓN NATURAL; **2h50min**). The Erroiarri Waterfall can be heard far below, but is not visible from here. Now the path remains level and eventually rejoins the **road** (**3h20min**), just before the point where we originally entered the forest at the start of the walk. Turn right along the road or parallel path to return to **Eskas** (**3h30min**).

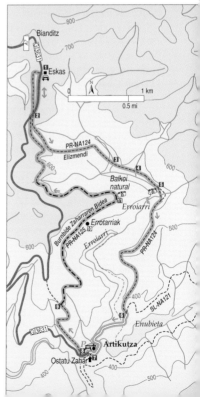

Walk 7: AIAKO HARRIAK (PEÑAS DE AIA) CIRCUIT

See also photo on page 17
Distance: 12km/7.5mi; 4h20min
Grade: ● moderate, with an overall ascent of 370m. This walk does not involve any major climbs, but there is a fairly steep zigzag ascent through the forest on the return section of the GR121 to Aritxulegi. The narrow path beside the Canal Domiko can be slippery after rain. Well waymarked; from Aritxulegi to Elurretxe on the PR-GI1010 (yellow and white), returning on the GR121 Gipuzkoa circuit (red and white).
Equipment: See page 55
Access: 🚗 Follow Car tour 2 on the Oiartzun-Lesaka GI3420 road. Park either by the Oiartungo Mendi hostel (**Arritxulo**; signposted from the road just before the cattle grid; 43° 16.339'N, 1° 47.761'W) and walk up the path by the info panel or, if there is space, park on the right-hand side of the road just before the tunnel at **Aritxulegi Pass**). 🚌 from Plaza de Gipuzkoa in Donostia-San Sebastián to the main square in **Oiartzun**, from where a taxi can be taken to **Aritxulegi Pass** (8km); alternatively take a taxi from Irún to Elurretxe/Castillo del Inglés, from where you can pick up the route at **8** or **10**.

Aiako Harriak (Peñas de Aia) is one of the most climbed mountain ridges in the Basque Country, and rightly so. Walking the whole ridge is exhilarating, but reaching the two 800m+ peaks of Txurrumurru and Erroilbide involves some serious scrambling and is not for vertigo-sufferers. The classic route from Elurretxe is described in *Landscapes of the Pyrenees*. The walk described here is a complete circuit of the mountain at between 400m and 500m, offering the chance to explore a curious irrigation channel, some beautiful forest and excellent close-up views of the near-vertical south face.

Start the walk from **Arritxulo** (**1**; 417m; www.arritxulo.org), a well-kept hostel open year round. Follow the path uphill and through a wooden gate onto the main road, turning right almost immediately up the gravel road just before the tunnel that marks **Aritxulegi Pass** (439m). Some 100m along, turn left onto a green/white marked path that rises to an electricity pylon. Then you come to a **cattle grid** (**2**; 492m; **10min**) to the right. This marks the border between the provinces of Gipuzkoa and Nafarroa, and there are great views back towards the sea and over the surrounding hills.

Turn left here for ELEZARRETA on the PR-GI1010 path, veering right downhill almost immediately. Descending initially through thick mixed woodland and then across open hillside, you pass through a gate to reach the **Bar/Restaurante Aialde** (**3**; **30min**), with a nice terrace overlooking the valley and **San Antón Reservoir**.

Turn sharp left ('ELURRETXE') on the path marking the start of the **Canal Domiko**. The new paving lain on the first part of this irrigation channel, comes to an abrupt end about halfway along (**4**; 356m; **50min**). From this point the path is narrow in places, so watch your step, although it is a beautiful meandering walk through the forest, with tantalizing glimpses down towards the **Endara Valley** and an impressive rocky outcrop, the **Risco de San Antón**, on the far side.

Leave the irrigation channel at a signpost for ELURRETXE, crossing the bridge to the left (**5**; 358m;

78

Rounding Aiako Harriak (left) and the Canal Domiko (right)

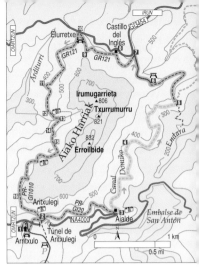

1h25min). The path zigzags up to a small **clearing** (**6**; 507m; ♒; **1h50min**) in this mostly oak and beech forest. Continue along the waymarked track to the right.

Just before the Oiartzun–Irún road, turn left onto a path marked ELURRETXE (**7**; 502m; **2h**), from where we now follow the red/white waymarked GR121. After going through mainly pine forest and past a couple of frog ponds, you come to the remains of a house in the forest, overlooked by several large twisted beech trees. This is the **Castillo del Inglés** (**8**; 495m; the Englishman's Castle; **2h20min**) — the former residence of an English engineer who owned the mining concessions in the area and who in the early 1900s would organize lavish parties here for the wealthy families of Irún.

Continue on the GR121 up through the forest to join the Aiako Harriak/Peñas de Aia summit trail, passing the **Elurzulo** (**9**; 'snow hole'; 537m; **2h25min**) — a hole in the ground used in ancient times to keep meat and other food cold. Then descend to the parking area of **Elurretxe** (**10**; 503m; **2h30min**).

To begin the return route, follow the path signposted ARITXULEGI, still on the GR121. The path hugs the immense granite rock face of the three peaks of Aiako Harriak very closely, and at this height is below the tree line. After an initially flat stretch, you pass through a **gate** (**2h35min**), after which the path starts to zigzag down through the

forest to to a small **outcrop/ledge** (**2h50min**) that affords glimpses of the valley below and the crags above.

Descending a little further, *ignore* a sign pointing to UNAILEKU (**11**; 439m; **2h55min**); continue straight on, to a second **outcrop** (**12**; 426m; **3h05min**). This makes a fine rest stop from which to admire the valley of the **Arditurri Mines** below, and beyond them, towards the coast. Soon after, the path crosses a **stream** (**13**; 389m; **3h10min**) with the peak of **Txurrumurru** towering directly above — another very pleasant shady rest stop.

From here it's a fairly steep climb up through the forest to a **rock overhang** (**14**; 463m; **3h20min**). Then, higher up the hillside, the path takes a sharp right turn by some clear waymarking (**15**; 549m; **3h30min**). You eventually emerge above the trees and round the grassy end of the ridge. A trilingual sign-post points the way to TONTORRAK/ CIMAS/CIMES (**16**; 578m; **3h55min**), the route up to the third and highest peak of Aiako Harriak/ Peñas de Aia. A short distance beyond here we begin the fairly steep descent down to the junction at **2** (**4h10min**) and back to our starting point at **Arritxulo** (**4h20min**).

Walk 8: AIZKOLEGI

Photos on pages 9, 19, 20
Distance: 20km/12.4mi; 6h
Grade: ● moderate-strenuous, with overall ascents of 750m. This fairly long circuit involves a gradual ascent to the highest point, Aizkolegi, and then a short, steep ascent of Azkua. The descent from the ridge back towards Etxalar is also fairly abrupt. Paths are generally clear; the section from 3h20min to Etxalar is well waymarked.
Equipment: see page 55
Access: 🚗 Park in the centre of **Etxalar** (the 46km-point in Car tour 2; 43° 14.037'N, 1° 38.364'W). 🚌 Donostia-San Sebastián/Elizondo buses stop at **Ventas de Etxalar** on the main road, from where it is a 4km walk into **Etxalar** itself.

This little-trodden route starts from the beautiful village of Etxalar and offers the chance to explore some of the most extensive beech forests in the region. There follows an exhilarating ridge walk just above the treeline, with great views of the Baztán region and an ascent of Aizkolegi, the highest point of the Señorío de Bertiz Gardens, with its abandoned wooden 'palace' on the summit.

Start out in **Etxalar** (**1**; 100m): follow the road to the right of the **church**, signposted to ZUGARRA-MURDI. You pass an explanatory board showing walking routes in the area and follow signs out of the village towards ARTAKO BIDEA. Cross the stream (**Sarriko Erreka**), head uphill and take the first right turn after **Xoraxuriko** *borda* (**2**; 135m; **15min**) — a lane signposted to several places including BAGOLEKO BORDA. The lane follows this pretty valley into the forest and is a fairly flat 4km walk. At the first main junction (**3**; 273m; **1h15min**) proceed straight on towards BAGOLEKO BORDA. Then take the next lane (**4**; 315m; **1h25min**),

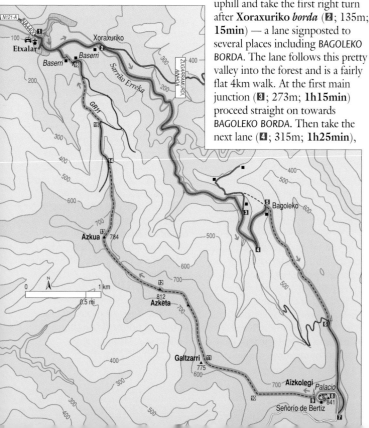

signposted to AIZKOLEGI, going steeply uphill and across a cattle grid, to reach attractive **Bagoleko** *borda* (**5**; 390m; **1h40min**), perched on the hillside. This, and a couple of other *casas rurales* in the valley, are used for holiday rentals.

Go through the **gate** to the left of the house, again signposted to AIZKOLEGI, and turn right immediately along a path which initially follows a **fence** and soon enters the beech forest (**1h50min**), climbing steadily. As the path starts to level out, the ridge along which we return to Etxalar is clearly visible on the opposite side of the valley. Then we re-enter a particularly beautiful section of forest. After a **stile** (**2h05min**) the path converges with a forest track beside a **cairn** (**6**; 600m; **2h10min**).

Turn left from the cairn and proceed along the forest track, which contours until reaching a **gravel road** (**7**; 728m; **2h40min**), where there is an information panel and some benches. Here we turn sharp right up the hill, to an abandoned caretaker's house. Although there is a chain across the steps to the left, ignore it (everybody does!) and climb the last few metres to the grassy summit of **Aizkolegi** (**8**; 841m; **2h55min**), with its observation board and the curious remains of the old wooden *palacio* 'palace' designed by a local Basque who made his millions in America and returned to invest his fortune in creating the **Gardens of Señorío de Bertiz** (see Car tour 2 on page 19), of which this is the highest point. Do not try to enter the building itself, however, which is badly decayed. The views from the top extend well towards the Pyrenees on a clear day.

Return back down the road and,

just before the first bend, turn left on a path beside a **wooden bench** (**9**; 795m; **3h10min**). Follow this as it winds through the forest clearly enough (though recently it has become somewhat overgrown). Climb over a **stile** (**10**; 801m; **3h25min**), to emerge on the open ridge, and follow the clear red/white waymarking alongside the fence — first downhill and then up again to the left, to the next grassy summit, **Galtzarri** (**11**; 775m; **3h45min**).

Still keeping the tree line just to your right, go on to the following summit, **Azketa** (**12**; 812m; **4h05min**), topped by a clump of rocks. A fairly sharp descent and even steeper ascent brings us to the top of **Azkua** (**13**; 784m; **4h40min**), with its large concrete summit marker. Below to the right is the valley we followed up to Aizkolegi.

Go straight ahead along this flat summit to the first **wooden pole** (still marked red/white) and guided by markers/poles, descend the mountain spur steeply, with Etxalar directly in front of you. Turn right on reaching a track (**14**; 532m; **5h10min**), and follow this until you come to a bend to the right (**15**; 452m; **5h20min**), where you leave it and continue following the red/white waymarking of the GR11 steeply down the hillside on a path through ferns and then woodland.

When you eventually rejoin the track left earlier, turn right and, almost immediately, left on a path beside a *baserri* (**16**; 249m; **5h40min**). This passes another, very old *baserri* (**5h50min**) and joins an asphalted lane. Follow this down to rejoin the ZUGARRAMURDI ROAD from the outward journey, where you turn left to return through **Etxalar**, back to the church (**6h**).

Walk 9: XORROXIN WATERFALL

Distance: 14.4km/8.9mi; 3h55min
Grade: ● fairly easy, with an overall ascent of 400m/1315ft. The route as far as Xorroxín Waterfall makes a nice short walk with children. The path to the waterfall is waymarked green/white; most of the circuit around the Iñarbegi Valley is waymarked yellow/white.

Equipment: see page 55
Access: 🚗 From the N121B take the NA2600 east to **Erratzu** (just past the 87km-point in Car tour 2). Park around the main village square by the river (43° 10.811'N, 1° 27.374'W). 🚌 bus from Donostia-San Sebastián or Iruña-Pamplona to **Elizondo**, then taxi to **Erratzu**.

This is a very pleasant, easy circuit starting from the picturesque village of Erratzu with its wood-beamed houses, typical of the Baztán region of Nafarroa, and the nearby beautiful Xorroxín Waterfall, deep inside a mainly oak forest. The rest of the walk involves a pleasant hike along the right bank of the Iñarbegi Stream to the valley head, mostly in the forest, and a return route along the hillside on the opposite bank offering open views of the surrounding mountains and pastureland dotted with farmhouses, via the equally beautiful village of Gorostapalo, also boasting some of the finest rural architecture in the area.

Start the walk at the main square in Erratzu (**1**; 288m), following the road beside the Hotel Kastonea signposted BAZTAN CAMPING. Leaving the village, cross the bridge over the **Aranea River** and turn right on the track marked XORROXIN (5min). When you come to some meadowland, note a curious WW2 bunker to your left and keep straight on beside a drystone wall on a path that soon returns to the river. Take the next signposted path downhill (**2**; 314m; **15min**) and cross the river on a small moss-covered bridge. Continuing on the path on the other side, fork left by a farm building, to return to the river and cross another bridge. Follow the XORROXIN sign up to the right (**3**; 312m; **25min**) and after a few metres cross a tiny footbridge. Fork right again, continuing alongside a fence until you come to some wooden steps that lead up to more meadowland. This path eventually joins a track and descends to a major junction of paths (**4**; 331m;

45min). Continue following signs to XORROXIN, passing a waterfall discernible through the trees to the right, and then fork left uphill (**5**; 362m; **55min**). After about 200m note an unmarked path to the left by the remains of a moss-covered **drystone wall** (**6**; 384m; **1h**). Do not take this path at this point; we will take it after visiting the main waterfall. (Notice the small wooden shrine-like object embedded in the wall here.) For the moment keep straight on alongside the river, crossing a couple of small streams, to reach the **Xorroxín Waterfall** (**7**; 371m; **1h05min**). Take the time to cool off in this idyllic sylvan spot.

Then retrace your steps to the old **drystone wall** and climb up to the right through woods, following the vestiges of a path, initially alongside this wall, until you reach a wider path — the yellow/white-waymarked PR-NA7 along the **Iñarbegi Valley** (**8**; 421m; **1h15min**). The walk is now a gentle climb on a clearly waymarked path

82

through a picturesque part of this mostly oak forest. To the left are meadows on the flanks of **Mt Autza**, which marks the border with France; several *bordas* (some occupied, some not) are passed along the route.

Emerging just above the forest, head right along the asphalt road (**9**; 568m; **1h55min**) which leads to the scattered *baserri* along the valley. Just off the road, to the left, is the **Dolmen de Sorginotxoa** (**10**; 619m; **2h05min**), a good vantage point for views of the valley. Return to the road and continue along it, turning right at the next crossroads down the lane to the right (**11**; 557m; **2h10min**), and then, when you come to a hairpin bend, fork right on an unmarked track (**12**; 520m; **2h15min**) — the lane that continues downhill is private and leads to the **Iñarbegi** farmhouses. Cross the bridge over **Iñarbegiko Erreka** (**13**; 493m; 2h20min) and proceed up the hill on the opposite bank on a track that initially climbs a bit above the river and then, where it veers to the left, veer right on along a trail beside the **fence** (**14**; 550m; **2h30min**).

We now follow this pretty winding path with views over the valley until the trail forks slightly uphill to the left (**15**; 544m; **2h45min**) and a little further emerges on a farm track, with the Barrenetxea *baserri* down across the meadow to the right. At the next main fork (**16**; 566m; **3h10min**), leave this meandering track and take the path down to the right. At the point where the path becomes enclosed by fences on both sides, continue around a further 50m to leave the yellow/white waymarking (**17**; 467m; **3h25min**), descending a path leading to the first houses of **Gorostapalo** and its main village square (**18**; 371m; **3h35min**). Stop to admire the fine rural architecture in this unspoilt village (in particular the large Dolorea *baserri* in the square itself) and then head past the *fronton* towards the end of the village, turning right to come to the roadside chapel of **Nuestra Señora de Dolorosa**. From here follow the road round to the left that leads back to **Erratzu**, crossing the river bridge to return to the main square (**3h55min**).

Xorroxín Waterfall

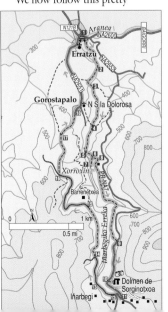

Walk 10: MENDAUR

Distance: 13.4km/8.3mi; 4h25min
Grade: ● strenuous, with an ascent of 930m (the final summit ascent is quite steep). Very well waymarked in yellow and white from Aurtitz to Buztiz Lepoa (part of the PR-NA104); the ascent from this pass to the summit, and the short descent (200m) from the Mendioder ridge to the reservoir are not waymarked, but are easily followed nonetheless.
Equipment: see page 55
Access: 🚌 to **Aurtitz** (the 116km-point in Car tour 2). Turn right off the NA170 at the second signpost for this village (when approaching from the N121A or Ituren). Park anywhere in or near the entrance to the village (43° 7.924'N, 1° 43.237'W). (It is also possible to drive the 5km from Aurtitz to the **Embalse de Mendaur** (43° 9.129'N, 1° 43.945'W) along a somewhat potholed track, thus reducing the walk to about 2h return. There is a nice picnic site at the far end of the reservoir(🅿P).

● This *reservoir and its picnic site* makes a nice *shorter out-and-back walk* from Aurtitz. 🚌 from Iruña-Pamplona to **Aurtitz** (request stop), via **Leitza**; otherwise more frequent buses from Iruña-Pamplona and Donostia-San Sebastián to Doneztebe/Santestaban, 6km away, then taxi.

Mendaur is the most prominent peak in the Baztán Valley, and this route is the classic one to the summit, via the small reservoir bearing the same name. The summit itself is topped by a small chapel dating back to the 17th century, and the whole route from Aurtitz is extremely varied and picturesque.

Start out from the entrance to **Aurtitz** (**1**; 192m), by a small square: turn left along a street running parallel to the main road, then go right at the signpost for *MENDAUR*. Just beyond the last house in the village, turn left along a lane, following the red/white waymarking out of the village and across a **bridge** over the stream. Cross the lane beyond this bridge (it leads to the reservoir) to a couple of GR11 info panels (**2**; 194m; **5min**) and continue along the path opposite (still red/white waymarking), which soon becomes cobbled. A little further on, turn left onto a track just before a **water pipe** (**3**; 236m; **10min**). Continue along this track, ignoring a path off to the left. On reaching a *borda*, the track veers sharp right (**4**; 261m; **15min**).

After a steady climb through pretty — mainly oak —forest, you emerge on a wider track (**5**; 405m; **35min**). Turn left here and, shortly after crossing a bridge beside a small **waterfall**, take the path to the right (**6**; 445m; **45min**), still marked red/white. A few metres further on a sign points to *MENDAUR* via the PR-NA104. Just after another *borda* and just before a concrete road, continue on the path to the right, which from here is well waymarked, and follow the stream as far as a small **aqueduct** (**7**; 500m; **55min**). Carry on uphill alongside the stream through a particularly pretty section of beech forest, to eventually rejoin the gravel road that ascends from Aurtitz, where you turn left to the reservoir **Arrustailegi Urtegia/Embalse de Mendaur** (**8**; 722m; **1h20min**).

Turn left to walk around this small reservoir, with the summit of Mendaur directly above it, to a shady **picnic site** on the far side (**9**; 729m;

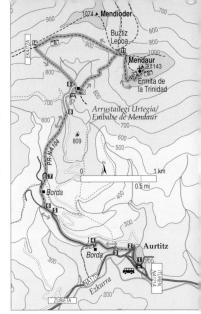

1h25min; ⼝P). Cross the stream and turn left at the next *borda* (⑩; 740m; **1h30min**), to climb steeply up the hillside. Once above the tree line, veer left, away from the summit of Mendaur, following the main path past the small fenced-off **Humedal de Mendaur** wetland towards a large **menhir-like boundary stone** marking the pass (⑪; **Buztiz Lepoa**; 942m; **1h50min**).

From the stone, take the path zigzagging uphill to the right. This brings you to the start of the **60 stone steps** (⑫; 1112m; **2h10min**) leading to the chapel on the summit of **Mendaur** (⑬; 1143m; **2h15min**). This chapel, the **Ermita de la Trinidad**, dating from 1692, was largely restored in 1963. From the cross behind it, there are wonderful views over the entire Baztán region, with the villages of Aurtitz and Ituren far, far below.

Descend either the same way or simply straight back down the hillside to **Buztiz Lepoa** (⑪; **2h35min**) and the **Humedal de Mendaur**, then take a different scenic route back to the reservoir: follow the path from the right-hand corner of the fenced-off area that rounds the hillside of the neighbouring mountain, **Mendioder** (1074m). Keep on this path until it joins the **ridge** (⑭; 969m; **2h55min**), from where there are excellent views down to Arantza village and valley on the far side. It is possible to continue west along the top of the ridge to the next mountain, Ekaitza (1047m), in about 30 minutes from here, but we descend the first spur just after reaching the ridge — following the vestiges of a path directly down to the picnic site by the **Embalse de Mendaur** (**3h15min**).

From here retrace steps around the reservoir, to rejoin the **path** (**3h20min**) back down through the forest to **Aurtitz** (**4h25min**).

Menhir-like boundary stone marking the pass, Buztiz Lepoa; below: steps to the Mendaur summit

Walk 11: GANEKOGORTA

Distance: 19.5km/12mi; 5h20min (from Plaza Zabalburu in Bilbao itself, but see also under 'Access')

Grade: ● strenuous and tough. The ascent of Ganekagorta — up, up almost all the way — is a long one, starting almost at sea level and reaching 1000m at the summit. Waymarking is quite good, and Ganekagorta is now well signposted at Pagasarri, Biberdi and the crossroads in between. *Important:* The summit approach should not be attempted if the top is covered in cloud, otherwise the walk presents no difficulties. ● **Shorter option**: a hike just as far as the pleasant, shady **picnic site of Pagasarri** which already gives a feel of being up in the mountains away from the city (3 to 3h30min round trip from Plaza Zabalburu, shorter still from Iberdrola or Igertu — about 2h).

Equipment: see page 55

Access *(see map):* 🚌 From Plaza Zabalburu in Bilbao's city centre,

drive south on Calle Juan de Garay. Take the third exit from the large **roundabout with the fountain** before the motorway, the **Avenida San Adrián**, signposted to SAN ADRIAN. Then continue up through the suburb of the same name. Cross the motorway bridge and veer left around the side of the **Iberdrola electricity substation**. When you come to another roundabout, continue straight ahead on a road that bends to the right and continues through **Larraskitu**. You pass Bar Athletic and come to a picnic site and car park at **Igertu** (4km from Bilbao; 43° 13.937'N, 2° 56.458'W). Driving here reduces the return walking time by nearly 2h.

🚌 No 76 city bus from Plaza Moyua to San Adrián. Get off at the Iberdrola stop (1.5km from Bilbao) and refer to the map; this reduces the return walking time by just under 1h.

G anekogorta is the only mountain reaching 1000m within the *comarca* of Bilbao. In fact, its real height is 998m, but a 2m-high summit marker has been built to enable it to attain mythical status among locals! The full, albeit long walk from the city centre is recommended to put things in their true perspective, providing an extraordinary contrast between the concrete jungle of the Basque Country's largest city and the surprisingly wild, green mountainous area immediately to the south — the high point of which is a superb ridge walk to the summit and distant views of the whole Bilbao conurbation to the north and mountains in every other direction.

Start the walk from **Plaza Zabalburu in Bilbao** (**1**). Follow the signs TODAS DIRECCIONES and SAN ADRIÁN by walking up the left-hand side of **Calle Juan de Garay** and when you come to the large **roundabout with fountain** before the motorway (**2**; 75m; **10min**), keep straight ahead across a busy road, following **Avenida San Adrián** and signs to SAN ADRIÁN.

Then continue up through the eponymous suburb.

Follow this road across the motorway bridge and take the first right turn. Then, just past the **No 76 bus stop**, take the first left up **Larraskitubidea** (**3**; 118m; **25min**), keeping the **Iberdrola electricity substation** to your left. At the top of this street, take the steeper right-hand fork with steps, emerging by the first houses of **Larraskitu**. Ignore the signpost here indicating a variant of the GR228 (the 'green Bilbao ring' walk): *PAGASARRI 7.23KM*. Instead turn right and, after the first bend, head left up **Pagasarribidea**, a steep lane (**4**; 158m; **32min**). This takes you back to the road, just before **Bar Athletic** (**5**; 196m; **40min**). You have now gained considerable height, and the views already extend well out towards the Bilbao estuary. Follow the road until you come to the picnic site and car park at **Igertu** (**6**; 252m; **50min**), where there is an information panel about the area. This is the place to leave the car if you are driving to the trailhead.

Keep straight ahead along the road beyond here (left leads to the church of San Roque, visible on the opposite hillside). Go through a **gate** (**7**; 298m; **55min**) and join the start of a forest track, closed to traffic. From here it's a steep climb to **Artabeko Bidegurutzea/Cruz de Artabe** (**8**; 413m; **1h15min**). From there take the signposted **Camino Viejo** straight ahead — a path which winds quite steeply up through the woods. Then turn right on rejoining the track (**9**; 548; **1h35min**), ascending to the meadowland and limestone rocks of **Pagasarri** (**10**; 634m; **1h45min**; ⊓*P*), where there is another information panel, a fine shady picnic site and a refuge serving drinks and snacks to the left (www.pagasarri.com; open daily ex Tue, 08.45-14.30). The city feels a

long way away from here!

The Ganekogorta ridge is now visible ahead in the distance. From the information panel, follow the track downhill; it's signposted *GANEKAGORTA 6.4km* — but like many distances shown on signs in this area, this is not reliable: it's

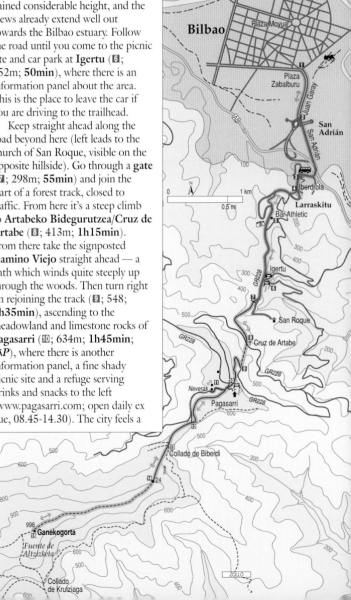

View down the Ganekogorta ridge from the summit

actually about 3.8km! (*Note:* if you need to fill up your water bottle, first take the track down to the right, through a gate. Continue downhill and after less than 200m you will come to two former *neveras* on the right (**11**). These basic constructions, known as 'snow wells' or 'snow pits' were once commonly used in mountain areas to store food; now they are covered with safety railings. Behind them some steps descend to a spring with delicious cold water).

To continue towards Ganekagorta, keep straight downhill on the track past another information panel (the track to the left of the one leading to the spring). Reaching a signposted **crossroads of paths** (**12**; 595m; **1h55min**), keep straight on until you come to a large electricity pylon and, just beyond it, a **concrete marker** at the bottom of the ridge: the **Collado Biberdi** (**13**; 613m; **2h**). Take the very steep forest track signposted 'GANEKAGORTA 2.4km' to the right here and zigzag up the mountain to

a grassy spur and **marker 24** (**14**; 703m; **2h15min**). From here a clear path ascends to the ridge and beyond, to the **summit marker of Ganekogorta** (**15**; 998m; **3h**). Horses and goats normally graze on and around the summit, and vultures are also frequently sighted.

Return back along the ridge to **Collado Biberdi** (**3h40min**) and from there back uphill to **Pagasarri** (**4h**). From the information panel at the picnic site, remember to take the track downhill to the right, signposted BILBAO (ZABALBURU), returning back down the **Camino Viejo** to Igertu (**4h30min**). (Although the descent on the red/white waymarked GR228 would eventually bring you to the same place, it is far longer than taking the **Camino Viejo**. At the bend just after **Bar Athletic**, also remember to return right down the lane through **Larraskitu** and retrace your outgoing route from there all the way back to **Plaza Zabalburu** in **Bilbao** centre (**5h20min**).

Walk 12: URKIOLAGIRRE • (ANBOTO) • LARRAONA

Distance: 10.7km/6.6mi; 3h05min (or 12.5km/7.8mi; 4h30min including the detour to Anboto)

Grade: ●▮ moderate. Fairly easy, then a steady (but not steep) ascent to Urkiolagirre followed by an extremely steep ascent of 300m/1000ft from Pagozelai to the ridge just below the Anboto summit. The final metres to the top are very exposed; you must be sure-footed and have a head for heights. The total ascent is about 600m, with a cumulative altitude gain of about 800m; it's 300m less for a basic loop.

Equipment: see page 55

Access: 🚗 Leave the A8 motorway at the exit for Durango (Car tour 3 at 28km). Then drive 13km south on the BI623 signposted to *VITORIA-GASTEIZ* and *URKIOLA*. Park close to the Bar/Restaurante Bizkarra (43° 6.053'N, 2° 38.788'W); if this car park is full, there is another parking area to the left above the *santuario*. 🚌 buses between Durango and Vitoria-Gasteiz stop at **Alto de Urkiola,** on the main road by the bar.

Anboto, while not Bizkaia's highest, is without doubt its most striking and renowned mountain. The basic loop to Pagozelai at its base, with a short side trip to the main ridge at Larraona, is a beautiful circuit providing fine views of the whole range, although a spectacular detour following the classic route from the Urkiola Sanctuary to the summit will give one the sensation of being in a mountain range the equal of the High Pyrenees or the Picos de Europa.

Start the walk at **Urkiola** (**1**; 712m). First visit the Information Centre (signposted from near the bar/ restaurant as 'TOKI ALAI 0.3KM'), for maps and details of many walks in the area. Then head up the road opposite, past the **Basílica de San Antonio** (more commonly called the **Santuario de Urkiola** and one of the most important pilgrimage sites for Basques). It is surrounded by a large and extremely popular picnic area (🏕P). At the end of this picnic site and second car park (**2**; 742m; **5min**), turn left up through the

woods, following the GR12 signpost indicating *URKIOLARRE* and *ASUNTZA/POL-POL*. Cross the **stile** and head up across the meadow, to a small area of **pine forest** (**15min**), then follow the path through the middle of this wood. You emerge on a hillside from where there are superb views to the north, to the lower limestone peaks of the Duranguesado Massif. Where the main path veers to the right (**3**; 919m; **30min**), head straight along the ridge to the orientation board on **Urkiolagirre** (**4**; 1005m; **45min**).

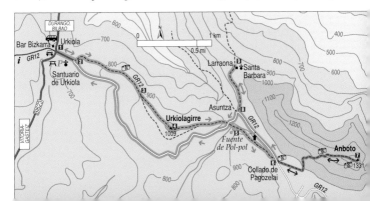

Left: Anboto's summit ridge; below: the Sanctuary of Urkiola

1h25min). There are fine views from just above this col over the eastern end of the massif. The detour to the Anboto summit starts here.*

From **Pagozelai**, return along the GR12 track to a signpost at the pass of **Asuntza** (**8**; 883m; **1h45min**). Take the path to the right for LARRAONA. Cut into the mountainside, this climbs gently up to the main Allutiz-Anboto ridge. Just below, on the north side of the ridge, is the small private refuge of **Larraona** and the tiny chapel of **Santa Barbara** to its right (**9**; 955m; **2h**). The views from this ridge extend all the way to the sea. From here retrace your steps to **Asuntza** (**2h15min**), then follow the main track back to **Urkiola** (**3h05min**).

From here there are superb views towards the rest of the Duranguesado chain, with the abrupt face of Anboto rising at the far end.

Descend the spur beyond Urkiolagirre — just beyond a peculiar **metal summit marker** embedded in some rock, crossing a stile and reaching a track (the return route to Urkiola). Cross this track to descend to the stream and make for the onomatopoeically-named **Fuente de Pol-Pol** (**5**; 878m; **1h05min**), a large natural spring enclosed by a fence. Follow the path on the right-hand side of the stream as far as the remains of a peculiar **brick structure** (**1h10min**), originally used for washing minerals mined in the area. From here ascend past an old disused **refuge**, to rejoin the track crossed earlier. Follow this (still the GR12) towards ZABALANDI as far as the **Collado de Pagozelai** (**6**; 995m; 90

*Detour to Anboto: Turn left at this col, following the sign to ANBOTO, and start climbing very steeply via rock and beech woods. This tough route is well marked in red. From the main **ridge** (**1h55min**) you have your first glimpse over the villages of the Atxondo Valley, 1000m below. Follow the ridge to the right; at first the way is quite safe and not too exposed. From a **marker** (**2h**) just below the summit, the views back along the ridge are superb. This may be as far as many will wish to climb: the last stretch, to the summit, involves a steep scramble up the exposed south face. While this is not as abrupt as the vertical north face, it *is* somewhat intimidating. If you do reach the summit of **Anboto** (**7**; 1331m; **2h10min**), you will enjoy a 360° panorama. From the top retrace your steps to the **Collado de Pagozelai** (**2h50min**) and from there follow the notes above back to **Urkiola** (**4h30min**).

Walk 13: BOSQUE DE OMA

Important Notes

1) The Bosque de Oma is currently closed to the public owing to the spread of a disease affecting pine in the forest. Please check at www.bosquedeoma.com to see when it will be reopening. It is still possible to visit the Santimamiñe Cave and to hike down the Oma Valley as far as the ruined Olakoerrota water mills (about 2h return).

2) To prevent further deterioration to the extraordinary paintings, a viewing platform has been built just inside the entrance to the Santimamiñe Cave (the only part of the cave that can be entered). All visits are in conjunction with a 3D virtual tour inside the San Mamés chapel beside the entrance. Prior booking is necessary. Contact santimamie@bizkaia.eus or tel 94 4651657/94 4651660. Tours year round Tue-Sun

at 10.00, 11.00, 12.00 and 13.00, with additional tours from 15/10 to 14/04 at 15.30, 16.30 and 17.30.

Distance: 6.7km/4.2mi; 2h30min

Grade: ● easy, with a gradual ascent from Lekiza and then from the village of Oma back to the starting point. Waymarked throughout in yellow and white (PR-BI180).

Equipment: see page 55; good trainers are fine for this walk.

Access: 🚗 From **Kortezubi** (northeast of Bilbao via Gernika; the 122km-point on Car tour 3), take the BI4244 east towards *CUEVA DE SANTIMAMIÑE* and *BOSQUE PINTADO*. Park beside or just beyond the **Lezika** bar/restaurant (a 2.5km detour from the main road; 43° 20.677'N, 2° 38.283'W). 🚌 the Bilbao/Lekeitio bus passes through **Kortezubi**; alight at the crossroads and walk or hitch the additional 2.5km.

T he beautiful Oma Valley is a wonderful retreat from the pace of modern life, highlights being the unspoilt village of Oma itself with its traditional *baserri*, the unique 'painted forest' — the work of local artist Agustín Ibarrola — and the Santimamiñe Cave, with the best-preserved cave paintings in the Basque Country.

Start out at the **Lezika** bar/restaurant (**1**; 47m): walk to the end of the road beyond the main car park. From here, 308 steps take you up via the **Ermita (chapel) de Santimamiñe** and a pretty **picnic site** (🎋P), through forest and limestone, to the entrance to the **Santimamiñe Cave** (**2**; 119m; **10min**). This is a magical place,

tucked inside **Mt Erenozar** and home to the Basque Country's finest cave paintings.

Back at Lezika (**20min**), head up the concrete lane to the right beside a large picture of the painted forest, the yellow/white-waymarked PR-BI180 signposted to *BOSQUE DE OMA/OMAKO BASOA*. The lane soon becomes gravel and winds its way

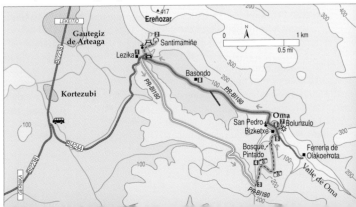

Bosque Pintado (left) and the artist's garden (above)

steadily up through the pine forest to another signpost (**3**; 222m; **1h**). Turn left here to plunge down into the forest until you reach the first painted trees of the **Bosque Pintado**. The largest concentration of trees is where the path levels out (**4**; 151m; **1h15min**), their trunks painted in all manner of strange designs — local artist Agustin Ibarrola's unique visual creation. Take the time to explore this unique forest before descending a little further to another signpost pointing to *OMA* (**1h20min**).

From here the path descends beside a small stream through a gate and to a road just beyond it (**5**; 54m; **1h30min**). You are now on the floor of the **Oma Valley**. (A short, five-minute detour along the road to the right would take you to **Olakoerrota** (62m), the remains of an old watermill, but there is not
92

much left to see and it is now attached to a large, fairly modern house.)

To continue the main walk, turn left at the road to enter the picture-postcard village of **Oma** itself, with its traditional stone *baserri* and verdant meadows full of grazing sheep and goats.

Opposite **Bizketxe** *baserri* (**6**; 44m, **1h35min**), cross a small **stone footbridge** over the stream beside an information panel about the karst landscape in this area, then follow a narrow path downstream. From here the garden of the artist Ibarrola, containing some of his works, is visible through the trees on the opposite bank, before you reach the remains of an old **watermill** in the forest. Just after this point, the stream disappears underground into a huge moss-covered hollow known as **Bolunzulo** (**7**; 42m; **1h40min**).

Return to the road (**1h45min**) and turn right to head out of the village, passing the **chapel of San Pedro** on your left and climbing out of the valley and onwards through undulating farmland, via **Basondo** *baserri* (**8**; 60m; **2h20min**), back to the starting point at **Lezika** (**2h30min**).

Walk 14: ITXINA

Distance: 10.6km/6.4mi; 3h45min

Grade: ● moderate, with a short, fairly steep ascent from the forest to Ojo de Axular, the entrance to Itxina. The return walk to Urigoiti involves a similar ascent from Supelegor cave back to Ojo de Axular. Itxina is a labyrinth of rocks and forest, and exploring beyond the waymarked path to Supelegor cave should not be attempted: it is *very easy to get lost*, especially if there is a danger of mist. Apart from a few small cairns, there is little waymarking from the MP16 boundary marker until you reach the large cairn at the base of Ojo de

Axular, but by keeping parallel to the wall of Itxina there should be no confusion.

Equipment: see page 55

Access: 🚗 Follow Car tour 4 to **Ibarra** (34km) and continue 3km on the BI4514 up the mountain to **Urigoiti**. Park on either side of the lane just beyond the village church (43° 5.236'N, 2° 50.620'W). 🚌 Bizkaibus No A3613 runs an hourly service every day from Bolueta and Atxuri in Bilbao to Orozko (8km from Urigoiti), two of which continue in the morning to Ibarra (3km from Urigoiti). You can also take a taxi from Orozko (8km).

I txina is one of the most fascinating landscapes in the Basque Country and is a truly magical place. It is a karst fortress on the north side of Gorbeia Parke Naturala, Bizkaia's largest nature reserve. Access to this world of strange limestone rock formations, dense forest and the location of the huge mythical cave of Supelegor is via a 'window' in the rock face known as Atxular Ate or Ojo de Axular — 'Atxular's Eye'.

Start the walk in the **church square** in the pretty hamlet of **Urigoiti** (**1**; 454m), where an old millstone table can be used for picnics (*P*). Continue

uphill along the lane signposted to the car park for about 500m, to a further car park and small picnic site at **Elezkin** (**2**; 500m; **5min**). There

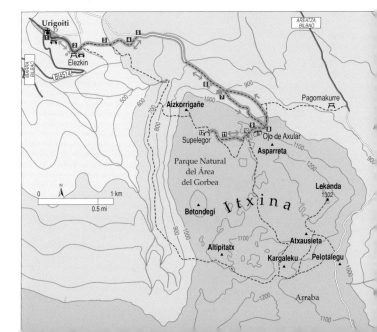

Left: view from inside Itxina looking out through the Ojo de Axular; below: Mt Aizkorrigañe at the northwesternmost corner of Itxina

is an information panel here about the **Gorbea Nature Park**, which covers the whole of Itxina and Mt Gorbea itself, the highest peak in Bizkaia. Continue on the path beyond here, crossing the cattle grid and following the sign to PAGOMAKURRE.

The incredible limestone wall of Itxina is directly ahead of you from here all the way up to mountain

pastureland. When you come to a small building, keep on the path to the right to climb fairly steeply up through pine forest to a **stile** (**3**; 577m; **15min**). Cross it to temporarily leave the woodland and continue climbing to a second stile. Cross this one as well and enter a field. Here the path seems to disappear but do not fear! Simply keep to the left of this field until you reach a fence bordering a gravel road, and follow the fence up to a third stile. Crossing this, you emerge on the open mountainside beside another **information panel** (**4**; 654m; **30min**).

Now on the gravel road, the route ascends gradually up the hillside through another **gate** (**5**; 678m; **45min**), after a short concreted section becoming a path that emerges by a clump of trees on some verdant pastureland at the foot of **Mt Aizkorrigañe**, the north-westernmost corner of Itxina. From here keep straight on following the vestiges of a path across this pastureland to a fence running parallel to the north-facing wall of Itxina. Follow this fence until you come to a **spring** (**6**; 839m; **1h05min**) and from there continue following the fence back into the woodland and on to **boundary stone MP16** just in front of a large overhanging **beech tree** (**7**; 868m; **1h10min**).

From here take the path to the right which winds fairly gently up through the forest towards the limestone wall. There are occasional small cairns to guide you, but as long as you remain fairly close to the wall and keep climbing, there should be no confusion. Eventually you will emerge at a clearing just beneath the wall itself, where there is a **large cairn** (**8**; 1023m; **1h35min**). From here turn right to head directly to what at first glance appears to be beginning of a scree slope but in fact becomes a path that zigags up to a beautiful natural 'door' in the rock face — **Ojo de Axular** (**9**; **Atxular Ate in Euskara**; 1095m; **1h45min**), a wonderful viewpoint.

From here you enter the fantasy world of **Itxina**; descend to a large hollow and circle round it, to a junction of paths (**10**; 1084m; **1h50min**). Follow the sign pointing downhill to the right to SUPELEGOR. Continue descending through the magical beech forest, following well-positioned cairns through a **natural passageway carved out of limestone** (**11**; 1036m; **2h**). Beyond here the path veers down to the right to a clearing strewn with boulders, leading on to the immense entrance of **Supelegor Cave** (**12**; 993m; **2h10min**). It is possible to go quite a way inside the cave, and it is a popular refuge for cows and sheep. This is just the 'tip of the iceberg' of an immense cave system, and Supelegor itself is the focal point of many legends in Basque mythology.

Remember to keep some energy for the return climb back to **Ojo de Axular** on the same path (**2h35min**). Return the same way to the **cairn** (**8**) first encountered at the 1h35min-point, from where you can take an alternative route back: head straight down the grassy spur ahead to the first fence and then turn left onto a path back to the **MP16 boundary stone** (**7**; **2h50min**). From this point simply return the same way to **Urigoiti** (**3h45min**).

Walk 15: TOLOGORRI

Distance: 8.2 km/5.1mi; 3h

Grade: ●: moderate-strenuous. The walk involves a fairly steep climb up through forest and is slightly vertiginous along the Senda Negra — a narrow, level path cut into the side of the Bedarbide mountain. Sporadic yellow waymarking, both in the forest and on the open mountain — not always clear, so explicit instructions are given in the text below for those points where you might be in doubt. Overall ascent 590m

Equipment: see page 55

Access: 🚌 From Orduña town centre (the 84km-point on Car tour 4), take the road which starts close to the main square signposted to *LA ANTIGUA* monastery and the villages of *BELANDIA/ MAROÑO* (BI3931). This road passes the railway station and the monastery. After 3.5km, turn left on the BI4532 to *LENDOÑO GOITIA*, passing a dolmen on the left and a small **picnic site** (🚓*P*), from where there are excellent views of Tologorri. Turn left 300m before Lendoño Goitia, by a large wooden sign, *'RUTA DE ITURRIGORRIA/ITURRI-GORRIKO BIDEA'*. Park at the end of the lane (6.5km from Orduña; 43° 0.726'N, 3° 3.362'W). 🚌 hourly service from Bilbao Abando station to **Orduña**, from where a taxi may be taken to the start of the walk near Lendoño Goitia. *NB:* By car you can continue 8km further along the scenic BI3931 from Orduña to 'Guzurtegi', a rustic *agroturismo* and bar/restaurant in the hamlet of **Maroño**, just above a small reservoir of the same name, one of the few places to eat in the area and a wonderful viewpoint for Tologorri and the whole Sierra Salbada (www.guzurtegi.com).

The magnificent twin prows of Tologorri are visible for miles around and form the most prominent peak of the Sierra Salbada — a long plain which drops away abruptly above the Orduña and Aiala valleys, forming a long cliff face of about 700m in height above the valley floor. This is the best-known and most scenic route up the mountain, following the famous Senda Negra (Black Path), so called because of the colour of the earth on this mountainside.

The twin prows of Tologorri

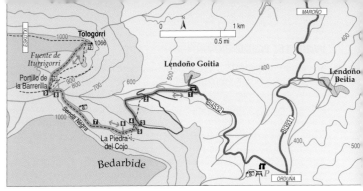

Start out at the end of the small **parking area** near **Lendoño Goitia** (**1**; 466m). Continue along the stony track, taking the first fork to the right and ignoring other, minor forks to the left or right. You pass through a **gate** (**8min**) and gradually climb through a large beech forest. At a three-way fork marked by a small **cairn** (**2**; 560m; **15min**), go straight ahead on the main (middle) track. The route then veers to the left, away from Tologorri, climbing more steeply.

There is occasional yellow waymarking from now, but it's not to be relied on. When you reach a **second cairn** (**3**; 699m; **30min**), turn right — by a rustic signpost marked RUTA ITURRIGORRIA. After 100m look for a **third cairn** (**4**), which marks the way up a leafy path to the left. After a short, steep climb, partially marked by yellow way-marking and small yellow ribbons tied to branches, carefully look for a jagged stone on the right, topped by a **further small cairn** (**5**; 736m; **40min**), to follow a path to the right. This path is not immediately obvious; there is also waymarking on a tree here, but it is quite faded.

Many rocks now invade the path, until we reach an especially large one with a plaque inscribed 'La Piedra del Cojo' (**6**; 776m; **45min**). *El cojo* (the lame one) was a local man who walked with a limp and would regularly stroll with his friends along this path and stop to rest at this spot.

The path soon emerges on the mountainside at the start of the **Senda Negra** (**7**; 822m; **50min**) which is cut into the rock face of **Bedarbide** (1037m). This is a beautiful path, with superb views towards Tologorri and down to the valley below, *but watch your step, especially after rain when the ground can be very muddy!* You will be relieved to reach a beech tree overhanging the precipice (**8**; 890m; **1h10min**), from where the Senda Negra zigzags up to the **Portillo de la Barrerilla** (**9**; 950m; **1h15min**), the only access point onto the top of this otherwise near-vertical ridge.

Go through the gate *(portillo)* and follow the path immediately to the right. As this levels out, the summit marker on Tologorri becomes clearly visible. From here it is an easy walk to the **Fuente de Iturrigorri** (**10**; Red Spring; 950m; **1h20min** — so called because the surrounding rocks are coloured by the high iron content in the water). Refill your water bottle, then carry on up a clear grassy path, over a stile, and on to the summit of **Tologorri** (1066m; **1h35min**).

In clear weather it is possible to continue walking all the way along to the end of the ridge for about an hour, to **Eskutxi** (1180m), the highest point; otherwise return the same way to the parking area near **Lendoño Goitia** (**3h**).

Walk 16: VALDEREJO NATURE RESERVE

See photo on page 28
Distance: 13.8km/8.6mi; 4h45min
Grade: ● moderate, with an overall ascent of 350m. Unusually, this walk involves an ascent on the *return* route, so conserve energy for this. On the plus side, the scenery in the Valderejo Nature Reserve is stunning, and the village of Herrán makes an excellent rest stop before heading back over the steepest section of the walk to Campas de Santa Ana. Waymarking, in yellow throughout the nature reserve, is excellent (except for the area between Campas de Santa Ana and Ribera). This walk can be extended over a full day, with a picnic lunch stop either in Herrán or on the way. ● *Shorter, easier alternatives* that avoid the rather steep return climb over Santa Ana

are out-and-back walks from Lalastra — to the abandoned village of **Ribera** (7.2km/2h), to the **Río Purón gorge** ('Desfiladero'; 10km/3h30min) or to the **picnic site** beyond the gorge (11km/4h).
Equipment: see page 55
Access: 🚗 15km south of the Puerto de Orduña turn west on the A2622 (the 108km-point in Car tour 4, signposted to PARQUE NATURAL DE VALDEREJO/VALDEREJO PARKE NATURALA). Turn left at **San Millán de San Zadornil** and then right in **San Zadornil** village, to continue to **Lalastra**, the main entry point for the park, 17km from the A2625. Park in the large car park just before the village (42° 52.569'N, 3° 13.710'W).
🚌 from Vitoria-Gasteiz to **Lalastra** Mon-Sat; change of 🚌 in Espejo

The Valderejo Nature Reserve is a paradise for walkers. There are many well-waymarked *sendas* (paths) within the park, details of which are available from the Casa del Parque/Parketxea in Lalastra, which also rents out binoculars for viewing the huge variety of bird life. The outward route described here is the classic one, visiting the abandoned village of Ribera and the beautiful gorge *(desfiladero)* of the Purón River, before ending in the village of Herrán in Burgos province. We return on a little-frequented path over the high meadowland of Santa Ana.

Start out from the car park just before **Lalastra** (**1**; 916m): walk through this pretty village, which has a large, pleasant picnic site. Pass Valderejo Etxea, a conveniently located *agroturismo* (tel: 945 353085) which also serves meals, and the church, worth visiting for its restored clock tower. Turn left by the **Casa del Parque/Parketxea** (**2**; 907m; **5min**), to follow SENDA PURÓN/GR282 towards RIBERA, with fine open views over the northern part of the park — pastureland surrounded by a semi-circular cliff face several kilometres long.

Just after entering the mostly Scots pine forest, fork right at the

first junction of paths (**3**; 905m; **25min**). (To the left is SENDA PORTILLO, which can also be used as a slightly longer return route from Ribera). About 20m further on, fork right again to descend through the forest. When you emerge on a wide track (**4**; 844m; **35min**), fork right following the yellow markers. You descend to a stream, the **Arroyo Polledo** (**5**; 819m; **40min**), and then follow the **Purón River**, eventually going through a gate (**6**; 757m; **50min**). Continue alongside the river. At the next crossroads, turn right over the river (signed SENDA PURÓN DESFILDERO 1KM) to a second crossroads (**7**; 761m; **55min**), with the abandoned village of **Ribera** to your right. The remains of some houses are being gradually covered by the ever-encroaching vegetation, but turn right here towards RIBERA ELIZA and then take the first right to climb up to the old church (**8**; 775m; **1h**), which still contains some frescos, albeit in an increasing state of disrepair.

Return to the main path and keep straight on past a small **picnic site** (**9**; 747m; **1h05min**; ⊟*P*) and across meadowland where there are usually plenty of cows and horses grazing. Pass through a gate, to enter more woodland and the entrance to the **Desfiladero del Río Purón** (**10**; 719m; **1h25min**). Shortly after entering the gorge, some **steps** to the left (**11**; 727m; **1h30min**) take you steeply down to the river, to a delightful spot close to a couple of small waterfalls.

Back on the main path, continue down through the gorge to a **footbridge** at the narrowest point. All too soon we round a bend and leave the gorge proper (**12**; 700m; **1h45min**) — although the scenery is no less dramatic, with the cliff on the opposite side of the river being one of several prime nesting sites in the park for Griffon vultures and other birds of prey. A clearing just above a **waterfall** (**13**; 674m; **1h55min**) is another viewpoint over the lower gorge. Continue past the junction with **Senda Sta Ana** (**14**; 654m; **2h**) and, as the path descends you come to a new **picnic site** (**15**; 622m; **2h05min**). Cross the river here to take a look at the **San Roque** chapel nestling in the cliff face. Continue by going through a gate and along a wider track, past another small, rather abandoned riverside **picnic site** (**16**; 591m; **2h15min**; ⊟*P*) and on to the pretty village of **Herrán** (**17**; 591m; **2h20min**).

Take advantage of this pleasant rest stop (although there is only one small bar that has sporadic opening times and serves no food), then retrace your steps to the junction with **Senda Sta Ana** (**14**; **2h45min**) and turn right to follow this narrow stony path. It zigzags fairly steeply up the mountain, with tremendous views back down to the Purón Gorge and beyond to the plains and mountains of Burgos. From **Campas de Santa Ana** (**18**; 912m; **3h15min**), a flat meadowland, follow the sign straight on towards RIBERA, looking out for yellow waymarking to guide you down through another Scots pine forest. Soon after the path forks to the left onto a main track, take the path to the right, still in the forest (**19**; 889m; **3h30min**), and continue onto the edge of a meadow (**20**; 837m; **3h35min**). From here follow the vestiges of a path across the meadow to join a track (**21**; 763m; **3h40min**), where you turn left to return to the bridge opposite Ribera (**3h50min**), thence retracing steps to **Lalastra** (**4h45min**).

Walk 17: ALONG THE RIO AYUDA FROM OKINA TO SASETA AND BACK

Distance: 10km/6mi; 3h
Grade: ● an easy walk along the Ayuda river valley, downstream to Saseta, and a gentle uphill return of 135m; the whole route is extremely well-waymarked in red and white (part of the GR38 Ruta del Vino y del Pescado).
Equipment: see page 55; trainers are fine for the walk along the Ayuda River.
Access: 🚗 From Vitoria-Gasteiz, the easiest way of reaching Okina is to follow signs east out of city to the

N104 towards IRUÑA-PAMPLONA and DONOSTIA-SAN SEBASTIÁN (the *old* road, *not* the dual carriageway). Turn right (2km) on A132 towards ESTELLA and then right again on the A2130 (4km) to the village of **Otazu**. Just past this village, take the signposted minor A3104 road towards OKINA. The road ends in the tiny village of **Okina** (17km from Vitoria-Gasteiz). Park in the village (42° 45.770'N, 2° 35.193'W). 🚌 *No public transport*

This walk offers the chance to explore the wild and unspoilt, forested Montaña Alavesa or, more specifically, the area forming part of the Montes de Vitoria. The main walk, along the Ayuda River between the tiny villages of Okina and Saseta, makes an extremely pleasant excursion from Vitoria-Gasteiz, just half an hour's drive from the city. But with the right footwear, the full walk up the Barranco de Arrola is highly recommended.

First look around the Romanesque village of **Okina** — and note the curious **fountain** in the main square. Then cross the square diagonally, to an info map about the GR38 — the 'Ruta del Vino y del Pescado', the old wine and fish trading route between the village of Oyón in the heart of the wine-growing area of Rioja Alavesa to the south and Otxandio to the north (**1**; 790m).

Start the walk by taking the lane to the left of the map, signposted DESFILADERO RIO AYUDA/SASETA. Now in the valley of the **Río Ayuda**, you go through a **gate** (**2**; 787m; **10min**) and enter a beech forest. The remains of an **old watermill** are visible on the right (**3**; 774m; **15min**) and, a little further on, to the left, a **refuge** where the cement road ends and the track begins; this also marks the border with the County of Treviño, a curious enclave belonging to the Castilian province

of Burgos within the Basque territory of Araba.

Just after this you come to a small wooden footbridge over the **Barranco de Arrola** (**4**; 756m; **20min**) from where you could make a pleasant, shady *detour* up this tributary of the Río Ayuda. It is possible to follow traces of a path close to this stream, the lower part of which passes through a small ravine. After about 25 minutes' walking, the path disappears altogether and the best option is to follow the bed of the stream over rocks. The going is practical up this valley as far as a **large yew tree** beside a **small waterfall** (**5**), although the latter may be a trickle or non-existent in summer). It is not really practical to continue beyond this point, as the old path — vague as it was — has now become impossibly overgrown.

For the main walk, cross the **bridge** over the Barranco de Arrola,

100

after which the path enters the gorge of the **Rio Ayuda,** the most beautiful part of the valley. We pass through a delightful forest, following the river's crystal clear-water downstream over small rapids. The whole valley is luxuriant with vegetation.

You pass a rock overhang (**5**; 746m; **30min**). There are many fine little picnic spots beside the river, including a particularly attractive **rock pool** (**6**; 745m; **35min**). A few metres further along the main path, take one leading off to the right for a view of a delightful **small waterfall** (**7**; 739m; **40min**). At times the path climbs fairly high above the river and at others runs just alongside it. The valley gradually opens out and the mountains of the Sierra de Toloño and Cantabria can be seen ahead in the distance.

After a fairly long stretch of path, you pass through a **gate** (**8**; 684m; **1h10min**) at a point where the route returns to the banks of the Ayuda, immediately after which you cross over a small stone bridge. After a further 250m the path joins a wide track (**9**; 689m; **1h13min**), which we follow into **Saseta** (**10**; 690m; **1h20min**). This village belongs to the County of Treviño. Having once been almost abandoned, some of the old farmhouses are now being restored as permanent homes. There is a small rustic bar with garden (Bar Larrein) to the right as you enter the village; it is open all year at weekends and daily in summer. You can usually get a meal but, in these fairly remote parts, it's best not to rely on this. (If you can speak some Spanish, call the bar beforehand to check: 945 403297 or 635 737710.)

From the village retrace your steps, taking care to fork left along the waymarked path where the main track ascends to the right (**9**; **1h30min**). As the walk is slightly

Near Okina

uphill on the return journey through the gorge, allow a little more time for this, following the same path back to **Okina** (**3h**).

101

Walk 18: BONETE DE SAN TIRSO

Distance: 8.9km/5.5mi; 3h20min

Grade: ●◗ moderate, with an overall ascent of 600m. A straight-forward, fairly gradual ascent up through the shady forest and onto the ridge all the way to the monolith and cave-chapel of San Tirso. The final 200m/yds of ascent to the summit itself requires care, and a couple of sections that demand a head for heights. All well signposted and waymarked throughout, but timings on the signposts are unreliable, so use timings given here.

Equipment: see page 55

Access: 🚗 For the most direct approach, follow Car tour 5 to the Venta de Armentia crossroads (14km) and turn left on the BU741 (later A2124) to **Bernedo**. Take the first right turn into the village, then turn right again immediately, on a lane marked Nᴬ SRA DE OKON. Otherwise follow the tour to **La Población** (69km) and turn left at the entrance to the village, following the sign to BERNEDO, on the north side of the range (NA7210, later A2126). Beyond the Bar Arrieta on the main road in **Bernedo**, at the end of the village, turn left and then immediate right onto a lane marked Nᴬ SRA DE OKON. In either case, leave the car at this chapel, at the end of the lane (1km from Bernedo), beside a picnic site and collection of old farm machinery (42° 37.418'N, 2° 30.671'W). 🚌 from Vitoria-Gasteiz to Bernedo, then walk 1km along the lane to Nuestra Señora de Okón.

T his is a beautiful walk up through predominantly beech forest to the top of a ridge and the huge rock monolith of San Tirso. Just below the summit is a cave-chapel. This is one of the more easily accessible and spectacular parts of the Sierra de Toloño-Cantabria. A short detour on the return route enables us to see some examples of traditional charcoal and lime kilns, some of which have been restored.

To **start the walk**, look for the old wooden signpost (**1**; 756m) to SAN TIRSO just before the chapel of **Nuestra Señora de Okón** and picnic site. (Just beyond the sign there is an information panel about *'La Ruta de los Caleros y la Carbonera'* (the lime and charcoal kiln route — a pleasant 3.2km circuit, waymarked yellow/white, which we can follow on our return. Several examples of the types of kiln tradition-ally used here have been restored in the forest.)

The *bonete* (mono-lith) of San Tirso is clearly visible on top of the ridge to the west beyond the restored chapel. Follow the wide gravel path up behind the picnic site until you come to the edge of the forest and a path junction (**2**; 791m; **5min**). Here we join stage 4 of the GR1 long distance path, linking Ampurias (Girona) on the Mediter-ranean with Finisterre on the Atlantic coast of Galicia. Turn right at the sign for SAN TIRSO, following GR1 red/white and

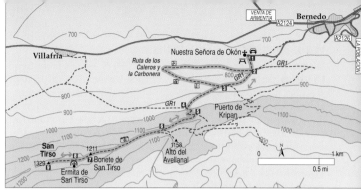

PR yellow/white waymarking. A gentle climb through beech interspersed with boxwood brings us to another choice of paths (**3**; 850m; **15min**). The first one, to the left and signposted 'Puerto Nuevo', is a direct route up to the ridge. A few metres further on, the signposted route down to the right leads to the lime and charcoal kilns that we will visit on our return loop.

Continue along the GR1 and at the next junction (**4**;**25min**), *leave* the main waymarked path (signposted to Villafria), forking left uphill along a path that narrows and becomes rockier in places. As we gain height, we get tantalising glimpses northward through the trees to the plain below and the rolling hills of Montana Alavesa beyond. At another junction (**5**; 1025m; **45min**), *ignore* the sign for 'Puerto Palo y Montorte' up on the ridge, instead keeping straight ahead. Just below the ridge itself, again *ignore* a cairn and a battered sign pointing left towards 'Puerto Kripan' (**6**; 1086m; **55min**); keep right. Some 100m further on there is another cairn marking a narrow path: continue straight on here.

Still among the trees, this beautiful path meanders gradually upwards until the huge **Bonete de San Tirso** (**7**; 1211m; **1h15min**) rock monolith comes into view directly ahead. From here the views

are spectacular — towards the plain of La Rioja to the south and the heavily forested Montaña Alavesa to the north. Continue past the monolith on a clear path to the rock face of Mt Tirso itself, until you reach the **cave** containing the ruins of the **Ermita de San Tirso** (**8**; 1244; **1h20min**). A *romería* (religious fiesta) takes place in this cave-chapel every year on 15th May. A very steep path zigzags up behind the cave and onto the exposed ridge above it. This becomes very narrow and vertiginous in places, as it ascends to the top of **San Tirso** (**9**; 1329m; **1h30min**).

From here retrace your steps to the signpost for LA RUTA DE LOS CALEROS Y LA CARBONERA just before **3** and turn left. After around 300m you come to an old lime kiln with info panel, accessible via some wooden steps (**10**; 852m; **2h45min**). Return to the path and follow the signpost SIGUE LA RUTA. A little further on, you come to a solitary picnic table opposite two charcoal kilns and another lime kiln behind them (**11**; 825m; **2h50min**). The path is well marked and, after entering a particularly thick section of forest, passes a huge lime kiln resembling a meteorite (**12**; 799m; **3h**). Our path now returns to the junction on our outward route (**2**) from where we return to **Nuestra Señora de Okón (3h20min)**.

Left: The Bonete de San Tirso, with a view down to La Población

Walk 19: IOAR

Distance: 7km/4.4mi; 3h

Grade: ● fairly strenuous, with a short but steep ascent of just over 600m from the Santuario de Kodes to the summit of Mt Ioar. There are no technically difficult sections and the route is reasonably waymarked all the way to the summit.

Equipment: see page 55

Access: 🚌 For the most direct route, take the A132 from Vitoria-Gasteiz to **Kanpezu**. Just before the village, turn right on the A2124 (later NA743) for 6km, then go left on the NA7200 to Aguilar. From **Aguilar** follow signs to the SANTUARIO DE NUESTRA SRA DE KODES, 3km beyond the village of **Torralba del Río**. Otherwise follow Car tour 5 to **La Población** (69km) and continue for a further 5km. Then turn right at the top of the pass, on the minor road towards AGUILAR DE CODES and PAMPLONA. From Aguilar, see notes above. Park in the car park on the right just before the **Santuario de Kodes** and guest house (42° 37.415'N, 2° 20.153'W). No public transport.

This route ascends Mt Ioar, the second-highest peak in the Sierra de Toloño-Cantabria/Sierra de Kodes range, on the border of Araba and Nafarroa. The climb is via the fantastic vertical rock formations known as the 'Gendarmes'. The going is steep, but superb scenery more than compensates for the effort, and the views from the summit are the best for miles around.

Start the walk from the car park just before the 16th-century **Santuario de Kodes** (**1**; 789m). A reasonably-priced *hospedería* (guest house) and bar offering simple meals and snacks are attached to the church (tel: 948378914). Continue about 100m up the hill to the left of it, past a shady picnic site, to where the tarmac ends and there is an info board about local historical sites. Follow the path behind the board (not initially waymarked) and at the first *borda* (**2**; 816m; **5min**), which has red/white waymarking on the side, keep straight ahead on the main track, ignoring the one that forks left. This heads fairly steeply up through a quite dense, mixed forest, with many young oaks.

When you come to a division of paths marked by a **cairn** and a faintly visible yellow arrow on a rock (**3**; 995m; **30min**), turn left. A little

View from the Collado de la Llana down past the Gendarmes to Torralba del Río

further on, you pass a beautiful solitary oak and emerge from the forest. The immense vertical rock pinnacles of the **Gendarmes**, guarding the entrance to the pass, now tower directly in front of you. The path becomes rocky and zigzags up the mountain, slightly to the right of these pinnacles. Look out for vultures circling around the Gendarmes and the summit.

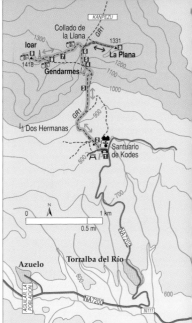

Once you are beyond the pinnacles, look for another **cairn** that marks the spot (**4**; 1094m; **50min**) where you follow the path to the right to avoid the scree slope straight ahead and briefly return to some woodland. When you come to a further **cairn** at a point where the path starts to level out (**5**; 1145m; **1h**), keep straight on to reach the next, large cairn at the **Collado de la Llana** (**6**; 1200m; **1h05min**), on the edge of a pretty moorland sandwiched between the peaks of Ioar and La Plana.

Take the unmarked path to the left* from the pass; this ascends the grassy hillside and offers increasingly open views across the heather-covered **moorland** towards the long, comb-like ridge of Costalera at the far end of the Sierra de Kodes behind you. The large TV mast on the summit of Ioar now comes into view and, as you climb, you enter a delightfully shady **beech forest** (**7**; 1286m; **1h20min**). Just after entering this forest, follow a visible path veering to the right, guided by sporadic cairns, passing some beautiful twisted beech trees.

Emerging by the **TV mast**, turn left for about 10-15 metres, above the mast, for the best views back down towards the sanctuary and the striking rock formations known as

View up to the Gendarmes

the **Dos Hermanas** (Two Sisters), at the base of the ridge directly below. (**8**; 1383m; **1h35min**). Then retrace your steps to continue to the large white summit marker of **Ioar** (**9**; 1418m; **1h40min**). Walk on just past the summit, to a cairn with a curious **mini-sculpture of a tree**, from where you will have the best views of the Sierra de Toloño-Cantabria and La Población to the west and towards the Izki Nature Reserve to the northwest.

Return the same way to the **Collado de la Llana** (**6**; 2h10min) and from there back down to the **Santuario de Kodes** (3h).

*From the pass you could take a *blue*-waymarked detour to the right along the main ridge to the summit of La Plana (**3**; 1331m) in 20 minutes.

Walk 20: SOILA RIDGE

Distance: 11.2km/7mi; 3h45min
Grade: ●❞ moderate-strenuous, with an overall ascent/descent of 550m/1800ft. A gradual ascent through forest, along the Korres Gorge and then on to the ridge of Mt Soila. Few people will find the initial descent vertiginous; it is perfectly safe and a rope is provided on this very short 50m section (see photo). The descent through the upper forest is steep and can be slippery after rain. Excellent nature reserve yellow waymarking throughout, with a series of numbered foot-paths (*sendas*). **A shorter alternative** is to follow **Bujanda path No 1** to **Korres** village and return on the **Antoñana path No 15** (2h20min).
Equipment: see page 55
Access: 🚗 For a direct approach, take the A132 from Vitoria-Gastiez to **Antoñana**. Otherwise, follow Car tour 5 to **Kanpezu** (82km) and turn left on the A132 to **Antoñana**. Park in the small car park at the village entrance (42°41.524'N, 2° 23.767'W), beside the bus stop. 🚌 Line 6 from Vitoria-Gasteiz (Estella bus) to **Antoñana**.

This is a very varied circuit around one of the most beautiful parts of the Izki Nature Reserve, a *parque natural* in the relatively little-known area of the Montaña Alavesa. Much of the walk traverses dense forest with yew, maple and ash, among many other species. The gorge and village of Korres are especially attractive, and the return along the Soila ridge spectacular.

Start out at the **car park/bus stop** in **Antoñana** (**1**; 588m), a beautiful medieval 12th-century walled village founded by King Sancho the Great of Navarre. Walk past the roundabout and follow the path under the bridge to the **Via Verde Centre** (restored railway carriages housing an info centre about the former Vitoria–Estella railway line, now a cycle track, which passes through here). Mt Soila is the long ridge directly ahead (although we will ascend the mountain from the other side). From here cross a road and follow the red/white-waymarked footpath of the GR1 and GR282 (**'Senda de Pastoreo'**). After about five minutes turn right to continue towards KORRES/GR282 and enter the **Parque Natural Izki** (**2**; 617m; 10min). Keep straight on; then, about 200m further on, turn left, following the yellow markings and GR282, to join a track that ascends to a multiple signpost (**3**; 697m; 20min). Turn left here for 'SENDA ANTOÑANA NO

15'. Turn left again at the next junction (**4**; 753m; **30min**), on a path signposted 'Senda Bujanda' (straight on is the return route for the short walk out to Korres and back). Ahead you have fine views of Mt Soila's steepest face.

The path descends to another junction at the start of the **Korres Gorge** (**5**; 645m; **50min**). Keep straight on, following this path up the heavily-wooded gorge, with the river barely visible below to the left. Divert 50m to the left, to the small **Aranbeltz Reservoir** (**6**; 657m; **1h**). As you reach the far end of the gorge (**1h05min**), turn right* up the lane to enter the pretty old village of **Korres** (**1h20min**) by a fountain. Take the first street up the hill to the right, to pass the 16th-century church of **San Esteban** (beside which is the start of the

---

*A left turn, downhill, here leads in five minutes to an excellent picnic site (🚻*P*) just outside the gorge.

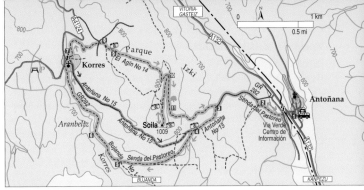

return path to Antoñana for the short loop), and continue along c/Mayor to the **Izki Nature Reserve information centre** (**7**; 719m; **1h25min**). Turn right here and then left on **Senda el Agín No 14**.

Always follow the yellow way-marking, ascending gradually through wood and scrubland. Go through a gate (**8**; 800m; **1h40min**), after which the path veers off to the left, still following the yellow waymarking, and then fork left again after 200m (**9**; 816m; **1h45min**). The terrain becomes rockier and the path zigzags up to the ridge, with increasingly open views towards the Sierra de Toloño-Cantabria. The **ridge top** (**10**; 968; **2h15min**) itself appears somewhat abruptly after a relatively gentle ascent, and affords great views down to Antoñana. Follow the **signpost** to the right along the ridge, to the summit of **Soila** (**11**; 1009m; **2h30min**), from where the Korres Gorge is now visible to the right. Vultures are commonplace there. Take the time to descend slightly, to a **natural window** in the sheer rock face (accessed via a hollow just below the summit).

Retrace your steps along the ridge to the **signpost** (**10**; **2h50min**) and continue along the narrow **Senda el Agín**, cut into the rock. The path turns sharp right after 50m

and plunges into the forest below the cliffs (a rope helps on this first section). You descend past ash and maple trees and reach a giant ancient **yew** (**12**; 885m; **3h05min**). The yew is now a protected species in the Basque Country. A series of steps takes us further down through this beautiful forest, until we eventually emerge at the junction first passed at the 20minute-point (**3h25min**). Turn left, to return along the track/path to **Antoñana** (**3h45min**).

Arriving in Korres (top) and the ridge descent from Soila on the Senda el Agín

Walk 21: RIO UREDERRA

Distance: 9km/5.5mi; 3h
Grade: ● easy. The walk follows the Urederra River, with a steady, gradual ascent of some 200m towards the end. Mostly within a nature reserve and clearly signposted from Baquedano. While the walk may be easily completed in the time shown, it's worth spending much longer, to enjoy the river and forest.
Equipment: see page 55; trainers are fine for this walk.
Access: ⛟ Fastest access from Iruña-Pamplona via Estella and the NA718. Otherwise, follow Car tour 5 to the NA718 (113km) and turn right towards ESTELLA. Pass through **Zudaire** and after 2.5km turn left in **Barindano** on the NA7187 to **Baquedano** (a detour of 5.5km from the car tour route). Cars must be left in a car park just to the left of the village (42° 46.996'N, 2° 23.767'W; €5 in summer/at weekends, at other times free); no parking is allowed in the village. *No* public transport.
Important note: To control numbers of visitors in the summer months/weekends, entrance tickets for the nature reserve (free of charge) now need to be booked via the website www.urederra.amesca.net.

The Urederra River is one of the most beautiful spots in the Sierra de Urbasa, with its turquoise pools and waterfalls, and most of this walk provides a wonderful shady escape from the summer heat (although this is also when it is most popular with local people, who love to picnic by the river). The route ends some way below the river's source *(nacedero)* — directly below the awesome cliff face of the Balcón de Pilatos. There are few more idyllic river walks in the Basque Country.

Start out from the **car park** at **Baquedano** (**1**; 596m): walk up through the village, following the sign 'UREDERRA' past the large *frontón* (pelota court) in the square (**5min**). Go past the **Bar/Restaurante Urederra**, which has a map of the Urbasa area on the wall and, once out of the village, ignore the GR282 path signposted to URBASA; instead take the left fork past some **picnic tables** (**2**; 631m; **15min**). Passing through a **green gate** (**3**; 626m; **20min**), the route zigzags downhill towards the river. A **second gate** (**4**; 559m; **30min**) by a wooden hut and info panel marks the end of the track and the start of the path through the nature reserve proper.

Continuing into the forest, steps to the left lead you to the **Río Urederra** (**5**; 579m; **40min**) and the first of the **waterfalls** with its turquoise pool. This, and the other most visited sections of the river, are roped off: visitors are discouraged from climbing down to the water's edge, although plenty do. Reclimb the steps and continue along the path closest to the river, mostly in the shade of a beech forest.

You come to an equally stunning second **waterfall** and pool (**6**; 582m; **50min**), then go through a **gate** (**7**; 608m; **1h**). The path now climbs gradually, gaining height above the river; wherever there is a path to the left beside the river, take it, as it always rejoins the main path further on and there are several fine viewpoints overlooking the various rock pools and waterfalls. Cross a small **bridge** (**8**; 608m; **1h35min**) and continue climbing through dense forest and over rock. Just before a much longer, **wooden footbridge** (**9**; 653m; **1h45min**), there is a viewpoint above the largest **waterfall**.

Cross this bridge and follow the path on the other side, with the river now to your right, until you reach a flat area, still in the forest, which is as far as walkers are allowed. Our walk ends here at another **waterfall** (⑩; 680m; **1h50min**), from where there is a view up to a rocky promontory reminiscent of a diving board jutting out from the top of the **Balcón de Pilatos** — several hundred metres directly above you (see Car tour 5).

Retrace your steps back through the forest and the **gate** passed earlier (**7**; **2h20min**), either taking the more direct path or once again keeping close to the river. Go through the **green gate** (**2h40min**), **Baquedano** village (**2h55min**) and back to the **car park** (**3h**).

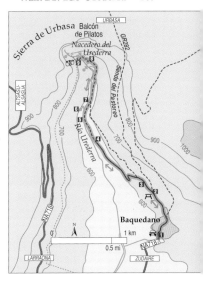

Emerald pool on the path to the source of the Urederra

Walk 22: IRUMUGARRIETA

Distance: 17.3km/10.8mi; 4h45min
Grade: ● moderate, with a gradual gain in height of 400m over several kilometres. *However, once above the forest, it is very easy to get lost on the high pastureland of the Sierra de Aralar when the mist comes down. The full circuit described here should only be attempted on clear days.* A **shorter, easier alternative** is the walk to **Igaratza** and back along the forest road (3h return). Waymarking is clear except in a couple of places on the return from Urdangoene, in which case detailed instructions are provided.

Equipment: see page 55
Access: 🚗 Fastest access from either Donostia-San Sebastián or Iruña-Pamplona to Junction 127 on the A15: turn off at Lekunberri and then take the NA-7510 signposted to Sierra de Aralar. Otherwise, follow Car tour 5 to the site of the former **Guardetxe/Casa Forestal de Aralar** (🏠). Leave the car in the large car park (42° 57.423'N, 2° 0.166'W).
🚌 Buses running between Donostia-San Sebastián and Iruña-Pamplona stop at Lekunberri, 13km from the start of the walk (taxis available).

This is a varied circuit through the beech forests, karst landscape and high pastureland of the central Sierra de Aralar, an area which is also renowned for its many neolithic remains. The walk culminates with an ascent of Irumugarrieta, the highest mountain in the range — quite easily reached without major exertion, since the walk begins at 1000m.

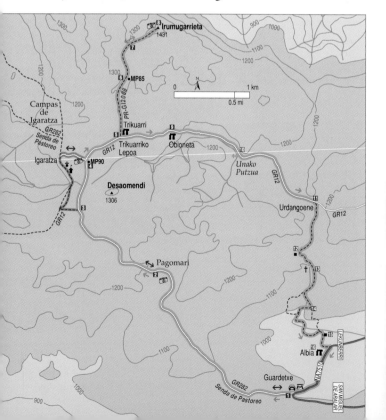

Horses grazing beside the GR12, near Trikuarriko Lepoa

Start the walk from the site of the **Guardetxe** (**1**; 1043m), the former forest guard's house, now demolished. There are a couple of picnic tables here. From the far end of the **car park**, go through the **green gate**. Follow the unsurfaced forest road (closed to unauthorized vehicles), the red/white-waymarked **GR282, Senda del Pastoreo**, a long-distance footpath that follows some of the old shepherding routes across Aralar. You remain in the forest until you emerge at **Pagomari** (**2**; 1170; **45min**), a flat area which provides the first open views of the karst landscape and mountains of the sierra. Continue climbing gradually on the main track, ignoring any minor offshoots, through some beautiful forest interspersed with limestone boulders, to come out on the open mountain.

When you come to a signpost to LIZARRUSTI (**3**; 1239m; **1h10min**), the GR282 forks left, and you can take a detour here: after around 15 minutes' walking, you would come to the refuge and chapel of **Igaratza**. The main walk, however, continues along the gravel road which now veers uphill to the right. When you come to the **MP90 marker** (**4**; 1266m; **1h20min**), if you haven't already made the detour on the GR282, take a few moments to climb up to the brow of the hill to look down on the refuge and chapel. From this point, practically the whole Aralar range can be seen.

Just after this marker, take the gravel road to the right which ascends from Igaratza, and following the red/white waymarked GR12, head across pastureland, directly towards the limestone mass of

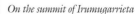

On the summit of Irumugarrieta

Irumagarrieta. On reaching a sign for the PR-GI2008 to IRUMUGARRIETA at the pass of **Trikuarriko Lepoa** (**5**; 1241m; **1h30min**), turn left to make for the remains of the **Trikuharri dolmen** (**1h35min**).

From the dolmen follow the clear red waymarking over the limestone, veering to the left at the **MP85 marker** (**6**; 1306m; **1h50min**), to rise onto the main ridge. Once there, just above another PR-GI2008 signpost, cross the **fence** (**7**; 1367m; **2h**) and continue to the summit of **Irumugarrieta** (**8**; 1417m; **2h10min**), from where the views over the valley 1000m below and along the whole ridge are awesome. The pointed peak to the west, at the far end of the range, is Txindoki, the summit climbed in Walk 4 and shown on page 56.

Descend the same way to **Trikuarriko Lepoa** (**5**; **2h40min**), then turn left to continue along the same gravel road on the GR12 for

'UNAKO PUTZUA'. Pass the **Obioneta dolmen** (**9**; 1212m; **2h55min**) and come to **Unako Putzua**, a fenced waterhole usually well frequented by the many horses grazing on this pastureland (**10**; 1175m; **3h10min**).

Remain on the gravel road, first descending slightly to the left and then climbing to **Urdangoene** (**11**; 1190m; **3h30min**), an *unmarked* pass beyond the end of the **Txameni** ridge. At the pass, fork right, away from the GR12, initially towards a clearly visible brown earth path. *(If you continue on the gravel road as far as a signpost to Baraibar, you have gone too far; return to the pass.)* But almost immediately fork right again to descend to a valley, following the vestiges of a path beside the stream whose source is just below the pass. Descend into the forest, passing a small *borda* to the right (**12**; 1122m; **3h45min**), beyond which there is some fairly clear red waymarking to show the way. Later you pass a **headstone** with a *lauburu* (**13**; Basque cross; 1090m; **3h55min**) to the right of some pine trees.

At a clearing with a faint junction of paths marked by an arrow (**14**; 1020m; **4h10min**), turn right. The path soon becomes wider and stonier, passes a second, much larger white *borda* (**15**; 991m; **4h25min**), and joins the road. Turn right, past the **Albia dolmen** (**16**; 990m; **4h30min**), and follow the road back to the **Guardetxe** (**4h45min**).

Map for Walk 23

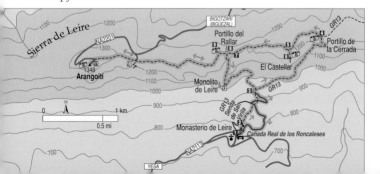

Walk 23: ARANGOITI

See map opposite
Distance: 9.2km/5.7mi; 4h35min
Grade: ● strenuous, with an overall
ascent of 700m. A steady ascent on
the GR13 to start (not always well
waymarked). On the ridge, especially
between the passes of La Cerrada
and El Rallar, waymarks are varied
(cairns, paint daubs, small ribbons
tied on trees). The path is quite
overgrown and rocky in places, so
the going is fairly slow. But by
heading more or less in a straight
line just below the top of the ridge
and using the large TV mast on the
summit of Arangoiti as a landmark,
there should be no problem. The
short-cut descent from El Portillo del
Rallar back to the monastery is
steep, but safe and not exposed. A
shorter alternative is an out-and-
back to **El Castellar** (3h), avoiding
the more overgrown section along
the ridge and the steep return
descent, but still with spectacular
views.
Equipment: see page 55
Access: 🚗 Fastest access from Iruña-
Pamplona via the A21/N240 to Yesa,
then see below. Otherwise follow
Car tour 6 to just beyond **Yesa**, then
take the NA2113 to the **Monasterio
de Leyre** (4km; car park: 42° 38.173'N,
1° 10.257'W). 🚌 Iruña-Pamplona-
Uztarroz bus to **Yesa**, then walk 4km
up to the monastery.

The Leire Monastery, perched high above the Yesa Reservoir,
provides the dramatic starting point for this walk, which
follows one of the old drovers' roads from the Pyrenean valleys
to the dry southern region of Nafarroa. An interesting section
along a ridge culminates in an ascent of Arangoiti, the highest
mountain in this part of central Nafarroa — with awesome views
towards the Yesa Reservoir area, the Aragón River and the
canyon of the Foz de Arbaiun.

Admire the ornately carved 12th-
century Romanesque portico and the
Gothic/Romanesque nave and vaults
at the **Monasterio de Leire** (771m).
Then **start the walk**: return to the
car park, and look for an info board
about the **GR13 Cañada Real de
los Roncaleses** — (**1**; 775m) one
of the most historic of the old
Pyrenean drovers' roads. Go up the
steps behind this board and follow
the **Senda de San Virila**. Where the
track bears left, keep straight on to a
derelict **shepherd's hut** (**2**; 792m;
3min), where we find the first red
and white waymarking. From here,
follow a gully marking the course of
a long-dried-up river bed. The
waymarking is a bit haphazard from
here on, but by following it up
through the forest, you can't really
get lost. Mostly holm oaks grow in
the gully, although these give way to
beech and pine as you climb.
    The going gets increasingly steep
and, immediately after crossing a
forest track for the third time,
passing a solitary holm oak, you
come to a rock bearing red
waymarking and topped by a cairn
(**3**; 905m; **25min**).
    Fork right at this rock, and after
a few metres, you will see another
waymarked fork to the left. This
provides a more direct ascent to
Arangoiti, but as it is very steep and
tiring, it is best left for the return
journey if you are planning to
complete the loop. Keep straight on
here to continue along the main
GR13 route which gradually climbs
up to the long ridge above. There is
a particularly attractive cobbled
stretch before you emerge on an area

113

Monolito de Leire

the ridge top. Climb over a stile and keep straight on, following the red and white dots and a 'coto público de caza' (hunting allowed!) sign on a tree (**7**; 1218m; **1h55min**). On coming to a small clearing with a cairn, marking **El Portillo del Rallar** (**8**; 1232m; **2h15min**), *take note of this cairn for the return journey, as it marks the start of the direct descent to the monastery.*

Proceed straight ahead on the path, still in the forest, before emerging temporarily above the tree line at a point from where the canyon of the **Foz de Arbaiun** (see Car tour 6) can be seen to the right (**9**; 1267m; **2h15min**). From here the path is clearer and better marked by cairns, as it runs along the top of the ridge with increasingly open views towards the Yesa Reservoir. Continue along a practically level stretch, to pass an **electricity transformer station** (**10**; 1249m; **2h40min**) and continue straight ahead on the path that ascends the final ridge fairly steeply. Here you join the private road coming in from the north and follow it for the last few metres to the summit of **Arangoiti** (**11**; 1348m; **3h05min**).

Return the same way to the **Portillo del Rallar** (**8**; **3h40min**), and turn right by the cairn. The path descends steeply through the forest, to emerge by a **promontory** (**12**; 1128m; **3h55min**) directly above the monastery — near the **Monolito de Leire**, a large rock monolith about a third the way down from the ridge top. Descending steeply, rejoin the GR13 and turn right, passing the **rock/cairn** at **3** (**4h15min**). Just below here, rather than heading back down the ascent route on the potentially slippery path, turn left on the track and zigzag back down to the **Monasterio de Leire** (**4h35min**).

of high meadowland at the **Portillo de la Cerrada** (**4**; 1214m; **1h25min**), a high pass marked by a rickety old sign. From here there are great views down to the monastery and towards the rock face of Castellar, topped by a large cross.

Here we *leave* the GR13 by making for some **boulders** to the west of the pass. Tiny cairns mark the ongoing path between these boulders, but they are usually no more than just a couple of stones, so keep your eyes peeled. Climbing up through the forest, keep a clump of large rocks to your right and, when you emerge at the **highest point** (**5**; 1274m; **1h28min**), divert left to El Castellar (**6**; 1282m; **1h30min**). This promontory offers the best views towards Yesa and beyond — Arangoiti, with its huge TV mast, is visible to the right.

Return to the ridge path. Some clambering over rocks is required, and the path is quite overgrown in places. normally cairns mark the most unclear parts, but basically keep contouring just to the right of

Walk 24: SELVA DE IRATI

Distance: 10.2km/6.3mi; 3h25min
Grade: ● quite easy, with an overall ascent of 450m. The walk, largely through forest, follows the Urtxuria River to the Koixta Reservoir. The path is quite narrow for the first 1km above the river, so take care until you have crossed the first stream. The steep descent on the return can be quite taxing on the knees. The circuit combines two well-waymarked routes among many around the Forest of Irati, in this case the SL-NA69 and SL-NA60A. In the main car park by the Irati River there is a kiosk staffed by park wardens (open daily 15/6-15/9; weekends only 1/4-15/6 and 15/9-30/11) where you can get a very good map of all the walks in the area for €2 (it's also available at the tourist office in Ochagavía). Even though this walk is relatively short, a whole day is recommended.

Equipment: see page 55
Access: 🚌 Make for Ochagavía, northeast of Iruña-Pamplona via the N135 and N140, then see below. Or follow Car tour 6 to Ochagavía (165km) and turn left on the NA2012, signposted to IRATI. This road crosses the long ridge of Mt Abodi. At the top (Tapla Pass; 1400m) there are maps detailing two more short, interesting walks along the ridge. The road then descends into the forest and ends by the **Irati River**, where there is also an excellent picnic site (🚐P). Park in the main car park by the river (42° 59.338'N, 1° 6.395'W; a 23km detour from Ochagavía). 🚌 daily from Iruña-Pamplona as far as **Ochagavía**, from where an option could be to follow the GR11 from the village northwards to the **Casas de Irati** (8h return). Otherwise there is *no* public transport.

T he Selva de Irati is one of the largest forests of beech and fir in Europe, extending over both sides of the Pyrenees. This circuit is perhaps the best in the area in terms of variety: not only is most of the walk inside the forest, but the route follows a scenic path beside the Urtxuria River to the small Koixta Reservoir nestling below the Mt Ori (2000m). We also visit the superb natural rock balcony of Akerrería above the forest and the interesting area around the Casas de Irati.

View down to the road to Casas de Irati from Tapla Pass

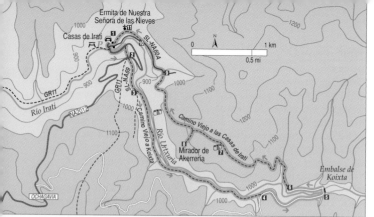

Selva de Irati

Start out from the **car park** by the **Irati River** (**1**; 848m): walk back up the road for about 300m, to the start of the **Camino Viejo a Koixta**. This old trail initially climbs steeply to the right, into the forest. At the point where the trail re-crosses the road (**2**; 913m; **10min**), the GR11 forks off to the right, but we follow the green/white waymarking of the SL.NA69 to the *left*. Soon after this path starts to narrow above the river (**3**; 919m; **25min**), *leave* the main path (which appears to carry straight on). Turn sharp left, to zigzag down closer to the river. The path is at its narrowest here, but this is the most beautiful section of the walk.

After crossing three tiny streams, the path emerges on a track (**4**; 1034m; **1h20min**) which we follow to the small **Embalse de Koixta** (**5**; 983m; **1h35min**). **Mt Ori** (2021m) looms directly above the reservoir, beyond the forest.

116

To return, cross the **dam** and turn left along a track, the **Camino Viejo a las Casas de Irati**. This initially runs parallel to the river, but then veers to the right, crosses a stream and ends (**6**; 1004m; **1h45min**). From here take a path climbing quite steeply up through the forest, to emerge in a **clearing** (**7**; 1156m; **2h15min**), with fine views towards the long, flat Abodi ridge. Cross some pastureland before re-entering the forest, and divert left to the **Mirador de Akerrería/ Akerriako Begiratokia** (**8**; 1138m; **2h25min**), a rock perched high above the river and a superb natural balcony over the forest.

Return to the main path, which descends very steeply to a forest track (**9**; 914m; **2h50min**), quite muddy in places. Follow the SL.NA60A signpost directing you back onto a small path (**10**; 876m; **3h05min**) which forms part of a short **nature trail**, along which the main types of tree in the forest are labelled.

The nature trail rises to the small hilltop chapel of **Nuestra Señora de las Nieves** (**11**; 894m; **3h15min**). From here descend past the ruins of the **Casas de Irati**, originally used as a fort during the Napoleonic wars and subsequently as a forest guard's house. The circuit is complete when we reach the **car park** by the **Irati River** (**3h25min**).

Walk 25: URKULU

Distance: 11.8km/7.3mi; 3h45min
Grade: ● moderate, with an ascent of 600m. A fairly gradual climb up to the Col d'Arnostegi is followed by a short but steep ascent to the summit of Urkuku. Waymarking is excellent throughout, partially following the Trans-Pyrenean GR11, but it is possible to get lost in cloudy weather in the somewhat confusing karst near the summit.
Equipment: see page 55
Access: 🚗 Make for Aribe, northeast of Iruña-Pamplona via the N135 and NA140, then take the NA2030 north and see notes below. Or follow Car tour 6 to **Aribe** and, after crossing the river, turn right on the NA2030, following signs to

ORBAITZETA. Continue through **Orbaitzeta** (5km), now on the NA2032. At the next crossroads (8km; where a right turn leads in 1km to the Mendilatz refuge (open Mar-Dec; beds, bunks and restaurant; www. mendilatz.com) continue straight ahead to the signposted **Fábrica de Armas de Orbaitzeta** (10km; 43° 0.563′N, 1° 13.639′W). It is also possible to drive beyond this point on an unsurfaced road to ❸, **Azpegiko Aterbea**, a small refuge (43° 1.936′N, 1° 13.636′W), reducing the walk by 4km/1h15min. 🚌 Iruña-Pamplona to **Orbaitzeta**, from where you must walk or hitch the last 5km.

T he Roman tower on the top of Urkulu, perched right on the French-Spanish border, provides a magnificent viewpoint over the Western Pyrenees. The shortest way to the summit is from the French side, from the Col d'Arnostegi, a route described in *Landscapes of the Pyrenees*. This walk starts from the Spanish side, from the curious remains of an old weapons factory used during the 18th-century Carlist wars, and also incorporates an interesting circuit of several important megalithic sites on and around the Col d'Azpegi.

Park the car just beyond the remains of the old **Fábrica de Armas de Orbaitzeta** (❶; 814m), at a small ramshackle collection of houses with an old church, the latter now being used to store farm machinery. It's worth looking around the eerie ruins of the old weapons factory, which are now quite overgrown, with the river flowing through the middle. The factory was originally built mainly to supply cannons to the army of Carlos III of Spain (Carlos V of Navarre) in the 18th century. Then **start the walk:** head along the unsurfaced road to the left of the **church**, and fork right beyond the last house, following the GR11 towards *AZPEGI*. This is a motorable road and in fact continues right over

the border into France, although most people leave their cars at the *fábrica*. Take the next right fork (❷; 850m; **15min**) and, following the course of the stream, come to **Azpegiko Aterbea** (❸; 966m; **40min**), a small emergency refuge with a spring and information boards about walks in the area.

Just beyond here, leave the road, forking left to follow the path signposted *RUTA MEGALÍTICA DE AZPEGI*, waymarked by small yellow dolmens. The scant remains of the first couple of **dolmens** are soon visible on the right, close to the stream. At the next signpost (just before a *borda*; ❹; 1028m; **50min**), turn left towards *SOROLUZE*. This is a pretty ascent up

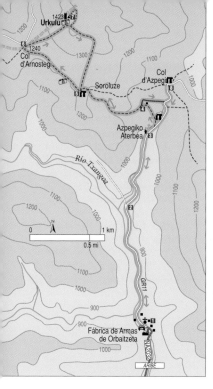

through mainly beech forest, following the course of the stream. The route then rises on the open fern-covered hillside, to enter a narrow pass and arrive at **Soroluze** (**5**; 1215m; **1h15min**). A well-preserved dolmen is just to the left

and another beside a tree a few metres further on.

Ignore the signpost to the right to Urkuku (this will be our return route); instead keep straight ahead, enjoying the open views towards Askozibar and the valley below and more or less contouring around the hillside to the **Col d'Arnostegi** (**6**; 1240m; **1h30min**). The mountain road which climbs up from St Jean-Pied-de-Port/Donibane Garazi ends here; there is a large animal drinking trough and the **205 marker** stone, on the French/Spanish border.

From here a clear a path ascends steeply, waymarked in yellow, to a flat area of karst rocks (**1h50min**) just to the right of the summit; make your way over these to climb up the steps to the summit of **Urkulu** (**7**; 1423m; **1h55min**), crowned by the impressive remains of an old **Roman watch tower**.

For the return, at first retrace your steps down towards the flat area, but then carry straight on through the karst landscape, taking care to follow the yellow waymarking until the path becomes clear as you descend the grassy hillside to **Soroluze** (**5**; **2h20min**). Turn left to retrace your steps, forking left at the signpost first passed at the 50min-point. Pass the *borda* (**4**; **2h40min**) and join a track which circles the *borda* and meets the unsurfaced road slightly higher up the valley.

Turn left to the **Col d'Azpegi** (**8**; 1055m; **2h50min**), just to the right of which is a well-preserved **cromlech**. From here return along the same road, past **Azpegiko Aterbea**, to the **Fábrica de Armas de Orbaitzeta** (**3h45min**).

Summit of Urkulu

Walk 26: LARRUN

See also photograph page 61
Distance: 11.8km/7.3mi; 4h30min
Grade: ● strenuous. The walk involves an overall ascent of 835m from Olhette, initially a steady climb along the GR10 to the Col des Veaux (563m) and then a fairly steep ascent to the summit at 900m. The descent is more gradual, except for a steep section from the ridge down to Venta Yasola.
Equipment: see page 55
Access: 🚗 For fastest access take the D810 from Biarritz to Urrugne,

then the D4 to **Olhette**. Otherwise follow Car tour 7 to **Olhette** (55km). When the road reaches the highest point in the village, opposite the Trabenia Hotel/Restaurant, take the country lane marked CHEMIN DU XURIEN BORDA to the right and, where the road ends, continue for a few metres on a gravel track to a large car park beside the river (43° 19.882'N, 1° 39.573'W). 🚌 St Jean-de-Luz/Donibane Lohizun to **Ascain**, then taxi to the start (4km).

Larrun is the last proper mountain in the Pyrenean chain before the Atlantic. The pronounced peak, with its large transmitter and collection of bars/restaurants (photograph page 61) is visible from far away and is one of the region's best known landmarks. Its funicular, which dates back to 1924, makes it easily accessible to day-trippers, and in high season and at weekends the top can get pretty crowded. Nonetheless, this itinerary is a beautiful circuit which follows two very scenic sections of the GR10 and then descends an exhilarating and surprisingly little used ridge.

Start the walk from the **car park** near **Olhette**: go to the far end of the car park where there is a map of the trail (**1**; 101m). Go through the gate/stile, waymarked by the red and white of the GR10 (where it says

DÉPART), and walk gently uphill through shady woodland. Turn right with the GR10 waymarking (**10min**), and you soon climb above the forest onto the open hillside — with your first clear view (**2**; 199m; **20min**) of the whole **Cirque de Larrun**, which we will follow in its entirety on this walk. This section of the GR10 also offers open views back towards the coastal French Basque towns and across to the Spanish side. Keeping to the left above the **Larrungo Erreka** stream all the way, the wide path ascends to the **Col des Trois Veaux** (**3**; 554m; **1h15min**), a major junction. The GR10 veers left here, down towards the village of Sara. Our route turns *right* just

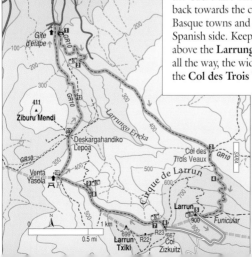

119

before the col (and the beginnings of a small pine wood), along a well-defined path signposted LA RHUNE 1.5KM: follow yellow waymarking and some arrows.

Beyond the edge of the wood, the path emerges on the mountainside (**4**; 631m; **1h25min**) and zigzags up towards the summit directly above you. There are several short cuts, but the main (less steep) path follows the yellow signs as far as the **funicular tracks**. Simply follow the tracks uphill to the summit area and cross them to the summit of **Larrun** itself (**5**; 900m; **2h15min**) with its large transmitter, bars/restaurants and orientation board. Take the time to enjoy the incredible views towards the coast and the Pyrenees and then, to escape the crowds, walk down the gravel access road which descends fairly steeply on the Spanish side beyond the **Udako Etxea bar** (**2h35min**).

Descend to **Col Zizkuitz** and continue along the path behind **border stone R23** (**6**; 667m; *not* waymarked; **2h40min**). Head for a small beech forest on the other side of the col behind R23 and follow the path round to the left, gently descending. On emerging from this woodland, you will be on the opposite (southern) side of the *cirque* to the GR10 route of ascent. A small **niche** in a rocky outcrop to the left (**7**; 627m; **2h45min**), with a carved white bird inside, makes a nice rest stop/viewpoint. The path, cut through ferns, descends gradually around the north side of **Larrun Txiki** (Little Larrun), affording great views towards the sea.

Join the ridge on the far (west) side of Larrun Txiki, from where an exhilarating ridge walk leads you down to a col at the edge of a **larch forest** (**8**; 533m; **3h10min**) on the left, from where a five-minute diversion to the right takes you up to a quite impressive **rocky outcrop** (**9**; 555m; **3h15min**). Return to the col (**3h20min**) and continue steeply downhill on a clear path, with the forest to the left, to **Venta Yasola** (**10**; 398m; **3h40min**; *⌂P*), a small refuge with picnic site, where you can buy drinks during high season and most weekends. From here a clear, less steep path continues down to **Deskargahandiko Lepoa** (**11**; Col des Contrebandiers; 276m; **4h05min**), where the path rejoins the GR10. From here a pleasant, easy descent with more fine views to the Cirque de Larrun on the right, brings us to a fork (**12**; 218m; **4h10min**), where we veer left. Just after passing the *gîte d'étape*, you come to a lane. Turn right here to cross the *Larrungo erreka* and return to the **car park** near **Olhette** (**4h30min**).

Larrun, and the tourist train (above)

Walk 27: MONDARRAIN

Distance: 11.6km/7.2mi; 3h45min
Grade: ● fairly strenuous, with an overall ascent of 700m. From the Col d'Amezketa to the summit of Mondarrain is a fairly steep climb of 270m, and the descent from the summit to the road directly below is also steep in places. Follow the notes below, to avoid a scramble up to and down from the summit. The upward route is fairly well waymarked in yellow beyond Col de Legarre, but only sporadically so until there; the return route is reasonably waymarked. The walk should not be attempted if cloud is obscuring the summit. **Shorter option:** simply do the loop from **Pas de Roland** to **Col de Legarre** and back down the escarpment through

Itxassou without the side trip to Mondarrain (around 2 hours)
Equipment: see page 55
Access: 🚌 Take the D932/D918 from Bayonne to Espelette; then pick up Car tour 7 at the 83km-point. Or follow the whole tour to the Hotel/Bar Pas de Roland (92km). If there is no space at the hotel, park up the hill to the left or beside the lane past the hotel, just after the *frontón* (43° 18.759'N, 1° 24.196'W) or, alternatively, at the small car park just before the entrance to the Pas de Roland gorge if coming from Itxassou (🄸 on the map; 43° 19.202'N, 1° 24.281'W).
🚂 Train from Bayonne/Baiona to **Itxassou**

D espite its fairly modest height, Mondarrain is one of the most interesting mountains to climb in the French Basque Country, and the circuit offers extraordinary views over this scenic area of hills and gorges. The beautiful summit itself is covered with old, twisted beech trees amidst a chaos of rocks.

Start the walk at the **Pas de Roland** (🄰; 77m) by walking along the road towards ARTZAMENDI — between the pretty Hotel/Bar Pas de Roland and its refuge. Before the *fronton*, take the first right turn, up Helenako bidea (🄱; 75m; **3min**). Then leave this lane where it descends left to a farm, and take the path straight on (🄲; 129m; **8min**). The rocky summit of Mondarrain soon comes into view towards the left as the path climbs the hillside. Continue straight on at a **crossroads** (🄳; 316m; **30min**) and then turn left at a sign for MONDARRAIN (🄴; 354m; **40min**). Go through a **gate** and turn right up another lane. This leads to the **Col de Legarre** (🄵; 378m; **50min**), where there are a couple of farmhouses.

Turn left along the path sign-posted CIRCUIT DU MONDARRAIN ET

DE L'ARTZAMENDI, alongside a fence and large red and white house, to circle the smaller **Pic d'Ezcondray** (550m), crossing a **cattle grid** (🄶; 450m; **1h**). Continue to the small pine wood on the **Col d'Amezketa** (🄷; 515m; **1h10min**). Go around the wood and start the steep climb up the grassy north spur towards the summit; the path is now clearly waymarked in yellow. You reach the pre-summit area of twisted **beech trees** and **moss-covered rocks** (🄸; 694m; **1h35min**). Keep to the right of the rock face, looking out for vague yellow markings, until a path emerges which you follow around to the right of the summit, when it starts climbing. The last part involves veering to the left to zigzag up through the rocks to the summit of **Mondarrain** (🄹; 815m; **1h50min**), where there is an old

121

Pas de Roland, with Mondarrain in the background

yellow and signposted ATHARRI/PARKING. Follow this path as it veers left and descends to a stile on the edge of the escarpment. From here there are great views over Itxassou and the rolling hills towards the sea. Turning left, the path zigzags down the hillside to enter woodland, eventually emerging on a country lane (**11**; 153m; **3h**).

Turn right along this lane, signposted ATHARRI. At the first bend, leave the lane and keep straight ahead on a path which re-enters woodland and traces a route cut between hedgerows, leading to a **junction** (**12**; 108m; **3h10min**). Turn right here, following the CIRCUIT DU VILLAGE sign. This woodland path descends gradually — ignore any minor paths to the left or right — until emerging on another lane. Keep straight on and after 50m, at another signpost (**13**; 54m; **3h20min**), you can either detour 300m to visit the beautiful church of **Saint-Fructeaux d'Itxassou** beside the Hotel du Chêne (an excellent bar/restaurant with garden, beside the church; tel: 0559297501) or continue straight ahead towards PAS DE ROLAND.

stone cross. The views across the valley to transmitter-topped Artzamendi and back towards the Pas de Roland are fantastic.

Retrace your steps back to the Col de Legarre (**6**; **2h35min**). Cross the road and follow the path beside the house opposite, waymarked in

At the next road junction, turn right to pass a small car park (**14**; 50m; **3h30min**) just before the gorge (a good parking alternative if there is no space around the Pas de Roland itself). Return on this narrow road beside the river to the **Pas de Roland** (**3h45min**).

Walk 28: PEÑAS DE ITSUSI

Distance: 11.2km/7mi; 4h30min
Grade:●❖ strenuous, with an ascent of 450m. The ascent on the GR10 between Bidarrai and Ainhoa is steep and fairly exposed in places, although no scrambling is involved. A 15-minute stretch of path from the GR10 to Martikoena at the beginning of the Peñas de Itsusi is narrow and demands a head for heights, but this may be avoided by going further up the GR10. The rest of the walk is straightforward, although once off the GR10, you need to look for occasional scarlet-coloured (and even more occasionally yellow) way-marking dots on rocks — and, on the descent from the ridge to the valley floor, there is *no waymarking* at all. The walk should not be attempted when there is a risk of cloud descending below the Peñas.
Equipment: see page 55
Access: 🚗 Take the D932/D918 from Bayonne to Espelette, then pick up Car tour 7 at the 83km-point. Otherwise follow the whole tour to the **Pas de Roland**. From there continue towards BIDARRAI. On

reaching the valley floor (about 300m past the 101km-point in the tour), ignore the left turn over a girder bridge (to the D918 which follows the river for 1km to Bidarray-Pont-Noblia, the lower part of the village and train station). Instead, turn right along the narrow lane up the valley of the **Baztán River**. You initially pass some typically colourful French Basque houses. The gorge offers numerous pleasant picnic sites (🍴P). After 2km, take the lower lane to the right, following the yellow GR10 signpost to COL DES VEAUX. Some 4km further on you cross a bridge and ascend 1km to the **Arouchia** farmhouse (the second of two farmhouses), where the tarmac ends. Park just before the farmhouse, by some rudimentary steps marked by a GR10 post (43° 15.795'N, 1° 23.067'W). 🚂 Train from Bayonne/Baiona to Bidarray-Pont-Noblia station below Bidarrai, but there are no taxis. It's a 6km walk from the station to the **Arouchia** farmhouse — only an option for the *very* fit.

The somewhat tough climb up to the Peñas de Itsusi is amply rewarded. You visit the unusual cave of Harpeko Saindoa, follow one of the more exciting sections of the GR10 as it passes through the French Basque Country, take a beautiful hike along the entire group of crags making up the Peñas de Itsusi (with the opportunity of seeing griffon vultures at close range), and you return along the wild and unspoilt Aritzakun Valley on the Spanish side of the border. There are many beautiful places to stop once you're up on the ridge, so be sure to allow a full day for this excursion.

Start the walk just before the **Arouchia** farmhouse (**1**; 252m), at the GR10 post beside rudimentary steps. Climb these **steps**, then keep left (**2**; 286m; **5min**) alongside a **drystone wall** as the path climbs the hillside. Follow the red and white waymarking to a series of **steps** leading to the cave of **Harpeko**

Saindoa (**3**; 350m; **15min**). This is a place of partly Christian, partly pagan pilgrimage, as evidenced by the bizarre collection of offerings — pieces of clothing, dolls and rosaries. The water dripping from the 1.23m-high stalactite just inside the cave to the left is believed to cure skin diseases.

Peñas de Itsusi from the Aritzakun Valley

Returning to the GR10, continue up and round the hillside; the path becomes steeper as it enters a **gorge** below the peak of **Zelahiburu** (**4**; 426m; **30min**), where care is needed in places, as you clamber over rocks. A slight scramble takes you up to a **ledge** (**5**; 497m; **45min**), a good rest stop.

Climbing higher, take the narrow path to the left (**6**; 544m; **1h**), *leaving* the GR10 and following some faint scarlet waymarking. This path crosses the stream and hugs the opposite hillside. It is quite narrow and a bit vertiginous in places, but should present no problem to the sure-footed walker. (Alternatively,

you can continue steeply up the GR10 to the Col d'Artzatey and, when you come to a junction of paths on the plateau at **a**, turn left on a path past border marker No 84 at **b**, rounding the highest point of the Peñas de Itsusi, to rejoin the route on the ridge.)

The **Peñas de Itsusi** begin at the grassy promontory of **Martikoenea** (**7**; 614m; **1h15min**), from where there is a view across the valley to the impressive pyramidal peak of Irubelaskoa. The path now continues upwards and along the top of this wonderful series of spectacular crags high above the Aritzakun Valley.

When you are parallel with a

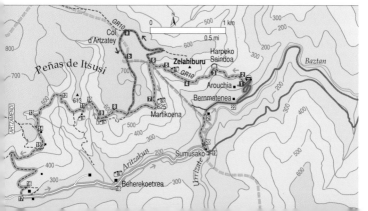

curious **dog-shaped rock** (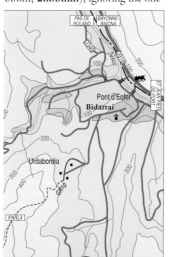; 632m; **1h35min**) below to the left, leave the main path and descend to it (9; 574m; **1h40min**). A large colony of griffon vultures can usually be seen on a ledge below this rock — and you are sure to see some at other points on the crags as well. Continue along the lower path to a **waterfall** (10; 541m; **1h50min**), which drops over 200m into the valley below. Cross the stream just above the waterfall, and keep on to a derelict **shepherd's hut** (11; 560m; **2h**), from where there are splendid views back to the waterfall and over the crags and valley below. Continue along the path that circles a drystone wall, to reach another ruined hut (12; 557m; **2h05min**). Then fork right, away from the valley, to cross another stream and follow the winding path around towards the final *peña*.

Just before a small shady oak grove, cross a further stream (13; 600m; **2h25min**), to follow the vestiges of a path over the brow of the hill. Descend past a couple of still-used **shepherd's huts** (14; 590m; **2h30min**). There is another, lower hut across the field to your left. A little below the upper huts, take the grassy path forking left (15; 556m; **2h35min**), ignoring the one

that doubles back sharp left towards the lower hut, to zigzag down towards the valley. About halfway down, cross a low, dilapidated fence (**2h50min**) and, once you are almost at the bottom of the valley and in the forest — just before the entrance gate to the field of a large white **farmhouse** (16; 324m; **3h05min**), veer right on a path that circles the property. From the main entrance gate, descend to a gravel road along the **Aritzakun Valley** (17; 285m; **3h10min**). This remote place is actually in Spanish Nafarroa.

Turn left and walk along the road, past a beautiful stone cottage (18; Beherekoetxea; 204m; **3h30min**), from where there are fantastic views back up to the Peñas de Itsusi. Beyond the old **Sumusako borda** (the last house in Nafarroa; 170m; **3h40min**) you reach a parking area and a bridge over the **Urrizate River**, which forms the border with France (19; 170m; **3h45min**).

Retrace your steps about 100m back past this house, then take the small path to the right (there should be some kind of simple waymarking here, but don't count on it!).

This descends to the **Aritzakun River** (called the Baztán River on the French side) just before the two rivers converge. Cross the metal **footbridge** (20; 165m; **3h55min**) and climb a path faintly waymarked in scarlet paint up through a beautiful forest and past a small waterfall. On reaching an old **stable** (21; 202m; **4h10min**), turn right along the track to **Bernatenea** farm (22; 191m; **4h20min**). To avoid going through this private property, follow the track round to the right, to where it emerges on a lane, and walk up this lane back to the **Arouchia farmhouse** (**4h30min**).

Walk 29: URSUIA

Distance: 11.4km/7mi; 3h45min
Grade: ● strenuous; a very gradual ascent to Col de Iramalda but quite steep from there to the summit. Clear yellow waymarking to the col, but no other waymarking on the walk. A **shorter, very pleasant alternative** (●) can be simply to ascend via the stream to Col de Iramalda and return via the ridge, making a return loop of about 2h30min

Equipment: see page 55
Access: 🚗 From Bayonne take the D932 to **Cambo-les-Bains**, then the D10 to **Urcuray/Urkoi** — or follow Car tour 7 to the village (the 124km-point). Park in the car park beside the church and *fronton*, just off the main road to the right (43° 22.074'N, 1° 21.257'W).
🚌 Bayonne/Baiona to Hazparren, then change of bus to **Urcuray/ Urkoi**.

The large rounded hill of Ursuia, being somewhat north of, and separate from, the main Pyrenean chain, is one of the best viewpoints from which to take in the whole range from a slight distance. This walk makes a very pleasant circuit, ascending via a beautiful stream through some delightful forest and returning along a grassy, fern-covered ridge.

Take the time to look around the village church at **Urcuray/Urkoi**, which has a half-timbered house curiously built onto its side! Then **start the walk**: from the car park (**1**; 79m) follow the signpost PLR NIVE ADOUR URSUYA, turning immediately left to head up the lane past several houses. The yellow waymarking is clear. At the first fork (**5min**) keep left and a little further along this lane, pick up your path by crossing a stile beside a **gate** (**2**; 115m; **10min**), where there is a

small information panel about Ursuia.

The path runs close by the stream for some way. At the next fork (**3**; 169m; **20min**), keep right to enter some delightful forest, soon reaching a small **waterfall** (**4**; 168m; **25min**). The path now skirts the stream as you gently ascend through cool, shady woodland. When you reach a '**crossroads**' (**5**; 238m; **40min**), keep straight on, still following the yellow way-marking (the track heading uphill

Col de Iramalda and (right) heading up alongside the stream

to the right is our return route).

Emerging from the forest, continue on an increasingly wide path up through the ferns, ignoring any tracks to the left and following the **line of electricity pylons** to a crossroads at the **Col de Iramalda** (**6**; 398m; **1h10min**). Turn left here and after a few metres left again by an old farmhouse (still waymarked in yellow) and follow the farm track uphill.

About 100m before a **ruined barn** (**7**; 438m; **1h20min**), fork right to follow the fence up the hillside. Where the fence veers right, now on the ridge, keep straight on through the ferns to a grassy spur and continue on the path ahead steeply up the ridge running parallel to the ridge of Ursuia to your right. Just beyond a small summit, you reach a **col marked by a few stones** (**8**; 563m; **1h40min**). From here there is a clear path straight up to the summit ridge, veering right to reach the large cairn at the summit of **Ursuia** (**9**; 675m; **1h55min**). Enjoy the extraordinary views towards the Pyrenees to the south (the mountain directly opposite is Baigura).

Descend the same way to **Col de Iramalda** (**6**; **2h25min**), but at the crossroads continue ahead for about 100m, to cross over a **stile by a gate** to the right, passing two old farm buildings. Follow the path that heads over the top of the **Iramalda Ridge** (428m), ignoring any lower tracks to the right and keeping the Pyrenean peaks to your left (the rocky summit of Mondarrain and the globe-shaped transmitter on Artzamendi are easily distinguished). Enter a gated field (**10**; 410m; **2h40min**; one gate at each end!), and after a gradual descent cross a **cattle grid** (**11**; 360m; **2h55min**). Keep straight on here and on

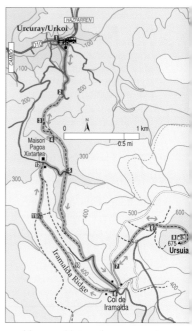

reaching an old stone house named **Maison Pagoa Xixtartea**, perched on a col and with a garden (**12**; 302m; **3h05min**), follow the farm track down to the right. This brings you back to the **crossroads** by the stream first encountered at the 40min-point in the walk (**5**; **3h10min**). From here simply follow the stream back to **Urcuray/Urkoi** (**3h45min**).

Walk 30: PASSARELLE D'HOLTZARTE

Distance: 12km/7.5mi; 4h25min
Grade: ● strenuous, with an overall ascent of 700m. The route to the hanging bridge of Holtzarte is quite steep in places, but a handrail helps on the steepest parts. Waymarked red/white (GR10) as far as the Plateau d'Arakotxia and again on the final descent to Logibar, which is extremely taxing on the knees.

The GR10 path as far as the bridge is well used, and a **shorter and extremely satisfying alternative** would be to just go there and back (● 4km/1h30min).
Equipment: see page 55
Access: 🚗 Follow Car tour 8 to the car park behind the bar/refuge of **Logibar** (46km; 43° 1.042'N, 0° 55.677'W). *No* public transport.

The Himalayan-style hanging bridge of Holtzarte, suspended over 200m above the Gorge of Olhadübi, is probably the best-known landmark in Xiberoa and a must for all visitors to the area. This circuit visits the bridge as part of a somewhat longer walk than the usual two-hour return trip, offering the chance to explore the Holtzarte Forest and the upper reaches of the Olhadübi Gorge, following one of the most spectacular parts of the GR10 on its journey through the Basque Country.

Start out from the car park behind **Logibar** (**1**; 403m), across from the signpost BOUCLE HOLZARTE ARDOKOTXEA on the far side of the river bridge. The path follows the GR10 along the river, and soon after crossing a wooden bridge starts to climb quite steeply over rocks; steps and a railing secure the potentially more slippery parts. The Holtzarte Gorge and the mountain peaks

beyond it come into view. Continue along this clear path until you reach the **confluence of the Holtzarte and Olhadübi gorges** (**2**; 596m; **40min**), where there is a spectacular viewpoint from a precariously balanced oak tree a few metres off to the right: the incredible **Passerelle d'Holtzarte** is seen to the left, above the Olhadübi Gorge.

When you reach the bridge (**3**;

600m; **45min**) cross it. Despite its swaying movement, no accident has ever been recorded here! It was originally built in the 1920s as part of a forestry exploration programme in the area, but it has been restored.

Once on the far side, take the path zigzagging up through the **Holtzarte Forest**, with tantalizing glimpses through the trees of the Holtzarte Gorge to the right. The GR10 red/white, and other scarlet waymarkings are clear.

On reaching a Y-fork with a wider path/track to the right (**4**; 711m; **1h10min**), turn left, following the sign to OLHADÜBI along a wide, level path which crosses a stream just below a small **waterfall** (**5**; 794m; **1h35min**). A little further on, a larger **waterfall** in the main Olhadübi Gorge is visible through the trees (**6**; 809m; **1h45min**), and we soon reach the small wooden **Olhadübi Bridge** (**7**; 822m; **1h50min**) at the head of the **Olhadübi Gorge**.

Cross the bridge, following the sign to ARDAKOTXIA/LOGIBAR along a

Below: Passarelle d'Holtzarte

path which leaves the forest and continues along the hillside with increasingly open views to the gorge. After crossing another stream (**8**; 848m; **2h15min**), the path gently climbs to a flat grassy area (**9**; 878m; **2h25min**) with stunning views. From here we veer right, up the hillside, to a track. Follow this to the left, to a GR10 signpost at the top of the **Plateau d'Arkatotxia** (**10**; (980m; **2h45min**), the highest point of the walk.

The GR10 forks right here, but we keep straight on following the signpost RETOUR LOGIBAR. This path descends gently towards Logibar and re-enters the forest. Turn sharp left on a waymarked path (**11**; 882m; **3h20min**) and go over a **stile**, emerging from the forest on a **grassy spur** (**12**; 722m; **3h45min**), with fine views down to the Larrau Valley ahead. The final descent, beginning at the bottom of the spur (**13**; 583m; **4h05min**), is rather tough going, but steps help over the steepest sections as the path enters the forest again and descends to the car park at **Logibar** (**4h25min**).

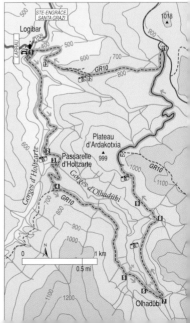

Walk 31: GORGES D'EHÜJARRE

Distance: 15.4km; 9.5mi; 5h50min
Grade: ● fairly strenuous and long, with an ascent/descent of 900m. The path up the gorge involves criss-crossing the stream, although there is usually only enough water to get wet up to the ankles in the lower reaches. Some steep sections in the upper gorge and up to the track at the start of the return; long descent through the forest back to Santa Grazi. The route as far as the descent through the forest to Santa Grazi is well waymarked in yellow, but leaves a bit to be desired from there on. A **shorter alternative**, still interesting, is to the entrance to the **Ehujarre Gorge** (●; 2h40min return).
Equipment: see page 55
Access: 🚌 Follow Car tour 8 to the 11th-century Romanesque church in Santa Grazi/Ste-Engrâce (64km; 42° 59.744'N, 0° 48.594'W). *No* public transport

The province of Xiberoa is famous for its immense canyons, and this tour of the Gorges d'Ehüjarre is an incredibly beautiful circuit which follows the bottom of the gorge all the way from the church at Santa Grazi to the high meadowlands of Erraitz. The walk returns along the top of the canyon via Mt Utzigaina, with a descent through the Utzia Forest.

Start from the **church** in **Santa Grazi/Ste-Engrâce** (**1**; 632m), where a map shows the route. Head down the lane and, after a **bridge**, turn right at the first fork, following signs to the gorge. Turn right again, over a **second bridge** (**5min**; left is the GR10), then cross a **third bridge** (**Pont de Gaztelugar**) and continue uphill. Ignore the lane off left at the brow of the hill (the access route for 4x4s to La Verna) and descend to the next bend. Cross the **stile** (**2**; 603m; **15min**) to the left and follow the narrow signposted path through lush vegetation reminiscent of more tropical climes, until the first **river** crossing, now in the **gorge** (**3**; 636m; **20min**). From here we cross the river several times, steadily climbing up the middle of the gorge, until the two branches of river and gorge converge, marked by a TOUR DES GORGES D'EHUJARRE sign (**4**; 1000m; **1h20min**). The shorter alternative can end here.

We now follow the increasingly narrow **Ehüjarre Gorge**, leaving the **Eruso Gorge** to the right. The path keeps quite high above the river and is fairly steep at times. We emerge from the forest and climb the hillside to the **Grottes de Molerse** (**5**; 1282m; **2h10min**), a couple of small caves inside the canyon wall — an ideal place to rest and contemplate the awesome views. The narrow path continues to follow the left bank of the stream, passes a

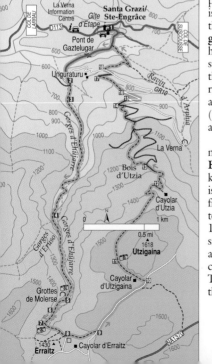

Above the cave in the Ehüjarre Gorge

beautiful **waterfall** (**6**; 1321m; **2h15min**) and then climbs up around the side of a second **waterfall,** to come out onto the open mountain with views ahead to Mt Lakora and other peaks straddling the border (**7**; 1380m; **2h25min**). This is a second place to end an out-and-back route — and also a sensible precaution if cloud cover is coming down.

To continue the main walk, cross the stream 100m further on and follow the waymarking up to the left, to the flat meadowlands of **Erraitz** (**8**; 1430m; **2h40min**). Keep to the left of a **sheepfold** before the **Cayolar d'Erraitz**, to climb up through a valley strewn with limestone and join a track (**9**; 1504m; **2h55min**). Follow it to the left and enter a forest, re-emerging on the mountainside by a **large rock** (**10**; 1537m; **3h10min**). From here your path forks left, to pass the **Cayolar d'Utzigaina** and ascend gradually around the west side of **Mt Utzigaina** (1618m). There are fine views back towards the Pic d'Anie and the Larra karst area, as well as the upper reaches of the canyon just walked. From its highest point (**11**; 1556m; **3h25min**), the path remains fairly level before starting the descent to the lower part of the canyon and the Santa Grazi valley and church, the latter clearly visible.

At the first sharp bend (**3h50min**) after a prolonged yet fairly gradual descent, you can look down onto the Cayolar d'Utzia just above the forest, but keep descending on the main path until you come to a verdant area on the hillside some way below the *cayolar* marked by a **cairn** (the yellow waymarking briefly disappears around here). Turn left at this point (**12**; 1362m; **3h55min**) to follow the grassy path down to a **beech tree and small bench** (**4h**). Just beyond

here you enter the **Bois d'Utzia** forest on a fairly wide path that becomes a track further downhill. At the first bend, fork left on a yellow-waymarked **path** (**13**; 1276m; **4h10min**). This is the first of several short-cuts down through the forest (keep watch for yellow and occasionally green and red waymarking on trees). In total the track is crossed three times (it's of course possible to stay on this track all the way down the mountain, but it will take longer) before joining it a fourth time just before a sharp bend, from where the canyon entrance is visible (**14**; 918m; **4h55min**). About 200m further downhill, you join a concrete lane (**15**; 880m; **5h**) which you descend for some distance until the path once again veers off to the left, marked between a couple of **large stones** (**16**; 829m; **5h10min**).

This straight path heads steeply down to the gated property that is the **Unguraturu** farmhouse and *cayolar* (**17**; 736m; **5h20min**), from where we turn sharp right along a track that rejoins the concrete lane. Turn left and after 200m right, back onto a path marked RETOUR STE-ENGRACE. This links up with the **GR10** (**18**; 707m; **5h35min**). Continue downhill to cross a river bridge and return to the junction with your outward route, and thence uphill back to the **church at Santa Grazi/Ste-Engrâce** (**5h50min**).

131

Walk 32: ARLAS

Distance: 5.6km; 3.5mi; 2h25min
Grade: ●❗ short but strenuous, with an ascent of 365m. The final section, to the summit and back, is steep but safe. Although short, this is the only walk in this book which exceeds an altitude of 2000m and so should only be attempted in clear weather. There is likely to be snow at this altitude from December to April. The only waymarking

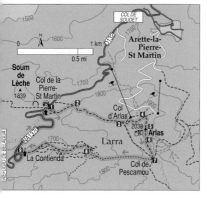

(yellow) is from the starting point to just below the Col d'Arlas, although on a clear day the rest of the route is fairly obvious as far as the ponds, and from there it is easy to follow the cross-country ski circuit.
Equipment: see page 55
Access: 🚗 Follow Car tour 8 to the **Col de Soudet** (1540m; 75km), and turn right towards *PIERRE-ST-MARTIN* on the D132. Turn right just before this small ski resort towards *ISABA* and the border, to the **Col de la Pierre-St Martin** (1765m), the French/Spanish border, marked by border stone 62 and an information panel explaining the history of the pass. Park on the left, by this information panel (a 3.5km detour from the Col de Soudet; 42° 58.173'N, 0° 46.045'W). The Refugio de Belagua, 7km below the col on the Spanish side (tel. 948 394002), offers meals and accommodation and makes a good base for exploring the area.

An ascent of Arlas provides a relatively easy and short way to reach a 2000m-high Pyrenean peak and enjoy superb views over the unique karst area of Larra — as well as towards neighbouring higher mountains such as the Pic d'Anie. The return walk, provided the weather is clear, is a beautiful amble through the Arlas valley which, being partly used in winter as a cross-country ski area, is one of the more accessible parts of Larra, a labyrinth of limestone rock formations and Spanish pine. The outward journey to Arlas follows the border while the return route as far as La Contienda is entirely in Spain!

From the parking area at the **Col de la Pierre-St Martin**, cross the road to peer down into a fenced-off, unmarked hollow — the seemingly bottomless abyss marking the entrance to the San Martin cave complex, one of the largest in Europe. Then **start the walk:** from the information panel (**1**; 1770m), take the clear path behind an **old refuge** signed COL DE PESCAMOU and waymarked in yellow. With the

pointed peaks of Arlas and Anie clearly visible ahead, follow this path over pastureland and through a small rocky valley, at first ascending, then gently descending to a **small pond** (**2**; 1783m; **10min**). From here you veer right to climb steadily up the hillside to the base of the mountain.

When the main, waymarked path veers right (**3**; 1903m; **25min**), head left on the upper path to the **Col d'Arlas**. Climb onto the brow

132

At the start of the walk, with the Pic d'Anie in the background

of the ridge and then, *ignoring* the path that goes straight ahead, turn right above a chair lift by a rudimentary **cairn** (**4**; 1920m; **35min**). Follow the cairns up the north side of the mountain, climbing steeply to the summit of **Arlas** (**5**; 2038m, **50min**). Below to the north is the ugly development of the Arette-la-Pierre-St Martin ski resort, but to the east and south is the extra-ordinary karst spectacle of Larra — its focal point is the abrupt north face of Pic d'Anie.

From the summit, watch your step as you descend steeply down the narrow ridge path on the opposite side of the mountain, to its base on the southern side (**6**; 1944m; **1h05min**), and then very briefly rejoin the yellow waymarked path at the **Col de Pescamou** (**7**; 1905m; **1h10min**). Pinpoint some ponds to the west, beyond which a gravel path is visible; at the beginning of the **Arlas valley**, and simply follow the

gully (there is no real path) down to the meadowland and the main **pond**.

Just to the right of this main pond is a panel about *urogallos* (grouse), quite common in this area, beside a map of the La Contienda cross-country ski circuits in the valley (**8**; 1718m; **1h40min**). Follow either Route 1 or the route behind the panels (they run parallel) which, outside the ski season, are pleasant rocky paths that meander through this karst landscape interspersed with Spanish pine. You eventually emerge at the **La Contienda ski hut** and car park on the main road road ascending from Isaba on the Spanish side (**9**; 1679m; **2h05min**) and are now about 1.5km inside the Spanish border. Follow the road back uphill. To avoid the long last bend, head straight up the hillside to **border stone 62** that brings you directly to the lower car park and your starting point at the **Col de la Pierre-St Martin** (**2h25min**).

Index

Geographical names comprise the only entries in this index; for other subjects, see Contents on page 3. **Bold face** type indicates a photograph; *italic type* indicates a map (both may be in addition to other entries on the same page).

134